Idylls of the Wanderer

Idylls of the Wanderer

Outside in Literature and Theory

Henry Sussman

FORDHAM UNIVERSITY PRESS
NEW YORK 2007

Copyright © 2007 Fordham University Press

All rights reserved. No part of this publication may be reproduced, stored in a retrieval system, or transmitted in any form or by any means—electronic, mechanical, photocopy, recording, or any other—except for brief quotations in printed reviews, without the prior permission of the publisher.

Library of Congress Cataloging-in-Publication Data

Sussman, Henry.
  Idylls of the wanderer : outside in literature and theory / Henry Sussman.
    p. cm.
  Includes bibliographical references and index.
  ISBN-13: 978-0-8232-2769-3 (alk. paper)
  ISBN-13: 978-0-8232-2770-9 (alk. paper)
    1. Outsiders in literature. 2. Outsiders in motion pictures.
  I. Title.
  PN56.5.O95S87 2007
  809'.93353—dc22
                                              2007018777

Printed in the United States of America
09 08 07   5 4 3 2 1
First edition

For Helen Tartar,

whose editorial practice contains a philosophy of books,
in admiration, solidarity, and gratitude
not only for her strategic assistance to the present volume,
but for her ongoing advocacy of critical theory, rigor, and invention.

CONTENTS

	Preface	ix
1.	Idylls of the Wanderer	1
2.	On the Butcher Block: A Panorama of Social Marking	43
3.	Exiles in Writing: Joyce and Benjamin	63
4.	James Baldwin's Exile: Theory, Circumstance, and the Real of Language	85
5.	William Faulkner and the Romance of the American Drifter	110
6.	The Afterlife of Judaism: The Zohar, Benjamin, Miller	130
7.	Modernist Night: Distortion, Regression, and Oblivion in the Fiction of Bruno Schulz	152
8.	Incarcerated in *Amerika*: Literature Addresses the Political with the Help of Ernesto Laclau	178
	Notes	205
	Index	231

PREFACE

The Moment When We Write

The exact moment and occasion of death are always attributable, in the post-mortem, to a concatenation of physico-physiological factors. Not so the precise moment when we set about writing, when the inscriptive instrument punctures or breaks a surface of blankness, or disrupts the continuity in a flow of electrons. In order to perpetrate this act, whose suddenness conveys a certain violence, the writer gathers herself in the interruption of a steady state or equilibrium that was going along perfectly well without her. Although compliance with deadlines is a staple of the academic modus operandi, writing, in the senses in which I am developing the term in this particular context, is rarely induced by someone else or produced under coercion. Equally seldom will the inscriptive process constitute a significant modification to the state of affairs under which it transpires.

Somehow, nevertheless, the onset, the onslaught, of writing happens. Why and when it should be initiated, just now and precisely in this manner, precisely which phrases and locutions set it rolling, is the great mystery, the glorious moment, the stillest hour, with the sweep and promise of the sublime, or of messianic possibility. It would be no exaggeration to claim that universes are opened, terrestrial limits are breached, with the onset of writing. Yet writing's punch, its upset of the status quo, is delivered in intense knots of verbal phrasing and abbreviation, striking the writer as much as anyone else with the intensity and reconfiguring suddenness of shock.

Yet the moment of first inscription is even more cataclysmic in its aftershock than was the event of phrasing that overcame us, taking us by surprise, gaining us however tenuous a foothold in a specific terrain of articulation.

The writing process having been initiated, the glide over the smooth space of language undertaken, all hell breaks loose, all experience and signs of life gather at the convergence between words and their horizon of expression. Being "in writing" characterizes an ontological state as different, possibly as heightened, as transporting, and as in earnest, as being "in love," and usually without the same costs and damage. What is authentically exceptional about the writing process as it runs its course is the focus, the meditative concentration, the "mindfulness" that it imbues to our quotidian interactions: everything of the moment converges at the finger-pads of a keyboard or the point of some stylus.

The state of writing makes us outsiders to our own existences, toward which we peer back in bemused strangeness. Our writing produces us as outsiders and exiles. "The Wanderer's country is not truth but exile," writes Maurice Blanchot in "Literature and the Original Experience." "He lives outside, on the other side which is by no means a beyond. He remains separated, where the deep of dissimulation reigns, that elemental obscurity through which no way can be made and which because of him makes its awful way through him."[1] Such is the price we pay for our turn into the climate of verbal fluency. It is to this condition of self-engendered strangeness, one as endemic to cultural critique as to poetic or narrative composition, that Friedrich Nietzsche, in *Human, All Too Human*, alludes, as something of a shibboleth, with the Wanderer, his own writerly shadow. Without a concerted withdrawal from the terms and most basic assurances of familiarity, writing simply doesn't get done, it doesn't *happen*.

Writing is a state, but bearing no nationality. Its citizens are precisely the stateless and the homeless. The state of writing is the radical alterity allowing phrases to form. The stunning surprise with which the articulations conducive to embroidering upon a particular occasion of thinking or cultural encounter emerge constitutes writing's considerable joy, one not without its sexual dimensions. It is indeed writing's power to *procreate* the words requisite to a rhetorical or performative situation that triumphs over its frustrations, its incipient tedium, and the indifference that the finalized and bound written artifact may provoke. Discharged, the turned text obviates the need for its programmer, indeed, exiles its writer back to the domains of conventional perception and sensibility.

The entrance to this state demands acquiescence in overcoming, a complicity in being overwhelmed, overrun. The trigger to an episode of inscription is less a grand idea, a motivating event, a state of affairs, than a convergence of lines of meaning that do not allow the unwritten to persist. This is what Blanchot terms an *exigency*.[2] Texts are written because in certain respects they have to be. They constitute by their very being a material resistance to the forces that would militate for their inchoateness. Whatever the intellectual or intellectual consequences, the writer places herself at the point of convergence where the concurrence of associations, suggestions, and resonances does not allow blankness (or the voids of ideology, rhetoric, bureaucracy, or careerism) to continue unscathed. She who has no capacity for surrender will not end up, even temporarily, in the writer's desk-chair.

The writer capitulates to an occasion or situation in all its arbitrariness, complexity, untenability, and conflicting messages. The critical task is not only to name and assemble the strands in the sociocultural predicament demanding illumination but to perform the emergence of this state of affairs and its potential revision, in pursuit of an enhanced sensibility. In assuming this repeated critical exercise, the writer, at the cost of a tangible detachment, marginalization, singularity, and disaffection—all attributes associated with the *outside* in the following study—also claims a certain *leverage*, whatever *torque* texts composed under the aura of a certain ethico-rhetorical sensibility can exert upon their readership.

Writing transpires within a profoundly democratic horizon of possibility. Language is, after all, equally and uniformly the property of all members belonging to its community of speech, inscription, and other media. The access that a particular community affords its members for exposure to and inculcation in the scripts and artifacts of cultural literacy—the quality, in other words, of communal libraries, museums, archives, and performing and media arts centers—is the Open welcoming its public into cultural literacy, participation, and dialogue.[3] There is no more compelling sociopolitical and cultural issue than the care afforded the quality of this Open, its maintenance, its updating, and its improvement.[4] Martin Heidegger is no doubt correct in situating this Open at the confluence of the pathways of poetic and semiotic decoding, encoding, and making, but I imagine the happening of this activity around an urban square, a regional arts center, or a university campus, rather than in the woods.

The quality of the cultural-semiotic Open into which we are free, with impunity, to wander is a decisive precondition for the cultural labor of devising a distinctive *style* for a particular project of writing and attending to the *display* of text and other signifying codes or materials on the page. It could indeed be argued that nothing is more political than the style, composition, memory, and citation embodied in texts and other communicative artifacts. And yet the obverse attitude and bearing of writing is not taken up by all. As Jacques Derrida demonstrated eloquently and convincingly at the outset of the still-current moment of theoretical inquiry, in the swings between the bearings that he associated with speech and writing, the resistances to whatever writing might highlight and disclose run deeply in the histories of Western philosophy and religion, and have counterparts in arenas of civilization seemingly far afield. The dynamic of auto-immunity that Derrida developed so powerfully in his later work[5] dramatically characterizes a running resistance to the disclosures of writing that may, through ideology and political theology, do more than merely neutralize its terse and shocking illuminations.

It turns out that writing is not an endeavor joyfully undertaken by all, whether in the roles of producers or of readers. The very academies and other institutions ostensibly dedicated to the reception, celebration, training, dissemination, and archiving of writing may well be, in their infrastructural configurations, constitutionally auto-immune, as Derrida puts it, to writing's implications and culture. The very social settings making writing possible in its solicitation and valuation may well muffle its higher and less harmonious frequencies. The moment when writing is initiated, then, is of decisive consequence on aesthetico-political as well as personal or communal cognitive and existential levels. In this microscopic paradigm shift is vested all the transformative potential and promise of an awakening.

At Home in Language

On the front burner of my ongoing commitment, obsession, and critical practice, the entire thirty-five years of teaching I have spent in classrooms ranging from the protected seminar room to the wide-open, high-tech lecture hall boil down to three postulates:

1. Teaching is encouragement. This is the only emotional tenor worthy of the atelier of formation and training. If education becomes a panorama of progressive impediments or filters to conceptual and aesthetic attainment, it disqualifies itself from the constellation of the viable enterprises of cultural literacy and diffusion.

2. Teaching is an excruciating attending to the individual members of a learning cadre while they are mostly silent, while you the teacher are speaking at them. (This is the Buddhist exercise.) The teacher constructs and opens up a temporary *home* in language for students who set out as aliens or relative newcomers to the dialect under study, as immigrants in a society whose idiom they have not quite mastered. Of course, the teacher has not achieved this overarching mastery either, but the language climate that she configures serves as base camp for bounded forays into uncharted terrain. The student's experience in a classroom that has been orchestrated well is an amelioration of the outsider's ongoing paralytic self-consciousness, sense of unfamiliarity, and dread of impending blunder and shame by the affirmative discovery of a hitherto unavailable facility.

3. The classroom is a vagrant or nomadic *home*, with all of home's uncanny but formative dissonance. Home may well be a haven of intimacy and of the aspirations we hold for our reproductive and familial lives. It is the primordial, and hence spectral, scene of nurturing and comfort, for which we imaginatively yearn when we are separated from it. In this sense, it is an imaginary homeland. But in the classical Freudian idiom of the Uncanny (*das Unheimliche*),[6] home is also a place where we can tell jokes, in their full prurient and aggressive content, where we let our hair down, where, in the privacy of *oikos* and domicile, we can share insults and derogatory nomenclature about our neighbors, those alters with whom we may share turf but not necessarily way of life. Home is the onerous-generative breeder of insult. At a particularly disturbing moment in global history, when large sectors of the planet are engulfed by sectarian violence and repression, which had presumably been checked through the rise and dissemination of secularity and the dismantling of theocracy in national spheres, we cannot be attentive enough to the culture of insult, which plays a definitive and structuring role in the interactions between organized religions, ethnic communities, and, yes, academic schools or "subdisciplines." The entire progression from local unrest to out-and-out warfare, whether of the "conventional" or "terrorist" variety, whether between sects and factions or recognized nations, follows the trajectory of an escalation of insults. It is through the study of speech acts, even such elusive ones as insults, that the critics and teachers of culture gain their most meaningful grasp of organized conflictual catastrophes.

Teaching, then, is a homemaking, even if of temporary duration or of the throwaway variety. Anyone with a constitutional aversion to this conditional nest building, say because it is undignified or not masculine enough, should stay away from teaching. The teacher invites the student to dwell, in the Heideggerian sense,[7] provisionally *within* a particular operating language, in full cognizance of the certainty that the student will venture into additional and different idioms and that she will expand and distort the usage of the language initially disseminated in the teacher's seminar room.

The critic is a perpetual outsider, culture's hermit crab, always in search of a discursive home. Always on the verge of exile from her own entrenched position, the critic is an expert in packing and unpacking, her book bag always poised on the threshold. To invoke Maurice Blanchot's trenchant eloquence: "Where I am alone, day is no longer anything but the loss of an abode, it is an intimacy with the outside, the outside that is placeless and without repose."[8] Constantly trucking in untenable positions, the critic shuttles between multiple dwellings, whose purchase she is always willing to consider even if permanent occupancy is out of the question. The critic has been invited into many households; her completed essay is a floor-plan for a tenable position of response to a cultural artifact. The position paper may or may not suit its reader. In its dispensability, the critical articulation is a throwaway formulated under tenuous circumstances in response to an artifact itself facing immanent cultural extinction, even if, by coincidence, at the zenith of its notoriety. It is incumbent on critics to engage with the evanescence of their considered positions, the instability of their footing, the frenetic rear-guard battle in which their readership is decisively engaged.

Once found, the critic's home, whether discursive or institutional, is as disorderly, as filled with cultural and attitudinal junk, as much in need of repair and maintenance, as any other. The critic is in an ongoing state of homing, of yearning for a home that, when realized, constitutes the single most pervasive and dangerous obstruction—among many—to her writing. The critical act is at once the location and the dismemberment of a home. The search for temporary shelter in particular current critical discourses and paradigms is unavoidable, as is the abandonment of each successive inscriptive perch or site amid the suspended self-correction of ongoing critical commentary.

Climates of Writing

It behooves us, at the current juncture of cultural commentary, to characterize the zone or setting of writing as a climate rather than as an integral system or an environment. So multitudinous are the factors giving rise to inscription, so intricate are the pathways and interfaces by means of which these impulses and influences interrelate, that we situate writing in the "open system" of turbulence, autopoiesis, and potential chaos rather than in the "closed system" of homeostasis.[9] Given its susceptibility to the broadest possible range of conditions and the volatility of the individual factors at play in its atmosphere, "climate" is a particularly useful and suggestive name for the opening of systematic constraints needing to transpire if writing is going to *happen*. The ethos and practice of critique at the present historico-cultural moment demand a particularly intense sensibility with respect to the complex interplay of the conditions allowing for writing: stimulating it, sustaining it, thwarting it, effacing it, stigmatizing it, and so on. The need to protect the ecology of writing, to implement controls on the damage already wreaked by such forces as the corporatization and governmental tracking of news and information, is as compelling a precondition to a vibrant public sphere enlivened by literate debate as are concerns regarding global warming and environmental pollution to the sustenance of a healthy terrestrial ecosystem. The delicacy of the ecology of writing is ordained by the sheer number of separate factors capable of squelching inscription; it is exacerbated by the multiple interactions between these factors, among them economic, technological, archival, ideological, educational, and political ones. It behooves us ethically as well as exegetically to treat writing as an impacted climate or ecology under habitual stress, to attain some consensus regarding the measures decisive to its protection.

Franz Kafka was hardly the first writer to acknowledge the cluster of tangible and conceptual conditions on which composition depends.

> Metaphors are one among many things which make me despair of writing. Writing's lack of independence of the world, its dependence on the maid who tends the fire, on the cat warming itself by the stove; it is even dependent on the poor old human being warming himself by the stove. All these are independent activities ruled by their own laws; only writing is helpless, cannot live in itself, is a joke and a despair.[10]

Even in view of writing's captivation and self-absorbing allure (Kafka composed his breakthrough story, "The Judgment," in one monumental overnight sitting between September 22 and 23, 1912), the writer acknowledges the full impact of tangential and even banal material conditions (most touchingly, the cat warming itself by the stove) on the very possibility of inscription.

Affected even by the meanderings of itinerant cats, the climate of writing is delicate indeed, requiring an auspicious conjunction of multiple support functions (socioeconomic, informational, archaeological in Michel Foucault's sense, architectural, and ecological). The inscriptive process can be disrupted and squelched by a disturbingly large array of factors. A Chinese encyclopedia of these would include the following: distraction, overwork, understimulation, ideological fundamentalism, interdenominational sectarian strife among "subspecializations" (remember that the culture of insult is as foundational to the academic division of labor as to organized religion), bullshit[11] (becoming an agent, for a variety of reasons, of Ernesto Laclau's "empty signifier"),[12] careerism and self-promotion, and institutional submersion and self-identification. It is almost as though the environmental thwarters of writing vie with one another for our attention and collusion.

To preserve and protect the climate of writing is to leach from it such toxins as these. Like the current ecological attentiveness, whose exigency has only become more pressing in the wake of persistent (even strategic) neglect, the maintenance of an overall climate of writing from one particular scene or setting to the next must be a collective project undertaken in the name of no particular interest. It must be a project contingent on each individual cultural programmer, whether through acts of composition, reading, or elucidation. And each anonymous contribution to the project of ecological sustenance and preservation incumbent upon the critical collectivity is attached to a singular inscriptive signature.

Nomadic Sociology

Amid current techno-political developments, the *address* of writing, its bearing as well as its destination, becomes all the more obscure, temporary, and translated into ever more elusive and virtually invisible traces. For all of the writing medium's intrinsic short circuits and other accidents and dysfunctions, forever queering its deployment as a dependable instrument or utility, the fact of its being keyed to an address, an implied receiver, endows it with an irreducible social dimension. The sociology of writing has much more to do with the points, interfaces, switches, and turntables along its trajectory than with the nature, habits, or behavior of its producers, consumers, apologists, or executives. To the degree that literary characters, even the "I" of purportedly neutral reportage or narration, are invariably figments of writing, we can say (and do) that the aggregate of literary characters and surrogates demands its own sociology as well as its encyclopedia, its typology, and its manuals of plot and rhetoric. This is particularly so at a moment of "reality TV" and a concerted strategy, among the corporate broadcasters and publishers of news, of blurring the boundaries between entertainment and information.

My renewed attentiveness to the anecdotal groundings and bearings of sociology, like so many discoveries, came about tangentially. It is my home university's great distinction to require of virtually all its undergraduate students a full year's program in world civilizations. Teaching the course demands no less than tracking the human experience on this planet in a staggered series of necessarily fragmentary snapshots. The growth of towns beginning in the late-medieval period, the advancement of trade both in outreach and acceleration, and the formation of professional classes of skilled craftsmen may count among the key material underpinnings of the broader modernity as it crystallized in Europe and elsewhere. I speculated on the writerly and cultural impacts of these developments in the interchapters to a study called *The Aesthetic Contract: Statutes of Art and Intellectual Work in Modernity*.[13] This is a setting that extends at least from *Hamlet* and baroque metaphysical poetry through modernism and the secret sharer that shadowed it ex post facto, in which the artist, in the most secular bearing permissible at the moment, personifies and negotiates impasses that were already the onus as well as the birthright of Shakespeare's signature tragic surrogate. Among these insurmountable conditions surely number: an impossible proliferation of loyalties and obligations, including the jurisdictions that monitor and enforce them; a widening fragmentation and overall crisis in the media of representation; and a polarization of moral values and positions following on metaphysical as well as professional isolation and individuation. Aesthetic values and deliberations still at play well into the twentieth century emerge in this context as a secular religion supplanting and filling in for theological institutions outmoded by urban density and the acceleration and violence of modern experience.

Having allowed myself, in the interstitial chapters of this study, to meditate more broadly and playfully than before on the overarching dynamics and vicissitudes of aesthetic processes, I came in my own trajectory upon a realization already evident in some degree to Kant so many generations before: namely, that an entire sociology hinges on the communality with which the artists of a certain setting and moment can acknowledge the specifications of the aesthetic horizon or paradigm under which they are working.[14] Furthermore, the dynamics under which the current system of art production is modified, resulting in discernible differences in the materials, styles, and very artifacts of art, entail collective agreements and understandings *between* the members of a particular artistic community. Through my own conceptual meanderings and hardly linear writing process, I had stumbled upon a position surely well-known to Niklas Luhmann as well: namely, that art is a play of meaning embedded in sociological subsystems of mutual recognition and strategic negotiation on the part of individual art operators.[15] Aesthetic production is both *of* sociology and *paradigmatic* of the compass and sway of sociological interactions in themselves. In the end, my intention to meditate further on the sociology of aesthetic production and reception was sidetracked by the auratic allure exerted upon me by literary texts. The discipline and honor of sustained theoretical oversight may have eluded me, I'm afraid, under the spell of aesthetico-critical stimulants.

It is no accident that the figure of the novelistic narrator merges, at the climax of *Swann's Way*, Marcel Proust's overture to his mega (eight-volume) *In Remembrance of Lost Time*, with that of the social-scientific fieldworker. At the very zenith of his despair regarding his lover and eventual wife, Odette, Charles Swann, the novel's paradigm and epitome of the manias for possession and control embedded in the ideology of monogamous marriage, drags himself out to a splendiferous *soirée* at the Saint-Euvertes' *hôtel*. Among other elements of the assembled crowd at this happening, he tracks the observers, the social novelists or reporters of the spectacular scene:

> And in these men by whom Swann now found himself surrounded there was nothing, down to the monocles which many of them wore (and which previously would at the most have enabled Swann to say that so-and-so wore a monocle)

which, no longer restricted to the general connotation of a habit, the same in all of them, did not now strike him with a sense of individuality in each. Perhaps because he regarded General de Froberville and the Marquis de Bréauté . . . simply as figures in a picture, whereas they were old and useful friends . . . the General's monocle, stuck between his eyelids like a shell-splinter in his vulgar, scarred and overbearing face, in the middle of a forehead which it dominated like the single eye of the Cyclops, appeared to Swann as a monstrous wound which it would have been glorious to receive but which it was indecent to expose. . . .

"Hallo, you here! Why it's ages since we've seen you," the General greeted Swann and, noticing his drawn features and concluding that it was perhaps a serious illness that had kept him away, added: "You're looking well, old man!" while M. de Bréauté exclaimed: "My dear fellow, what on earth are you doing here?" to a society novelist who had just fitted into the angle of eyebrow and cheek a monocle that was his sole instrument of psychological investigation and remorseless analysis, and who now replied with an air of mystery and self-importance, rolling the "r": "I am observing!"[16]

The monocles donned by the scene's roving socialites serve as the instruments and insignias of its heightened visual awareness. They transform a school of social fish marked as a species by the tuxedo into *hommes très distingués*. An invitation to the Saint-Euvertes' is hard to come by. Just being on hand at the *soirée* is a considerable distinction. To *assist* at the spectacle is to observe carefully and to be seen. The opening up of an aquatic depth and fluidity is the primary narrative motor powering the aesthetic revelations punctuating and occasionally redeeming the banality in which all the major characters, narrator "Marcel" as well as the likes of Swann, Charlus, Albertine, and Charlie, are for the most part submerged. The social novelist, whose trilled pronunciation pretends to a measure of distinction even beyond what has been made graphic by his monocle, belongs to a class of observers or fieldworkers that the reveling throng precipitates, in an instance of Hegelian self-reflexivity on a sociological plane, the social element both in and outside of its class.

"When it was the little phrase that spoke to him of the vanity of his sufferings, Swann found a solace in that very wisdom which, just a little while back, had seemed to him intolerable when he fancied he could read it on the faces of indifferent strangers who regarded his love as an insignificant aberration."[17] It is absolutely crucial to note that, in this emblematic scene of art's vindication—as embodied in the "little phrase" from Vinteuil's sonata—of love's psychological and psychosomatic torments, the ostensibly stationary and neutral *observer* is as much a moving target as the characters, spaces, costumes, and decorations under scrutiny. Any possibility of taking in the scene, of registering its minute dynamics and developments, is made all the more exasperating and untenable by being engulfed in the ongoing turbulence of communal time and history.

Whether Proust's highly refined social novelist or Nietzsche's forbidding Wanderer, whose shadow is his ultimate trace and expression, a philosophical incarnation of the horrors concentrated in Frankenstein's monster, the writer, at least the one caught up in the Moebius strip careening between modernism and its "post" supplement, is invariably a nomad. And the phenomena under her purview are largely of a situational and social provenance and significance. Whether explicitly marked or not, then, the writer, she who resides in the position and posture of critique, is a nomadic sociologist, never at home in the commentary she renders, dispatched as it is to destinations unknown and in all likelihood nonexistent or otherwise imaginary.

It takes a mobile sociologist, one never at home, one whose only home is the unceasing flow of variants in language and social form, to make sense of the concoctions that we, collectively and communally, we who are fated to live in close if not intimate proximity, cook up for one another on a near-daily basis. These social epiphenomena, noteworthy not merely on intellectual grounds but because they structure and limit our social interactions, range from mutations in the forms of polite address and civil interaction, to media of telecommunications and the new interactions they program, to (always increased) thresholds of verisimilitude in visual, phonic, and cybernetic media and the assumptions and expectations that they engender. The nomadic sociologist owes her almost instantaneous rapport with unfolding trends to the smooth space that Gilles Deleuze and Félix Guattari figured for the amalgamated flow of goods and materials, value (in its monetary, commodity, and symbolic forms), energy (immanent, i.e., sexual as well as virtual) characteristic of interaction and exchange under late capitalism.[18] Heir to the Baudelairean *flâneur* spotlighted by Benjamin as the avatar of the hip cosmopolitan with global outreach, the urban sociologist sizes up an emergent situation, takes definitive note of it, while on the run. As the current cliché regarding the critic reads, the nomadic sociologist is all of us; we who live under the current state of economic and teletechnic conditions are thrust, willy-nilly, into her posture.

It is no accident, then, that theoretically astute sociology is making preliminary gestures at circling back to its foundations in narrative and memoir. Indeed, with due respect to academic specialization and territorial strife at the level of the "disciplinary subspecialties," what sociology or, for that matter, anthropology sundered from its base in anecdote and reminiscence would we wish to imagine? Sociology begins in a relentlessly pluralistic account of the conditions prevailing in government and other large organizations, one extending to every relevant point of view. (It is this inclusiveness that grounds its initial claim to scientificity.) As in the meandering sequence of novels composed by Emile Zola, the vicissitudes of the fall guys and victims of institutional life are as essential an element to the early sociological phantasmagoria as the high deeds of the movers and shakers operating within the same picture. Having run its course as a technocratically domesticated discipline, replete with surveys and statistical spreadsheets, sociology is reasserting its common cause with a literary sensibility and aesthetic considerations in designing discourse.

The work of sociological upstarts such as Stephen Pfohl, Derek Sayer, Allen Shelton, and Jackie Orr reverts to personal travels and memories long metabolized in orchestrating an appeal to the core sociological sensibility, with its distinctive blend of empathy and acuity, as epitomized by such foundational writers as Karl Marx, Max Weber, Georg Simmel, Walter Benjamin, Siegfried Kracauer, Elias Canetti, Herbert Marcuse, and Erving Goffman.[19] It is only by opening up the foyer of domestic experience and private language to sociological thinking, as Pfohl, Sayer, Shelton, Orr, and their compeers demonstrate, that sociology can fulfill its empathic mission and its fish-eye visual scope.

Literature is, then, not a dysfunctional cousin to sociology at irreducible loggerheads with its pretensions to methodological and at least quasi-scientific rigor. It serves, rather, as sociology's best-wired electronic database and memory. Indeed, all the facets of the literary performance that make it appear most inefficient and out of synch—its semantic ambiguities, its stylistic excesses, and its generic transgressions—in fact comprise its most useful feedback.

Coincidentally, at the very moment when the sociologists of memoir acknowledge literary composition not only as an indispensable source and database but also as an unavoidable element in their own accounts and transcripts, a spate of recent literary artifacts acknowledges its motivating forces and internal narrative agents to be nomadic sociologists. There is a point at which the literariness of retrospective inscription segues directly into the sociological purview of mobile annotation. This may be a particularly auspicious perch for surveying the wide compass of fictive innovation attributable to the diverse projects of W. G. Sebald. Like the contemporary sociologists of memoir, Sebald is content to leave his narrative medium with a rough finish, as an amalgam whose consistency is none too fine. Sebald regularly inserts old photographs of telling locations encountered by his surrogates and facsimiles of documents relevant to their travels in the silences and blank spaces where the verbal adumbration of these memorable scenes gives out.[20] His fictive narrative fitfully fluctuates between personal reminiscence, "objective" reportage, and the opening up of visual windows. The result is less a literary recreation than a sociological account, seemingly (though looks can be deceiving) assembled in the haste occasioned by perpetual movement, between perspectives as well as locations. The discursive podium in Sebald's fiction fluctuates between his narrators, fictive characters assigned explicit "identities," and the odd historical figure (e.g., Kafka) that he occasionally mobilizes.[21] But the movements of these surrogates invariably bespeak the abrupt and discontinuous inscription occurring under battle conditions of truncated memory and constant displacement. Writing in the current climate of inscription, we find ourselves at a juncture, then, when the social (or "human") sciences' reclamation of their integrity through an explicit embrace of discourse's literary features coincides, in the camp of the "humanities," with a salutary blurring of the distinctions between invention, memoir, and virtual memory.[22]

The nomad's sleeping arrangements are invariably transient. While it might be far-fetched to assert that inscriptive mindfulness transforms every writer into a Buddhist, writing entails a sustained focus and concentration amid transitory conditions. This is the state toward which the congenital writer is constantly striving. There is no end point to inscription. Its Buddhist moment happens only along the way. The way of inscription is a mindful tracking, consolidation, and interfacing of semiotic input often arising from sociopolitical conditions of aggravated turbulence. It is hardly the writer's task to institute serenity or resolution. But a pronounced peace of sensibility is an indispensable catalyst to writing's synthesis and emergence.

In Gratitude and Solidarity

Even at this late phase of my studies and ongoing inscriptive record, J. Hillis Miller and Richard Macksey are inexhaustible, ongoing sources of inspiration, support, and moral education. Carol Jacobs remains an indispensable model and advocate of minute attention to detail, not only in reading but in all meaningful registers of being. Ewa Plonowska Ziarek and Krzytof Ziarek have infused the Comparative Literature Department at Buffalo, where I've now taught for almost three decades, with an unprecedented intellectual openness and effortless sociocultural instinct. Their return to Buffalo has been an enhancement to long-standing commitments and innovations by Rodolphe Gasché and Shaun Irlam, and a catalyst of important new initiatives and energies emanating from David Johnson and Kalliope Nikolopoulou.

Years of informal theoretical discussion and analysis of the academic profession and its role in promoting/stifling critical innovation and creativity with Tom Cohen have been decisive to any sense of the climatic conditions and environment for inscription communicated in the preceding and following pages. I have found Cohen's particular map (or Benjaminian constellation) of technological, media-related, material, ideological, and rhetorical factors impinging on the general economies of inscription and critique to be state-of-the-art and authoritative at the present juncture. Much of my current work is dedicated to the elaboration of coordinates whose designation and placement are the result of his vision. It is a particular pleasure for me to orient certain of my current musings to this interstitial landscape as Cohen and I initiate a newly founded Institute on Critical Climate Change, its conferences, and its projected publications. I hope that readers of the present volume will keep an ear tuned to the collective efforts of this strategically marginal community of discourse, perhaps with an eye toward collaborative participation.

Ongoing intellectual friendship and exchange with James Bunn, Cynthia Chase, Joan Copjec, Jonathan Culler, Paul Fry, William Galperin, Rodolphe Gasché, Werner Hamacher, Neil Hertz, Martha Hyde, Tom Hyde, Richard Lee, Susan Lee, Carla Locatelli, Christian Moraru, Rainer Nägele, Brigitte Peucker, Haun Saussy, Allen Shelton, Laurence Shine, Howard Stern, Garrett Stewart, Jim Swan, and Christina Zwarg have been indispensable to any currency I've been able to maintain with the critical debates and arguments most important to me. The influx of ideas that they've sent my way has been a lifeline to whatever intellectual vitality I've managed to sustain.

My students, both at the University at Buffalo and Yale University, furnish me with an inspiration and an affirmation that enable me to continue at the task of cultural exegesis. I could never thank them enough for their patience, vitality, idealism, and creativity.

Pivotal release time from customary duties was made possible, in 2001–2, by an NEH Humanities Fellowship, a residential grant by the Camargo Foundation in Cassis, France (Spring 2002), and a sabbatical leave from the University at Buffalo. Under paradisiacal conditions of research leave (especially in Cassis), I was able to think with particular vividness about the exiles in the present volume (James Joyce, Walter Benjamin, and James Baldwin); also to compose the material about deconstruction and religion in my recent *The Task of the Critic* (New York: Fordham University Press, 2005). I am particularly grateful to NEH and the Camargo Foundation for having opened the panorama of open-ended thinking and writing to me on multiple occasions. For those of us who disseminate the broader cultural literacy at public institutions, NEH is a particularly critical bulwark of sensibility and support.

Helen Tartar has not only been a patient purveyor and supporter, in every sense, of my own work. She has been the very earth of dedication in the English-speaking world to the mega-experiments of contemporary critical theory over the past quarter-century. It is, then, in gratitude for her relentless intellectual creativity and leadership and her unstinting personal generosity, and in cognizance of the many edifying editorial partnerships in which I've been fortunate to participate, that I dedicate *Idylls of the Wanderer* to her.

Acknowledgments

I am grateful to the Art Museums of San Francisco for their gracious permission to reproduce as the cover art to the present volume Vija Celmins's *December, 1984*, of which I was first made aware by Tamara Sussman.

The following chapters first appeared in the pages of other publications as articles:

"On the Butcher Block: A Panorama of Social Marking" (Chapter 2), in *New Centennial Review*, 4 (2004).

"The Afterlife of Judaism: The Zohar, Benjamin, Miller" (Chapter 6), in *Provocations to Reading*, ed. Barbara Cohen and Dragan Kujundzic (New York: Fordham University Press, 2005). A close variant of this chapter also appeared in *Actualities of Aura*, ed. Dag Petersson and Eric Steinskog (Svanesund, Sweden: Northern Summer University Press, 2005).

"Modernist Night: Distortion, Regression, and Oblivion in the Fiction of Bruno Schulz" (Chapter 7), in *Bruno Schulz: New Documents and Interpretations*, ed. Czeslaw Prokopczyk (New York: Peter Lang, 1999).

These publications and their editors have my sincere gratitude, first in disseminating my writings and then in allowing them to be gathered in *Idylls of the Wanderer*.

ONE

Idylls of the Wanderer

And when, after finishing his work in the shed, the coachman went across the courtyard in his slow, rolling walk, closed the huge gate, and then returned, all very slowly, while he literally looked at nothing but his own footprints in the snow [*in Betrachtung seiner eigenen Spur im Schnee*]—and finally shut himself into the shed; and now as all the electric lights went out too—for whom should they remain on?—and only up above the slit in the wooden gallery still remained bright, holding one's wandering gaze for a little [*der Spalt in der Holzgallerie hell blieb und den irrenden Blick ein wenig festhielt*], it seemed to K. as if at last those people had broken off all relations with him, and as if now in reality he were freer than he had ever been [*als sei er nun freilich freier als jemals*], and at liberty to wait here in this place, usually forbidden to him, as long as he desired, and had won a freedom such as hardly anybody else had ever succeeded in winning, and as if nobody could dare to touch him or drive him away, or even speak to him; but—this conviction was at least as strong—as if at the same time there was nothing more senseless, nothing more hopeless, [*gleichzeitig nichts Sinnloseres, nichts Verzweifelteres*] than this freedom, this waiting, this inviolability [*diese Unverletzlichkeit*].[1]

The passage from Kafka's *The Castle* not only marks a transition in the protagonist's relation to the village he will haunt but never quite join; it is emblematic of the outsider's status among the collectivities to which he belongs, of the fictive character's exaggerated situation of detachment, of the writer's status as an outsider, of the unique combination of freedom and constraint attending this position, and of the bizarre hybrid of exhilaration and depression that this bearing or posture occasions. The novel places this figment of its own impossibility and belabored deliberation in a position that can only be described as untenable. K. has been summoned to the village for motives that are unclear and by agency that cannot quite be determined in order to perform a surveying task—the work of critics, journalists, and photographers as well as of engineers—whose need is by no means certain. The novel has thus commissioned K. not only to follow in the paths of so many characters and protagonists before him, going back to Don Quixote and beyond, whose movement and encounters supply the text in which he figures with a motive and framework. It has designated him as the exemplary outsider, the outsider of outsiders, the character theoretically and explicitly assuming the burdens—and license—of the outside figured and dramatized by writing, of the outside somehow inveigled in the very impulse to and occasion for inscription. K. descends from the likes of Poe's Man of the Crowd, Melville's Bartleby, Dostoyevsky's Underground Man, and Nietzsche's Wanderer.

Kafka invests the figure of K. in this scene with nothing less than auratic fascination. The electric lights may have gone out on him, but he is framed by the openness of the courtyard. The slit in the wooden gallery is not only his diminished visual access to the Herrenhof inn,[2] it is the viewfinder that the novel furnishes in order to keep him in focus, to accentuate his centrality to the visual and conceptual fields. The conditions of the novel unfold from the bittersweet opening that K. encounters. He is "freely freer" than he has ever been before, but any relation between himself and the village or its inhabitants has been "broken." Through K.'s circumstance of whimsical but lonely detachment, readers experience the sociocultural and writerly conditions making the novel possible. K. mirrors the writer's solitary stance, which serves as the novel's precondition, its framework. It is when he is outside the Herrenhof in the snow, before he has entered the sociological negotiations that will, in effect—by determining his working conditions and communal activities—define his putative or fictional role, that he most embodies the openness and emptiness out of which his tale can be told and the novel written.

The outside that is K.'s native land and the premise upon which much of the succeeding fictive invention relies are both familiar and forbidding. The exclusion that they betoken, whether imposed or self-administered, is figured in the coldness of the winter landscape. But there is something calming and reassuring in this distance, the detachment of the writer, the critic, as well. A distinctive comfort attends keeping a distance from all communal and familial complexities and trivialities in the name and interest of rendering commentary and judgment. The writer projects himself outside in order to write; his script configures itself in part as the strokes and caresses of self-engendered consolation and comfort. The words, phrases, marks, and subverbal elements that the writer discovers in the course of the compositional process seem to issue from an outside. They are strange, often unheard of, unprecedented. Yet there could be nothing more private, secret, sequestered, *internal* than the place from which the phrases emanate. Writing continually figures the oracular source of its articulations as a New World, an outside, a setting apart, an extraterrestrial satellite or planet, yet these otherworldly messages loop back to a Holy of Holies, a private interior known only to the solitary initiate, a secret spring. The very demarcation of an outside—which we should consider, for purposes of the present investigation, not as a supernatural or divine externality but as a moment, perch, or perspective in the trajectory of writing—the very experience of this outside summons forth a vigorous, renewed appeal to all the mysteries of the inside, whether understood as selfhood, presence, or truth.

Kafka renders the intimacy/disorientation of writing in such exquisite relief that we cannot overlook this initiatory gesture. There are any number of explanatory factors for his indispensability to the projection of the writer's dysfunctional marginality and intimacy. He achieved a stunningly explicit and concrete vocabulary for the writer's placement and invention at a moment of both the culmination and the breakdown of imperial and national hegemonies and administrative systems; of the introduction of invisible and immediate technologies of communication and informational transfer; of the application of the philosophical operating systems of the sublime, dialectics, and the phenomenon to the language of subjectivity and the very conception of the self; and of the reemergence of sexuality, in its polymorphous variants and forms, on the docket of public articulation and deliberation. There was something quite strange and generative about the moment in which Kafka elected to make his scriptural interventions, and he seized the singularity of his instant, his perch, with an unrelenting vigor belying the frailty of his physical constitution. He affords us, then, a marvelously precise glimpse not only of the chilling yet consoling isolation of his wanderers, whether Karl Rossmann of *The Man Who Disappeared* or the K.s of *The Trial* and *The Castle*, but also of the incomprehensible screeching that is the only language that traveling salesman Gregor Samsa, transformed into a monstrous insect, can produce. This is the patois as well of the thinking rodents who burrow through the Kafkan underworld, whose very premise challenges widespread received assumptions regarding the human, the spiritual, the sentient. The writer is not only fated to pay for the linguistic events or surprises that overcome him with isolation, possibly under the onus of social ostracism; he is fated to communicate in a speech that can only be apprehended as weird and inhuman:

> "Oh dear," cried his mother, in tears, "perhaps he's terribly ill and we're tormenting him. Grete! Grete!" She called out then. "Yes, Mother," called his sister from the other side. . . . Did you hear how he was speaking?" "That was no human voice," said the chief clerk in a voice noticeably low beside the shrillness of the mother's. "Anna! Anna!" his father was calling through the hall to the kitchen, clapping his hands, "get a locksmith at once!"[3]

The Kafkan writer, who is not as remote from the nineteenth-century Parisian *flâneur*, the Baudelairean poet, the Benjaminian critic, and the Barthesian semiotician as it might seem, has truly been hit with a double whammy. He is a fictional surrogate temperamentally endowed with the torments of solitude, isolation, and unrelenting disaffection. Linguistically, he has been wired to communicate in a language that no one else can understand. Indeed, in this extract, Kafka links the discovery of Gregor's linguistic incomprehensibility, the first discernible sign of his overall disfiguration, to the plot of the conventional monster narrative. "We're no longer dealing with any human son/sibling," the family, in the guise of the naïfs charged with first encountering the monster, discovers.[4]

Gregor's utterances, once his exceptionality has been given the literal figuration of an oversized beetle carapace, emigrate not only beyond the pale of known languages but outside humanity itself. His language, the most intricate of his human workings, is literally out of this world. Emanating from a creature debilitated by shame, these efforts at standard communication, at convention itself, provoke unrelenting public embarrassment. In the world of Kafka's fiction, the designated writer is imprisoned in a double and complementary respect: by dint of the monstrosity, disfiguration, or other visual insignia of his solitude and exclusion; and by being relegated to a language and an idiom in which no one else can communicate. He imprisons at the same time as he is imprisoned: he embodies the outer reaches of humanity, the limits beyond which personhood cannot stray, and he is incarcerated within the isolating singularity of his private idiom.

The notion of the outside is one of those hopelessly murky constructs—like justice or kindness—on which our basic senses of situation, identity, and propriety feed, but which are inherently damaged. A projection of the outside is a structural buttress against which many—rigorous philosophy would contest all—domains of normality, as they have evolved under Western metaphysics, are founded: presence, selfhood, form, purity, integrity, health, justice, immanence, intuition, communion, community, persistence, fate, futurity. Each of these notions is rooted in an implied experiential scene that cannot even be imagined, let alone invoked, in the absence of inside/outside markers. Even the terms with which we characterize the centrality of these core metaphysical terms—saying they are "integral," "basic," "unavoidable"—rely on the outside as the framework, buttress, *Gestell*,[5] upon and within which they operate.

Perhaps because of this familiarity, centrality, and pervasiveness, which make the outside something like a major donor or civic booster within the community of Western values, it is a fundament of the conceptual operating system under serious architectural stress. Louis Althusser cannot formulate the structuration and impact of ideology except in terms of its relations of interiority and exteriority, both to disinterested critique and to itself. The relations of uncritical espousal and disavowal prompted by ideology project a panorama of spatial parallaxes or optical illusions:

> What really takes place in ideology seems therefore to take place outside it. That is why those who are in ideology believe themselves by definition outside ideology: one of the effects of ideology is the practical *denegation* of the ideological character of ideology by ideology: ideology never says, "I am ideological." It is

necessary to be outside ideology, i.e., in scientific knowledge, to be able to say: I am in ideology (a quite exceptional case) or (the general case): I was in ideology. As is well known, the accusation of being in ideology only applies to others, never to oneself. . . . Which amounts to saying that ideology *has no outside* (for itself), but at the same time *that it is nothing but outside* (for science and reality).⁶

Ideology, in Althusser's parlance, can only express and realize itself in a rhetoric of mutually exclusive interior and exterior compartments. There are, in other words, performative effects of the figurative language of belonging and not-belonging through whose mediation ideological discourse scores its fundamental definitions and limits. The almost unavoidable rhetoric of spatial boundaries, to which ideology reverts in its figurative underpinnings, segues seamlessly into the spirited adversarial posturing of political partisanship.

It is not by accident that the notion of a virtual and operative outside, whether appealed to explicitly or implicitly, relatively more concretely or more figuratively, reverberates throughout Derrida's position papers for a deconstructive project. In demanding that deconstruction question starkly binary logic, among an interrelated complex of metaphysical constructs inherited from Western philosophy, Derrida required from the outset a conceptual space lending itself more to the finessing and leverage of spatial boundaries than to their reinforcement. A preponderant portion of the thought to whose decentering and destabilization Derrida addressed himself, thought-work that arrived at historical progressions and patent logical distinctions, was deep-rooted in the spatial compartmentalization apparent in Althusser's basic ideological formulations.

It is not by chance that, at the outset of his deep-seated and polymorphous project, Derrida felt impelled to address this issue of the spatial provenance of writing, its putatively immanent or extrinsic dimensions. As he himself recounts in later work, in essays such as "Ulysses Gramophone" and "A Silkworm of One's Own,"⁷ Derrida emerged from the marginality of an Algerian, Marrano, Judeo-Islamic background into a long and rigorous apprenticeship at the heart of the French intellectual and cultural scenes: with the guiding lights of French philosophy, criticism, and literature, on and off the faculty of the École Normale Supérieure. Derrida took considerable pains, in advance, to survey and announce the impact of his writing and literature-inflected project on the prevailing conceptual paradigms of his moment.

It is in the immediate context of his tribute to / leave-taking from linguistics that he formulates some of his memorable early articulations of the aporias of the inside/outside as they relate to language. "The Outside Is the Inside," Derrida declares at the head of a memorable section in his extended methodological introduction to *Of Grammatology*.[8] He arranged in this work a counterpoint between an exposé of the vestigial humanism persisting in the prevalent *sciences humaines*, skewing their field of vision, and a critique of structuralism's instrumental and thematic assumptions regarding language. One could argue that, of the trio of books Derrida orchestrated in 1967—the others being *Speech and Phenomena*, his extrapolation for a general audience of the implications of Husserlian phenomenology to contemporary intellectual issues and practices,[9] and *Writing and Difference*, an exportation of deconstructive perspectives to a wide range of cultural scenes of writing, including psychoanalysis, theatricality, the Judaic, and literature in general[10]—*Of Grammatology* takes on the role of deconstruction's early comprehensive "impact study." It posits a direct connection between the repugnance to language's less inspirational, edifying, and illuminating effects in Rousseauian ideology and certain of the blindspots limiting the perspicacity of contemporary structuralism and linguistics. This work culminates in the painful as well as clarifying gesture of taking Claude Lévi-Strauss, the venerable cultural anthropologist and reigning icon of the French intellectual world, to task for the condescension toward anthropological subjects and for the ethnocentrism in his own classic studies, made possible by Rousseauian scenarios of natural human sympathy, sensibility, and pity. *Of Grammatology*'s brash announcements of a rigorous deconstructive approach to the roles of language and literature in philosophy thus result in a double indemnity: discrediting two mainstays of French cultural identity, pride, and conceptual practice separated by half a dozen generations—Rousseau and Lévi-Strauss.

It is the very specificity with which the modern social science of linguistics, itself arising, to some degree, in the tradition common to Rousseau and Lévi-Strauss, treats the structural, functional, and cultural dimensions of language that enables Derrida to extrapolate and critique some of the West's dimensional assumptions and assertions regarding this medium. Derrida discerns in Ferdinand de Saussure's foundational *Course in General Linguistics* (1909) a compartmentalization of an even more venerable provenance between the outside and inside of language.[11] Derrida's initial survey of the breadth and impact of logocentrism gravitates to such Saussurian formulations as the following: "Language does have an . . . oral tradition that is independent of writing" and "Language and writing are two distinct systems of signs: the second exists for the sole purpose of representing the first."[12] "Has it ever been doubted that writing was the clothing of speech? For Saussure it is even a garment of perversion and debauchery, a dress of corruption and disguise, a festival mask that must be exorcised, that is to say, warded off, by the good word."[13] Indeed, the consummate product of Derrida's investigations into Husserlian transcendental psychology and its linguistic implications, supplemented by intense readings across the range of Western philosophy, is a reversal of the customary division of labor, which makes writing an instance of language. On the contrary, insists Derrida: language owes its full potential to the discriminations and dissonances traced by writing, the poetically constituted cultural medium irreducible to the pronouncements of ideology or the strictures of morality. "Let us ask in a more intrinsic and concrete way, how language is not merely a sort of writing. . . . Or rather . . . let us ask how language is a possibility founded on the general possibility of writing."[14]

Derrida's comment about the compartmentalization to which Saussure resorts in order to sustain the Western quarantine of the unsanctioned scriptoral accidents and insults of language betrays a good deal of the potential he finds in a theoretically astute reworking of language's spatial field:

> The meaning of the outside was always present within the inside, imprisoned outside the outside, and vice versa.
>
> Thus a science of language must recover the *natural*—that is, the simple and original—relationships between speech and writing, that is, between an inside and an outside. It must restore its absolute youth, and the purity of its origin, short of a history and a fall which would have perverted the relationships between outside and inside.[15]

It's not that outside and inside are entirely dispensable categories. Too much hinges upon them. (We will return soon to the Derridean figure of the hinge.) A rigorous examination of these boundaries will of course reveal that they are powerfully interpenetrating, imbricated, invaginated in each other. These lines derive from the outset of Derrida's address to dialectical situations in general. Instead of reinforcing the tradition of polarization, separation, and purification instated by philosophy's battery of logical implements, Derrida highlights the ironic reversal between putatively counterpoised categories or compartments. By insisting on the congenital difficulty, and to some degree absurdity, of the spatial compartments that metaphysics offers as an unavoidable way of expressing conceptual and linguistic relationships, Derrida throws a wrench into linguistics' aspirations, akin to those entertained by logical analysis, to a neat and edifying readout of language's properties and capabilities. In this passage, history and the built-in Western teleological scenario of a fall serve as the bad guys, queering the possibility of a limpid and unproblematical language. It is perhaps not excessive to speculate that, in light of future work, including "Ulysses Gramophone," had Derrida been pressed to specify which fall he was referring to, he might well have specified the fall of Babel, the fall from transparent language into many local variants, all fraught with a contingency also celebrated in Joyce's *Finnegans Wake*, rather than the moral and existential falls specified in Genesis 1–4. The amazing diversity of languages and the investigation, in Genesis and other core texts of Western theology, of the exasperations of their interlinguistic translation, furnish Derrida's "Des Tours de Babel" with its occasion.[16] The present study, while grounded in the always-shifting and emergent optical illusion of an outside, takes its cue from Derrida's seminal skepticism, important to so many fields, intellectual investigations, and writers, of any spatial boundaries or categories of an a priori, essential, iterable, or other than contextual nature.

Derrida not only subjects the interior and exterior of spaces of language to a rigorous investigation, he builds his grammatological alternative to this deployment of language within the cultural division of labor—one so deeply traditional as to have achieved invisibility in many quarters—upon this architecture. He supplements the traditional notion of language as a divinely sanctioned medium or mediator between upper and lower realms, endowed with characteristics perfectly fitted to inherent human perceptual and cognitive capacities, with the figure of language as an irreducible trace indifferent to and autonomous from the metaphysical "spin" that cultures inevitably impose on it. The difference between the Derridean infrastructures that have been so meticulously assembled and extrapolated by Rodolphe Gasché[17]—among them the arche-trace, but also including *différance* itself, the supplement, and the margin—and the appropriation of language for spiritual and metaphysical purposes performed by the likes of Plato, Hegel, and Saussure is precisely this: the infrastructures of deconstruction are immanent to linguistic process itself, bear the imprint of specific usages and contexts, and therefore resist extrapolation into linguistic laws that themselves encapsulate the spiritual/ideological biases of the Western tradition. Derrida, just as he embarks on a constellation of infrastructures, or key tropes, whose primary effect will be resistance to the pervasive urges to codify and constrain language with the pieties of religion and morality, the violence of political ideology, and the positivism of naïve science and disciplined learning, lights upon the figure of the hinge (*la brisure*, a substantive linked to the French verb for breaking) to characterize spatial relations within the system and between it and its grammatological investigation.

A hinge embodies a fluctuating pattern of falling in and out of the traditional terms and images, whether "justice" or the inside/outside distinction itself, that have conditioned Western (and non-Western) thought.

> Writing can never be thought under the category of the subject; however it is modified, however it is endowed with consciousness or unconsciousness, it will refer, by the entire thread of its history, to the substantiality of a presence unperturbed by accidents, or to the identity of the selfsame [*le propre*] in the presence of self-relationship. And the thread of that history clearly does not run within the borders of metaphysics. . . .
>
> Spacing as writing is the becoming-absent and the becoming-unconscious of the subject. By the movement of its drift/derivation [*dérive*] the emancipation of the sign constitutes in return the desire of presence. That becoming—or that drift/derivation—does not befall the subject which would choose it or would passively let itself be drawn along by it. As the subject's relationship with its own death, this becoming is the constitution of subjectivity. On all levels of life's organization, that is to say, of the economy of death. . . .
>
> Within the horizontality of spacing, which is in fact the precise dimension I have been speaking of so far . . . it is not even necessary to say that spacing cuts, drops, and causes to drop within the unconscious: the unconscious is nothing without this cadence and before this caesura. . . . This hinge [*brisure*] of language as writing, this discontinuity, could have, at a given moment within linguistics, run against a rather precious *continuist* prejudice.[18]

I cite at length this passage, on a "cadence" and a "caesura" between the "inside" and the "outside" of the fundaments of Western metaphysics occasioned by writing's spacing—implemented by the figure of the hinge—because it is indicative of both the breadth of interrelated core concepts and the momentous nature of the issues that Derrida is willing to entertain and splice together in this foundational phase of his project. These lines assign a preeminent importance to the dimension of space and to the negotiations of spacing within the philosophy of writing. Derrida is surely not in denial regarding the philosophical centrality of notions of time and temporality. Indeed, delay and deferral are from the outset dimensions and effects of *différance*, and historical schemes and evolutions are often experienced by Western metaphysics as corruptions of its originary scenes of founding and sanctification. But as the passage suggests, space, as in Heideggerian Being, maintains a privileged role in the deconstructive survey of writing's suppression and sustained potential destabilizing effects.

In light of the marked specialization in the theoretical field that has taken place since 1967, a specialization prompted, if nothing else, by the sheer volume of discourse that models such as deconstruction and Lacanian psychoanalysis have elicited, the easy transition between the spacing that Derrida imagines for a writing underscoring language's contingency and poetic arbitrariness and the lacunae in an unconscious of a certain psychoanalytical derivation may seem striking today. Yet Derrida does not hesitate to extrapolate, during his grammatological moment, the psychoanalytical implications of a logocentrism, a grand cultural sublimation of linguistic discrimination: in the wake of this correction, we can think of the subject only as a stabilized figment of writing, not the reverse. In the above passage, it becomes possible to think of the inevitable cultural fluctuations between the metaphysics of presence, in which language is a communicative subaltern, and the "language's eye view" brought into focus by writing as the "lapses" or "absences" that happen to consciousness or that, in a psychoanalytical idiom, betray the workings of an unconscious. Also in this passage, Derrida links absences in consciousness (to which the swings outward toward writing are akin) to the hidden instinct, the thirst for death or death-drive that Freud was able to fully acknowledge only in the aftermath of World War I.[19]

In keeping with the *Auseinandersetzung* or coming to terms with Heideggerian ontology that Derrida is undertaking in this epoch, it is telling here that any realization or development effected by the emergence of writing as the informing dynamic of language and culture is characterized not as a "becoming" or "coming into Being" but as "drift/derivation [*dérive*]." For reasons apparent in such essays as "Différance" and "*Ousia* and

Grammē,"[20] in his discourse of this moment characterizing the subordination of ideology to the accidents of language, Derrida is substituting an idiom of writing-immanent movement (threading, dropping, stopping and starting, Mallarméan pulsation, beating, dancing, and swerving) for the rhetoric of recurring to or emerging from Being or the essence. A subtle and elaborate conceptual dance enables Derrida to thread his hybrid discourse of writing between such blockages or obstacles as the exigencies of the Freudian subject (whose philosophical history runs at least as far back as Plato) and the understated implied essentialism persisting in Heideggerian ontology.

The figural destination of this major recalibration of rhetorical as well as conceptual torques or drifts effected by early deconstruction is the hinge. If this figure is fitted out to *break* the prevalent Western momentums or gravitations to presence, subjectivity, spirituality, and moral as well as epistemic purity, it performs this function through a movement no more momentous than swinging. The hinge is the possibility of an intermittent and recurrent release from the strictures of Western metaphysics, possible only on the basis of a meticulous reading that discloses the rhetorico-conceptual foundations of ideological constriction. To the degree that there is a fluidity and freedom to the action of an ultra-sensitive exegetical spring-mechanism, the figure of the hinge implements a *release* of the spatial categories or compartments determining such parameters as "outside" or "inside." Yet the release from this thinking, this encomium to deploying spatial categories in the performance of cultural exegesis only with the utmost rigor and responsibility, still draws upon the possibility of the outside and the figure of the outsider.

One marginal aside, a footnote really, to this section. Derrida—as his own vast writerly production occasionally placed him in a position to define and account for himself, and in spite of the considerable mindfulness and sensibility he lent to the serious consequences of our everyday and common impulse to think and express in terms of inside/outside categories—often described his own adventure and development in terms of his having been, always and everywhere, an outsider. It was thus possible for Jacques Derrida—who so brilliantly and generatively exposed the profound stakes in one of philosophy's and everyday usage's expressive gut-reactions, to speak in terms of insides and outsides of situations—to experience himself as the quintessential outsider. In the interview that Maurizio Ferraris conducts in *A Taste for the Secret*, Derrida identifies himself as an outsider to family:

> I do not identify myself with a linguistic community, a national community, a political party, or with any group or clique whatsoever, with any philosophical or literary school. "I am not one of the family" means: do not consider me "one of you," "don't count me in," I want to keep my freedom, always: this, for me, is the condition not only for being singular and other, but also for entering into relation with the singularity and freedom of others. . . . The fact is that I have a predisposition to being not one of the family, it wasn't just my choice. I am a Jew from Algeria, from a certain type of community, in which belonging to Judaism was problematic, belonging to Algeria was problematic, belonging to France was problematic, etc. So this all predisposed me to not-belonging; but, beyond the particular idiosyncrasies of my own story, I wanted to indicate the sense in which an "I" doesn't have to be "one of the family."[21]

Being Jacques Derrida, whether the man or the writer—although it may well be that the man existed only as the writer or as the collation of texts—is inimical to belonging, to belonging even to the most fundamental and *natural* unit, the family. It is not difficult for Derrida to find words for his congenital outsideness and estrangement to all belonging. He seems to pursue and be pursued by this surface tension in relation to others wherever he wanders. We might imagine that, being a consummate writer, whose most important hours were consumed by reading and writing, Derrida would at least find commonality with his linguistic community, with his fellow readers and writers of French. Yet as the interview proceeds, he takes explicit issue with this alternative as well:

> My signature is the moment of highest responsibility in a deep irresponsibility. When I say that, basically, I write for those with whom I share a language, culture, place, home, it is not a question of "belonging" to communities, of property or ownership, because I would say about language what I have just said about the signature. French, for example, is "my" language, I have no others, but at the same time it is radically foreign to me—it does not "belong" to me, it is not my property. It is to this extent that "I have my" idiom. Place, family, language, culture, are not my own. There are no places that "belong." . . . I know perfectly well that I write on the basis of my age, culture, family, language, but my relation to these seemingly communal structures is one of expropriation, of disownership. I no more belong to these things than they belong to me; my point of departure is there where this belonging has broken.[22]

It is ironic in the most productive sense that the writer who did, on a conceptual level, by dint of meticulous philosophically driven readings, the most to "out" the multifaceted violence performed by Western metaphysics's "inside" and "outside" boundaries, definitions, and thresholds defined his sphere of operation and his relations to his inevitable social environment only in terms of a consistent not-belonging. This irony, a creative and generative one, is an exemplary initial stepping-stone for the present study. The notion or sense of the outside is compromised from the very outset. Its parameters, location, orientation, and perspective are questionable from the start. They crumble upon any rigorous testing.

Yet the outside occupies a certain place within the dynamic of the compositional process, which was, in the end, the only way in which Derrida could couch his existence, activity, and impact. The outside is a shifting margin or window "within" the compositional process itself. It may well be an optical illusion, but it is also a delusion, the very margin for the de-concealment of unknown and unanticipated language, indispensable to writing. Without this provisional and always-shifting prospect or margin, writing cannot transpire, it cannot meander its way into thinking and being. The outside is at best a moving target. When it briefly flits into our sights, it is highly contingent and arbitrary. The current project will fulfill itself if it can occasionally, in the context of several writers themselves captivated by inscription, catch sight of the opening of the outside, particularly as it allows some of their distinctive productions to come into language.

To invoke the outside at all is to acknowledge that the outside inscribes itself only as that which has too many sides, for its good and our own. The outside presents "more sides than a seal."[23] Its multiple dimensions morph into one another without in any way marking the transitions. In this respect, the outside comprises a loose and uncanny Moebius strip, with related yet jarring features, one that even meanders into "the life of things,"[24] into "the heart of the heart of the country."[25]

Yet impossible as the figure of the outside inevitably is, cultural articulation and inscription are stymied in the absence of its possibility, projection, invasion, and intervention. It shares a significant share of its logical and figurative traits, then, with the deity of the Abrahamic religions. As slippery as the outside may be, Western mythology, religion, and visual and pictorial representation don't get "off the ground" without its play and intercession.

It can be said that the moment when we launch into writing, when an aimless, interconnected, and unbounded tangle of phrases, remarks, introjections, and ejaculations crystallize as we go about our lives and thinking, is the cross between an accident and a miracle.[26] The ensuing artifact is fated never to get over the happening, the event, that serves as the inevitably occulted pretext for the writing project to follow. The utterly arbitrary and unannounced moment of inscription is invariably an encounter with the outside, its incursion within a context or region, whatever the outside may be. We experience the outside that sets us to writing as freshness, a surprise, a discovery, but this is merely one facet of one of the outside's dimensions, the phenomenological.

If the truth be told, the outside is a surface, a membrane, a shell, a husk, a skin—in Derrida's memorable reading of Mallarmé, a hymen—but also a boundary, bourne, border, perimeter, limit, and also a margin, an abyss, a netherworld, a frontier to which the threatening, alien, or untoward may be ascribed. Sociologically, it configures itself as the gateway of toleration and acceptance. It is the possibility of ethno-racial profiling, discrimination, exclusion, deportation, genocide, but also, then, of "Immigration and Naturalization."

Contemporary critical theory's half-century journey has gone for naught if we do not understand and acknowledge that the prototype for entrance into / exclusion from various communities, for naturalization into a country, religious conversion, declaration of political, institutional, or gender affiliation, is inculcation into a language or languages. The acquisition of languages not only entails the discriminations and obstacles involved in the mastery of a national or regional tongue, in achieving maturity in that language, which amounts to coordinating a range of arbitrary specifications emanating from the grammatical, semantic, syntactical, and dialectical registers joining that speaking community. Language acquisition and mastery also highlight the unavoidable tension along the continuum leading from the sanctioned, public (and hence collatable, codifiable, standardized) meanings and values of the elements of language to the highly individuated, personal nuances people attach to signifiers by dint of their irreducibly singular experience and (semiological as well as psychological) associations.

So only the briefest of intervals, the way we do business in the West, lies between the metaphysical intuition of inside/outside articulations, those marked, at the microlinguistic level, by prepositions, and the structure of national and communal institutions. Citizenship and membership in religions, the processes of emigration, immigration, conversion, and exile, derive their specific character and "delivery" from the construct of the outside, which is not only cognized but intuited, sensed, and perceived. The outside occupies a privileged place in those fields and disciplines devoting their attention to the components and gradations of experience. Experiments on the thresholds of sound, light, and touch still occupy a prominent place in the subfield of psychology known as perception and in cognitive science, itself arranged on the interface between philosophy, linguistics, experimental psychology, and computer science. The possibility of the outside thus becomes the possibility for the very discourse, let alone science, of experience.

Indeed, the crystallizing subject of sociology, the science of society, may well be the boundaries around and between different communities of language users and operators, as well as within the language operator himself. As I have elsewhere elaborated, from a sociological point of view the drama of art is the tension it stages between the highly individuated, personally inflected language of the artist and/or fictional or poetic surrogates and the patois of a more broadly understood and used communal or local idiom.[27] Protagonists of novels not only negotiate a barrage of states or categories generated along legal, class, ethnic, gender, and racial lines, they swerve back and forth between linguistic contexts or neighborhoods at relatively greater or lesser extremes of singularity. The artifact may not resolve the tension between the irreducibly idiosyncratic and institutionalized dimensions of linguistic expression, but it always stages the drama. Aesthetics, then, as I've argued, is as much a purview on the shifting borderline between individuated and public expression at specific moments of cultural configuration as it is the study of various genres constituted according to formal specifications. The artist is anything but an outsider. His practice transpires only within the parameters of a contractual understanding: of the contemporary issues or terms still up for grabs or at stake in aesthetic dramatization; of the margin of activity accorded to artistic intervention at the moment; of the extreme outer linguistic limits of what public expression or deliberation will sustain. From this contractual perspective, at least since the Romantic epoch, the artist in the West has been more of a negotiator of the extremes and limits between personal and public expression, between linguistic idiosyncrasy and normativity, or between the deviance or sociability of language than the intuitive "original genius" conjured for the Enlightenment by Kant. Never entirely outside the fold, then, the artist who has presided over the broader modernity has been intensely involved in surveying inside/outside boundaries.

The centrifugal/centripetal tension engulfing the social subject is for Georg Simmel one of the fundaments of sociology:

> Sociable man, too, is a peculiar phenomenon; it exists nowhere except in sociable relations. On the one hand, man has here cast off all objective qualifications of his personality. He enters the form of sociability equipped only with the capacities, attractions, and interests with which his pure human-ness provides him. On the other hand, however, sociability also shies away from the entirely subjective and purely inward spheres of his personality. Discretion, which is the first condition of sociability in regard to one's dealing with others, is equally much required in one's dealings with oneself: in both cases its violation causes the sociological art form of sociability to degenerate into sociological naturalism. One thus may speak of the individual's upper and lower *"sociability thresholds."*[28]

In this passage Simmel characterizes human social participation as a negotiation between the "upper" and "lower" limits of sociability. We might generally define sociability as the compromises or trade-offs the individual is willing to make in payment for the price of admission to his particular social sphere or spheres. Sociability constitutes itself as the overall readiness to engage in social interactions; among other items, its shopping list surely includes amiability, politeness, and discretion. In Simmel's own terms, sociability is quite specifically the result of an exchange. It is the product of the axiom "that each individual should *offer* the maximum of sociable values (of joy, relief, liveliness, etc.) that is compatible with the maximum of values he himself *receives*."[29] Yet this exchange of "sociable values" that is Simmel's version of the social contract is possible only against a backdrop of dramatic design and aesthetics. Getting along well in society is tantamount, in the above passage, to an "art form." The breakdown of the constructed scene of amiability in which social connections, deals, and exchanges are made while humiliations and other indignations are avoided is "sociological naturalism," something sounding, in its particular context, like "the law of the jungle." In Simmel's scenario, the exchanges and constructs of sociability become the law of the social interior, the safe zone in which the norms of mutual oversight, protection, support, and sanction prevail.

From within the framework of Simmel's overarching perspective on society, his aspirations to synthesizing its laws, the misfits who have somehow skirted the conventions and protections of amiability are still in intense rapport with the community; they have not been marginalized into a state of terminal outsideness:

> The isolated man does not suggest a being that has been the only inhabitant of the globe from the beginning. For his condition, too, is determined by sociation, even though negatively. The whole joy and the whole bitterness of isolation are only different reactions to socially experienced influences. Isolation is interaction between two parties, one of which leaves, after exerting certain influences. The isolated individual is isolated only in reality, however; for ideally, in the mind of the other party, he continues to live and act.[30]

The sociological treatment of the outsider is no more simplistic and rooted in binary logic than the philosophical or the literary. Indeed, Simmel's scenario of the *isolato* and the community reaches toward the poignancy achieved by that other great allegory of sociopolitical relationships, Hegel's "Lordship and Bondage" passage.[31] The outsider is he who has left, or never arrived, but not without leaving a mark. In this case, it is the social roster or register that serves as a tablet for inscription, not a history or narrative. But the outsider is a trace element who delivers further traces; however mythical and involuted his status may be, he joins in the inscriptive process of culture. Indeed, he is the very locus and focal point of this process. Culture is the exchange between outsiders who leave traces and the community of readers who take them in and interpret them.

In the domain of sociology as well as that of critical theory, the outsider is the deviant or the scapegoat who assures the effectiveness of the norm on the interior, however it happens to be defined. This point reiterates itself in different contexts in Howard S. Becker's classic *Outsiders: Studies in the Sociology of Deviance*.[32] And yet, I would argue, the outsider's deviance, in the world of critical as well as social discourse, is less one of substance than of *perspective*. The outsider threatens and transforms less by virtue of what he does than what he highlights. He functions as a mobile visual viewfinder importing the intransigent, the inadmissible, and the unacknowledged into the field of vision. His crime is invariably foregone even if unknown. The outsider has incriminated himself, if by nothing else, through his links to unwanted images.

It is no accident, then, that the dramatic stage and its conventions are among the pervasive tropes in twentieth-century sociology, brought to apotheosis, perhaps, in Erving Goffman's frame-specific analyses of productive and dysfunctional social interactions. For Goffman, the dynamic in which situation-specific actors remain in role while they collectively perform a task or negotiate a predicament, at the same time being observed and evaluated by an audience, is hardly limited to the theater. This process is the model for structured interaction throughout society, whether it assumes the form of optimal public cooperation between restaurant employees, shuttling back and forth between the kitchen and the tables they serve, or between the "insiders" and the "outsiders" at a political convention. Goffman imagines a social sphere in which "interaction rituals" transpire less as an island surrounded by an exterior than as a panorama of backdrops in which social action in one situation can morph into audience participation in the next.[33] Social experience is a fluctuation between staying in role within the context furnished by a particular "frame" and joining the audience, between being an actor and an observer, being "inside the action" or somewhere else, being in the "back room" or the adjoining corridor.[34]

Social experience meanders through so many different kinds of settings as to justify Goffman's intense scrutiny of frames, the situational determinants specific to different interactions. The social situation you—cast in the detached position of an observer—are observing is impenetrable to you, argues Goffman, until you have a clear picture of the frame in which the event transpires. The time and care that Goffman devotes to the specific context, boundaries, and perspective attaching to a wide range of social theaters—encompassing, for example, industry, education, and the military—results in a sensibility closely akin to the wisdom of intense drama criticism or speech-act theory. Like its dramatic analogon, the sociological theater invoked by Goffman is a bounded space. "Onstage" action and reality are nuanced considerably by what goes on offstage. Indeed, one way of describing the development of theatrical technology over the millennia is as the history of access to offstage action. The very possibility of sociological observation is configured through insider/outsider shifts in the status of actors and observers. Like the writer, the sociologist is distinguished and stigmatized by the distance, or "outsideness" of his perspective. The sociologist is a descendent of the writer by way of scientific protocols of human observation introduced during the nineteenth century's rapid advances in administrative organization and social surveillance and control.[35]

When one is engaged in an extended project of writing, the features of experience are so intensely pitched that it would not be far-fetched to declare writing to be a distinctive ontological state. In keeping with the specter of outsideness, one is either "in" this state or not, "within" the particular condition of mindfulness that attends writing or "outside" its parameters. This is an elaborate way of saying that life passes differently when one is writing and when one is not. While I suppose that one does not have to be "empirically" or "clinically" composing text in order to "enter" the ontological state of writing, the hyperattentiveness to semantics, diction, syntax, and the material features of language demanded in the act of programming language for discourse constitutes a prominent feature in the neighborhood, climate, or ecology of writing.

What a terra incognita we enter when writing conditions existence rather than the reverse! The premium is on assessing the words, on entering an informed partnership with their flow. When writing transpires, the words enunciate themselves to us as much as we "dig them out," and we are not "hearing voices." Only in a state of lurid or uncanny attunement on our part do words announce themselves, make themselves known, as hits or bytes rather than consequential phrases. To live writing is the quest for a setting, nothing as intimate or reassuring as a home, to synthesize a setting that does not entirely mute its resonance, dissonance, *Klang*, or *glas*, which is how words initially articulate themselves, make themselves discernible. The quest for a setting for the words—their rough sequence, their dramaturgy within the abyss of the text—transpires from day to day, over the duration of a writing project. From day to day, when we exist as writers, we render ourselves susceptible to the happening of words; we agonize over the arrangements, among the words themselves and between us and words, that will allow them to instigate thinking in their arbitrariness, surprise, and clangor. Because we and words, whatever our ages, amount to consenting adults, there is a vast range of arrangements that can be worked out between us and telling words, among telling words themselves. The central issue is to arrive at the right, that is, felicitous, arrangement for words. There is by no means a plethora of possible arrangements, though there are no doubt several. The ethics of writing, as it has been explored by Derrida, Miller, and others,[36] accentuates the difficulties in this task of arriving at the right configuration of words, making viable arrangements for the words that have emerged to us because we have submitted to the susceptibilities of writing. The ethics of writing underscores the responsibility and commitment that such compositional arranging demands.

We arrange our lives according to the maximum play and percussion of words, in the interest of maintaining a susceptibility to language and cultural articulation that may well disadvantage us in existential spheres demanding greater socio-economic, functional, and proactive circumspection. This is a far cry from what most psychologists, philosophers, and behavioral scientists mean when they set about characterizing human existence. Susceptibility to words, to the semantic incongruities, systematic setbacks, and existential absurdities that writing occasions, augments our vulnerability on many scores. The extent of projects of cultural programming, the persistence of writing over time, suspends our aggravated vulnerability. Precisely at the point where our susceptibility to words and our vulnerability to the dissonance or *différance* that words drag with them become intolerable, no longer sustainable, we cease and desist from writing.

By the time that Friedrich Nietzsche arrives at programming his *Human, All Too Human: A Book for Free Spirits*,[37] he is aiming at nothing less than a philosophy of the sociocultural configuration or, in Benjamin's terms, constellation of his day.[38] The very project of this work is inconceivable: the philosophy, the most conceptual and systematic working through possible, of a *situation*, a confluence of forces and factors, defined precisely in its contingency and arbitrariness. This is both the most horrendous degradation of philosophy, its corruption by the *actualités* of its moment, and its most formidable and noble possible extension. It is not only the priests, the ultimate social incubator of state religion, who hold a "most comprehensive regard for *all human actuality*,"[39] in that strand of the work aiming for a historico-anthropological account of contemporary institutions, including the courts and the military. In extending philosophy to the pressing concerns of a very finite and specific occasion or moment, the captioning or *Unterschrift*[40] of *Human, All Too Human* takes an omnibus approach to the fields and venues of human achievement and folly. Although a certain nobility or benevolence by which humanity overcomes its predilections for triviality and retribution remains an ongoing ethical horizon of the work, it goes to great pains to demonstrate its involvement in the tangible socio-conceptual conditions composing the pith of human life:

> It is the mark [*Merkmal*] of a higher culture to value the little unpretentious truths which have been discovered by means of rigorous method more highly than the errors handed down by metaphysical and artistic ages and men, which blind us and make us happy. At first the former are regarded with scorn, as though the two things could not possibly be accorded equal rights: they stand there so modest, simple, sober, so apparently discouraging, while the latter are so fair, splendid, intoxicating, perhaps indeed enrapturing. Yet that which has been achieved by laborious struggle, the certain, enduring and thus of significance for any further development of knowledge is nonetheless the higher; to adhere to it is manly and demonstrates courage, simplicity, and abstemiousness. Gradually not only the individual but all mankind will be raised to this manliness, when they have finally become accustomed to valuing viable, enduring knowledge more highly.[41]

Not only does this paragraph underscore the orientation toward a comprehensive overview of *cultural actualities* that will structure so many of *Human, All Too Human*'s specific traits; it condenses a good number of the distinctive tropes and images tantamount to its signature. The work's nobility, the perspective or moral superiority that is the aim or orientation of philosophical meditation, will be achieved by its concern for the "little unpretentious truths which have been discovered by means of rigorous method." The "laborious struggle" not only results in a calm sobriety that is philosophy's distinctive mark, even at the cost of occasional tedium and boredom; the "ship of thought"'s[42] voyage also releases an energy and vitality that are, in the above passage and throughout the treatise, gendered masculine. (I believe that the emphasis in Nietzsche's valuation is more on the release of the life-force from within the moralistic and ideological constraints of civilization than on masculinity. In placing the release of a certain free and active expression of the life-force on the masculine side, Nietzsche is following some of his Indian and Chinese sources.)

The above early passage also condenses some of the work's unique temporal setting. The philosophical struggle that the work at once chronicles, describes, and performs will result in liberation, on a human scale, whose time-posture is futuristic. In appealing to the *eventuality* of culture's rise toward the manly, Nietzsche opens philosophy to the possibility embodied both by the Heideggerian *Ereignis* or happening and the deconstructive event and surprise.[43] Philosophy becomes a *khōra* or domain of the possibility held in abeyance by the institutional outgrowths of Western metaphysics and by the multifaceted ideological restrictions operated at the philological level of language.

Human, All Too Human is a philosophical treatise articulated entirely in the fragments and aphorisms developed into an art form by the German *Frühromantik*. Nietzsche, who may well write at the apogee of stylistic elegance for the entire history of philosophy, surpassing Kierkegaard, upon whose experiments he drew, in concentrated rigor, Heidegger in pointed finality of articulation, and Derrida in the sustained singularity of his writerly voice, claimed for philosophical ends and purposes the new discursive medium put to literary uses by the Schlegels (August, Friedrich, Caroline, and Dorothea), Novalis, Schleiermacher, and Tieck.[44] Nietzsche will place the literary shock whose potential was explored by his German Romantic predecessors at the service of his wide-ranging and interstitial philosophical investigation of the current predicament in which European human animals find themselves.[45] What he says of the maxim, whose tradition he traces back beyond La Rochefoucauld to its sources in classical philosophy and literature, therefore pertains to his own project:

> It was, moreover, by no means accounted easy to say something with true distinctness and lucidity; how else would there have been such admiration [*Bewunderung*] for the epigram of Simonides, which presents itself so plainly [*schlicht*], without gilded figures or witty arabesques but saying what it has to say clearly, with the reposefulness of the sunlight, not the snatching at effects of a flash of lightning. It is because striving toward the light out of an as it were inborn twilight characterizes the Greeks that a cry of rejoicing goes through the people when they hear a laconic maxim, the language of the elegy, the sayings of the Seven Wise Men. That is why the promulgation of laws in verse, which we find so offensive, was so well loved: it represented the actual Apollinian task for the Hellenic spirit of triumphing over the perils of metre, over the darkness and obscurity that otherwise characterizes the poetic. Simplicity, suppleness, sobriety, were *extorted* from the people, they were not inherent in them—the danger

of a relapse into the Asiatic hovered over the Greeks at all times. . . . We see them sink, we see Europe as it were flushed away and drowned—for Europe was very small in those days—but always they come to the surface again [*gute Schwimmer und Taucher wie die sind, das Volk des Odysseus*].[46]

I am certainly not the first to observe the centrality of matters of style, the degree to which the very *manner of writing*, could assert a strategic torque upon the wide-ranging critique of prevalent cultural, sociopolitical, ideological, and theological conditions in Europe undertaken by Nietzsche.[47] The style of cultural inscription is indeed *everything* to a deconstruction of prevailing cultural mores that can only transpire between the lines, in the marginal notations appended by Nietzsche in the persona of the last European man, the ultimate wanderer, shadow, and outsider to the Great Tradition. It one respect, it can only seem crazy that one of the rigorous and erudite philosophers of his age devotes extended passages to the stylistic idiosyncrasies of the likes of Goethe, Sterne, Wieland, and Herder. Yet on closer consideration, style emerges as the only plane from which corrections to the retribution motivating the courts, the hypocrisy engulfing organized religion, and the self-interest pursued by the political parties will issue.

In this passage, Nietzsche appeals to the plain talk, sobriety, and suppleness achieved by Simonides in the classical maxim as ethical values as much as stylistic achievements. Indeed, for all the reproaches of forked and oppressive moralism that the text of *Human, All Too Human* unleashes, at key junctures the work's persona casts its lot inextricably with the promulgation of a sensibility-enhancing morality that we now associate, under the aura of Levinas, with the ethical. The redemptive (if not quite yet messianic) improvement of Europe's cultural and political conditions is tantamount to an upgrading in the style, philological richness, poetry, and inherent drama of its written medium or notation. Indeed, in the above passage, Nietzsche is willing to write off some of the maxim's potential thunder and lightning in the name of its potential rigor and lucidity. The morality of Europe is at one with the ethical quality that can be implanted in the script that Europe secretes. Conditions for the morality of "high style" emerge when "Every word, every idea, wants to dwell *only in its own company*."[48] "To write better, however, means at the same time to think better; continually to invent things more worth communicating, and to be able actually to communicate them; to become translatable into the language of one's own neighbor; to make ourselves accessible to the understanding of those foreigners who learn our language; to assist toward making all good things common property and freely available to the free-minded; and finally, to prepare the way for that still-distant state of things in which the good Europeans will come into possession of their great task: the direction and supervision of the total culture of the earth."[49] A great measure of humanity's capacity to improve its state and ethos hinges on the ability to write better, a task that Nietzsche succeeds in exemplifying throughout much of *Human, All Too Human*. We wince today at Europe's "direction and supervision" of a global "total culture" and need to remind ourselves that these words enter a characterization of a world tangibly improved (in Judaic parlance, redeemed) by the eschatological and ontological (messianic, in the Judaic sphere), of a philosophy scored with exquisite care to its immanent linguistic roots and drift.

Nothing could seem more arbitrary and aesthetic in the whimsical sense than a topical overview of prevalent sociocultural conditions in the latter decades of the nineteenth century, a philosophical treatise calibrated in Schlegelian fragments. The relative brevity of the fragments, ranging from one-liners to three or so pages in length, highlights the combinations possible within and between the chapters, themselves extended compendia of related formulations. I'm suggesting that *Human, All Too Human* (as well as similarly configured works in the Nietzschean canon), although of Romantic provenance in formatting and in the collusion between sublime disinterest, wit, and an irony pervading tone and style, is premodern in its overall gathering into a permutation-generator of perspectives in and formulations of its still-Wagnerian *Leitmotive*: politics, religion, culture, morality, the human condition (always with a view toward the animal), sexuality, and freedom, to the extent that the latter remains possible under ideological constraints. The peculiar language games of Romantic fragmentary style, the poetic prose in which the formulations are couched, furnish the only expression appropriate to the multifarious conditions of modern life. And the fragments, in their culmination, expression, coming, emission also transport the writer closer to the very ur-conditions or deep roots of writing.

In its formal aesthetics, in other words, *Human, All Too Human* anticipates the dimension of modernism that consists in an illustrated generation of new possibilities out of existing premises. This happens again and again in cubist painting, jazz improvisation, and film montage. Under the illumination cast by Nietzsche's literary appropriations and stylistic and generic innovations, we witness, in other words, the interstice at which the philosophy of the event, the surprise, the happening, the future, and therefore of possibility itself joins, in the aesthetic sphere, with modernist experimentation. We learn of modernism, by the same token, that it was as much concerned with surveying and marking possibility as it was with structures, myths, excavations, polymorphous sexuality, and kaleidoscopic variation.

For all its concern with and play upon the philosophical fragment, *Human, All Too Human* is systematic in its purview and denouement. In almost businesslike fashion, it proceeds from the most abstruse and general metaphysical preconditions inflecting the moment ("Of First and Last Things") to the much more tangible implications of political parties and their ideological fingerprints, in "A Glance at the State." Between these two philosophical horizons, which span almost the totality of volume 1, Nietzsche added pointed and arbitrarily closed formulations on the philosophico-ideological conditions of European public life that were his obsessions. He proceeds from the state of contemporary morality to religion, art, its aesthetic simulacrum and replacement, and the play between mainstream and decadent or obverse attitudes in the evolution of culture, and he completes the sequence with meditations on the ethics of sexuality as coalescing around "Woman and Child," a topic that few male philosophers would have the forbearance to broach directly, even in our contemporary world.

Volume 1 of *Human, All Too Human* proceeds, in other words, in businesslike fashion from one thematically linked collation of fragments and brief statements to the next. They are all directed at specific areas of contention in the public sphere of contemporary European culture and dedicated to the linguistico-conceptual disclosure and decontraction of their ideological underpinnings. In many respects, volume 2 announces itself as the earlier segment's shadow. It is divided into only two extended segments, and these are not further subdivided. The first of these, "Assorted Opinions and Maxims," distinguishes itself precisely by the manner in which it scrambles the thematic organization of volume 1. What we find here is instead a potpourri of fragments that segue into one another according to a variety of resonances: rhythmic, tonal, stylistic, as well as substantive. This process of opening up the initial platform for articulation in volume 1 only continues, to the point of poetic hovering and discombobulation, in the ultimate fragment-body, "The Wanderer and His Shadow." The fact that this chapter openly speculates on the future of philosophy as well as on the work's immanent performance only increases the tenuousness of its own speculations, the obscurity of the futuristic haze in which it enshrouds itself. *Human, All Too Human*, by submitting itself to the incertitude and intractability of its own investigation in this section, highlights the features of its own persistence and extension inhering in the process of writing itself. The ultimate revelation of "The Wanderer and His Shadow" may well be the prevailing of the writerly and the possibilities it customarily encompasses at the outer limits of philosophical achievement and protocol. If this imposes any obligation or limit on philosophy, it is to be well—that is poetically, intensely, and surprisingly—written.

From a sheer quantitative point of view, the main part of the performance in *Human, All Too Human* is as frivolous as a contemporary review or feuilleton of the conditions of modern life in philosophical terms. The *sense* of Nietzsche's observations owes as much to the mastery of the conventions of fragmentary discourse as it does to his vocabulary or the substance of his observations. The production or achievement of this long preliminary exercise within the compass of *Human, All Too Human* is nothing more than "Man Alone with Himself" and "The Wanderer and His Shadow." I am suggesting that the end or result of Nietzsche's multiperspectival review of his times is the writer's withdrawal from the sociocultural state of affairs with and about which he has been in communication. The writer's exile from his own writing, the apotheosis of writing's trajectory and potential in the writer's banishment from all he has witnessed and observed, in the writer's metamorphosis into a shadow, is all the more striking given the intense engagement with his immediate cultural surroundings and with human psychology that the persona of *Human, All Too Human* amply and repeatedly demonstrates. The figures of Zarathustra and of the wanderer, invoked at the end of *Human, All Too Human*, may conjure up the sublime distance and detachment enshrouding the poetically expressive philosopher. But the ground they walk on is of an intensely psychological composition, making Nietzsche, even though he avoids the dramatic and narrative scenarios of the case history, a shadow, a secret sharer in the Freudian discoveries of psychoanalysis. Preempting the rift between psychology and rigorous philosophy instituted by the Husserlian critiques of experience and auto-affection, and in a long-standing idiom of conceptual markers rather than personal experiences, Nietzsche demonstrates a close productive collaboration between philosophical tradition and intense psychological and sociological insight.

I want to pause for a moment at the razor-sharp insight, fully equaled by a trenchant manner of expression, manifested by a philosophical writer whose existence ended in a pronounced state of derangement and whose self-selected alter-egos included the two above-mentioned odd and uncanny literary alter-egos. Nietzsche's epigrammatic pronouncements may seem to issue from a domain of sublime and inhuman remoteness, but his intimacy with the very odor of humanity supplies them with their pith and punch.[50] Both the outreach of his insight and the social pain discernible in the background of such acuity reach a crescendo in the chapter "Man in Society," where we encounter, toward the terse extreme of Nietzsche's expression: "*Demanding pity as a sign of presumption.*—There are people who, when they fly into a rage and offend others, demand firstly that it should not be held against them, And secondly that they should be pitied for being subject to such violent paroxysms. Such is the extent of human presumption."[51] Nietzsche's text here reserves the privilege of morally pronouncing on a particular social type, but most noteworthy of all is the terse psychological acuity with which Nietzsche "has" his character.

Nietzsche is no less acute in assessing both the redemption and stumbling blocks afforded by friendship, a crucial element in the human condition elaborated by this work. The poem with which he sums up volume 1 of *Human, All Too Human*, "Among Friends: An Epilogue," is bisected, each brief part culminating with the refrain: "Shall we do this, friends, again, / Amen, and *auf Wiedersehen!*" The abruptness with which the greeting *auf Wiedersehen* truncates the assertion of continuous and repeated amiability between friends graphically demonstrates the treacherous ambiguities of friendship, on which so many of the possibilities for human redemption are staked. It comes as no surprise then that the text, in a slightly more extended arc of statement, takes on the typological challenge posed by the evolutionary peculiarities that result in different modes of friendship:

> Among men who possess a particular gift for friendship two types predominate. One is in a continual state of ascent and for each phase of his development finds a friend precisely appropriate to it. The succession of friends he acquires [*erwirbt*] in this way are seldom at one with one another and sometimes in dissonance [*Mißhelligkeit*] and discord. . . . Such a man may jocularly be *called* a ladder.—The

> other type is represented by him who exercises an attraction on very various talents and characters, so that he gains a whole circle of friends; they, however, establish friendly relations between one another, their differences notwithstanding, on account of being his friend. One can call such a man a *circle*; for in him this solidarity between such different natures and dispositions [*Charaktere und Begabungen*] must in some way be prefigured.—For the rest, the gift of having good friends is in many men much greater than the gift of being a good friend.[52]

In this exposition, Nietzsche not only demonstrates deep psychological insight into the makeup of different psyches, he displays a sense of the social ramifications—in friendship—of the psychological predispositions he has teased out. His distinction between the "ladder" and the "circle" is not only catchy, it sticks. We are most appreciative of this type of characterization when, in a literary context, we encounter it in the narrative of Tolstoy or Proust. But Nietzsche has claimed this intense mindfulness of the dynamics linking psychological to social conditions in crystallizing a philosophical overview of his historico-cultural moment for philosophy.

The fact that we are left alone with the writer and the shadow, or afterimage, of his writing at the end of *Human, All Too Human* suggests a withdrawal from the compositional process itself. The culmination of the polymorphous meditation and its inscription is the throw-away husk or shell (or carapace) of the writer.[53]

> That author has drawn the happiest lot who can say as an old man that all of life-engendering, strengthening, elevating, enlightening thought and feeling that was in him lives on in his writings, and that he himself is now nothing but the grey ashes, while the fire has everywhere been rescued and brought forward.—If one now goes on to consider that not only a book, but every action performed by a human being becomes in some way the cause of other actions, decisions, thoughts, that everything that happens is inextricably knotted to everything that will happen, one comes to recognize the existence of an actual *immortality*, that of motion.[54]

So decisive is the integrity, justice, poetics, and sustained intensity of the writing process itself to the very possibilities of philosophy and cultural criticism that the writer emerges from it as a secondary factor, as the burnt-out residue and slag. He may have been, for a time, a medium for the fire that is not only a figure for vitality and creativity throughout *Human, All Too Human* but far and away the most prevalent literary image in the book, a lexicon that includes a menagerie of animals, insects as well as flowers, odors, and perfumes. But the fires of the life-force and of human invention in *Human, All Too Human* yield the body of the writer as exhausted wastematter as much as they generate a full range of artifacts and institutions. The only possibility for a transcendental persistence in the face of this transformative process, one both demanding and consuming vast reserves of energy, is reserved for motion itself.

The author/philosopher exists primarily as the vessel of the fire out of which his language is forged. The cultural fire or energy concentrating in the author both antedates and survives him. It is a flow motivating the Chinese and Indian systems of medicine and surfacing, among other places in the West, in the writings of Zeno and Heraclitus. It is of little consequence that the author slakes off this dynamic precipitation, emerges as its inert and inorganic residue, for the process itself—whose ultimate format is writing—is decisive to Nietzsche. The only immortality bequeathed by this process inheres not in the artist, the artwork, or the original genius, all subjected to extended debunking throughout *Human, All Too Human*, but in conceptual-compositional motion. This work is dedicated as an extended prayer to the sensational-perceptual-cognitive-phenomenal-writerly motion out of which civilization fashions and endlessly revises itself. If not exactly the priests of this evolution, writers and thinkers are the loners, the outsiders, the homeless ones, those exiled from the various homelands that civilization demarcates. Reduced to waste-product by the fire of his invention, the writer emerges in exile as a stranger to his own writing, to the only home he has managed to fashion. Writers and thinkers crystallize the very terms in which sociopolitical, cultural, and aesthetic organization and development transpire; they furnish an ongoing annotation on the uses and abuses of human civilization, but at the price of planned marginality, of quarantine and relegation to the nonstrategic sector. *Freedom* is the phenomenological and aesthetic dimension in which writers and thinkers experience their systemic marginality, and a tenuous situation this is, for it involves the constant demand of a reformatting and reformulation of actuality. *Human, All Too Human* is as much a chronicle and testament of this difficult freedom as it is a prayer to motion.

If writing is fulfilled, or fulfilling, in the completion of its self-guiding trajectory, this does not amount to the aggrandizement of the author. Indeed, almost in a Buddhist sense—remembering that Nietzsche and Heidegger entertain more openly than deconstruction the supplements to

Western conceptual models dwelling in Eastern religions—the trajectory of *Human, All Too Human* facilitates an embrace of the writer's postinscriptive emptiness.

A treatise on the conditions of modern life entirely set in Romantic fragments effects a transference and a translation of the urban concussions, sensory and informational overload, and offsetting multiple affiliations and commitments of modernity into a prose medium every bit as truncated, discontinuous, arbitrary, and shocking. Such a project is grounded in a direct apprehension of the wear and tear that modernity exacts from its denizens. The fulfillment of the draining task of translation and transcription that Nietzsche takes upon himself in *Human, All Too Human* is nothing less than a direct, if not immediate, communion with the shadow of writing, with the lonely posture that the act of writing demands of its practitioners. The isolation of the shadow of writing is death or peace, in the sense of the Freudian death instinct in *Beyond the Pleasure Principle*, in which the tumultuous process of fragmentary inscription issues. This is tantamount to living in untimely times. The reconciliation with the specter of writing that Nietzsche achieves by writing *Human, All Too Human* is rather a *Schriftstode*, a death in writing, rather than a Wagnerian *Liebestode*.

It is in the figure of the wanderer that thinking's inevitable isolation, with its attendant muses of melancholy, irony, exasperation, and impatience, coincides with writing's marginal critical annotation. Only a spirit endowed with the wanderer's momentum, detachment, and tragicomic disposition rises to the task of cultural inscription, which drains, exhausts, obliterates, and effaces him. It is only toward the end of Nietzsche's astonishingly innovative and productive run as a sane thinker that he can draft the wanderer as his critico-scriptoral alter ego, as the central character in a modern allegory of human realization in an apotheosis of freethinking and dense, theoretically astute, poetically nuanced prose. As Nietzsche constructs the modern-day legend surrounding this figure, on whose shoulders still rests a considerable share of the potential for disinterested, linguistically dynamic criticism within the public sphere, he unleashes a cultural persona whose potentials were seized upon by the contrary outsiders of twentieth-century literature. Kafka's K.s, I would like to suggest, among many other characters, are literary reappropriations of the Nietzschean wanderer, itself made possible by Nietzsche's attention to the philosophical potential of the literary emendations made to discourse by the Schlegels and their *Athenaeum* cohorts. The stranger who, in Jorge Luis Borges's "The Circular Ruin," first attempts a mythological, then a literary act of creating one of his fellow beings, emerges out of nowhere, from the "unanimous night."[55] In the utter groundlessness of this character, Borges takes his cue from William Faulkner, whose Sutpens and carpetbaggers emerge as if from nowhere. Faulkner joins the other odd authors encompassed by the present volume, among them James Joyce, James Baldwin, Bruno Schulz, and Moses ben Shem Tov de Leon, author of the Zohar, whose characters spend years in the wilderness before disappearing into the night. These literary figures not only serve as splendid vehicles for tall stories set amid a fluctuating aimlessness, they serve as indices of the shifting boundaries demarcated and violated by textual production. They are dedicated creatures, if not citizens of the texts in which they meander,[56] the illegitimate siblings of Nietzsche's wanderer.

I cannot overstate the importance of the figure of the wanderer both to the vividness of twentieth-century literary invention, which understood itself as a review of the entire prior tradition, and to the very possibility of memorable and transformational critical commentary.

> He who has attained to only some degree of freedom cannot feel other than a wanderer on the earth—though not as a traveler *to* a worldly destination: for this destination does not exist. But he will watch and observe and keep his eyes open to see what is really going on in the world; for this reason he may not allow his heart to adhere too firmly to any individual thing; within him too there must be something wandering that takes pleasure in change and transience. Such a man will, to be sure, experience bad nights, when he is tired and finds the gate of the town that should offer him rest closed against him; perhaps in addition the desert will, as in the Orient, reach right up to the gate, beasts of prey howl now farther off, now closer to, a strong wind arise, robbers depart with his beasts of burden. Then dreadful night may sink down upon the desert like a second desert, and his heart grow weary of wandering. When the morning sun then rises, burning like a god of wrath, and the gate of the town opens to him, perhaps he will behold in the faces of those who dwell there even more desert, dirt, deception, insecurity than lie outside the gate—and the day will almost be worse than the night.[57]

Nietzsche's wanderer is a denizen of Western metaphysics's apocalyptic night. Yet his inherently anomalous position—free but not absolutely so, oriented, but to "no fixed abode"[58]—affiliates him as well with a Buddhist position of nonattachment. Wandering is the allegorical scenario of becoming.[59] The wanderer's qualification to suffer and endure the night not of negativity but of intensified becoming is precisely his relentlessly intermediate position, his constant slide on the extremes encompassed by a continuum. Marked by the stigmata of freethinking and alterity, the Nietzschean wanderer is spurned at the gates of his native city, in whose stifling intimacy he discovers a violence and disillusionment more stark than the existential insults he has witnessed during his forays on the wild side. A Buddhist of the West, Nietzsche's wanderer is prone to intense suffering—the dislocations and detachments that freethought makes inevitable—but this pain pales before the violence of retributive justice, sexual and political repression, and religious hypocrisy, all stops on Nietzsche's deconstructive tour of European actuality.

The extended section "The Wanderer and His Shadow" is a final, ultra-speculative, eschatological, and futuristic stop on this tour. It is bracketed by two dialogues between its title characters, who relate to each other with a fatalistic irony, a gallows humor regarding ultimate questions, reminiscent of the apocalyptic tone of negative theology or the sublime discussions held by the rabbis in the Judaic afterlife opened up by the mystical literature. This spectral afterlife, pervaded by the ironies of unflinching dialogic commentary, is the subject of chapter 6 of the present study. "Only now do I notice how impolite [*unartig*] I am to you, my beloved shadow," confesses Nietzsche's wanderer in the dialogue opening this section. "I have not yet said a word of how very much I rejoice to hear you and not only to see you. You will know that I love shadow as much as I love light. For there to be beauty of face, clarity of speech, benevolence and firmness of character, shadow is as needful as light."[60] The collusion between the writer and his deconstructive edge here is as unsettling as any benighted collaboration we find in literature, whether between the dying Hunger Artist and his rapacious impresario at the end of Kafka's story or between Oberlin and Lenz in Büchner's *Lenz*. For this sublime dialogue Nietzsche synthesizes a style apposite to the tenuous trajectory of the wanderer, riddled with alienation and suffering but nonetheless furnishing the process of writing with a functional index of its intensities, inebriating revelations, and despairs. The literary style of the wanderer and his wanderings that Nietzsche devises for *Human, All Too Human* brings writing face to face with its intrinsic limits as much as it documents the encounter between philosophical negativity and the engulfing night of the human soul.

Although fluid, the wanderer's relentless motion is exacting. It brings him up against the limits of his will to write. His heart "grows weary of wandering." And yet, as the passage continues, compensations emerge in the course of the limit-experience:[61]

> Thus it may be that the wanderer shall fare; but then, as recompense, there will come the joyous mornings of other days and climes, when he shall see, even before the light has broken, the Muses come dancing by him in the mist of the mountains, when afterwards, if he relaxes quietly in the trees in the equanimity of his soul at morning, good and bright things will be thrown down to him from their tops and leafy hiding-places, the gifts of all those free spirits who are at home in mountain, wood and solitude and who, like him, in their now joyful, now thoughtful way, wanderers and philosophers. Born out of the mysteries of dawn, they ponder on how, between the tenth and the twelfth stroke of the clock, the day could present a face so pure, so light-filled, so cheerful and transfigured:—they seek the *philosophy of the morning*.[62]

For all that this passage is exaggerated by the sylvan setting, prophetic style, and Romantic rhetoric that Nietzsche crystallizes in order to usher in an age of cultural largesse, toleration, and exploration, it also functions as a hub for the interests that he relates to the climate and temperament of writing. The passage culminates volume 1 of *Human, All Too Human*. It issues in a prayer as well as a tribute to the "philosophy of the morning," to conditions of writing allowing for and initiating surprise, rethinking, and discovery; an eyes-wide-open embrace of humanity in its frailty that will initiate a repudiation of the most destructive pretenses and an authentic encounter with the other. In anticipation of this joyous apotheosis, the passage marshals everything constructive that Nietszche has unearthed in his no-holds-barred sociological critique. Muses summoned for the occasion furnish the inspiration requisite for the poetic dimension of memorable, thought-restructuring prose. Nietzsche invokes as well a redeeming human benevolence: "Good-naturedness, friendliness, politeness of the heart are never-failing emanations of the unegoistic drive and have played a far greater role in the construction of culture than those much more celebrated expressions of it called pity, compassion, and self-sacrifice. But usually they are neglected and undervalued, and there is, indeed, very little of the unegoistic in them."[63] His back bowed under the burdens of rigorous thinking and inventive language, relentless motion, isolation, and social ostracism, Nietzsche's wanderer will nevertheless encounter the mornings of his fulfillment. At the same time as he tallies the liabilities of compulsive script, Nietzsche declares the dawn of an era of terse, poetically inflected, epigrammatic, philosophically motivated cultural criticism. This is not work for the faint-hearted or the socially needy.

Writing thus constitutes a benign banishment or release from the automatic programming of selfhood. In this fashion, under writerly conditions, the writer ventures "outside" her "self." For purposes of the present elucidation, selfhood is best understood as a complex of stimulus-response reactions achieving the patent-ness of repetitiveness and automaticity. Indeed, the literatures of behaviorism, Skinnerianism, and empirical experimentation in psychology take off from the apprehension that learning is above all a matter of conditioning, and that the self or identity resulting from this repetitive process is analogous to a printing block toward the end of its run, when the finest details and stylistic traits have been worn away. The more the environment maneuvers us into thoughtless, that is, definitive, non-negotiable patterns of response to desires, needs, and the constraints of our sociological, professional, and material existences, the clearer and more recognizable the features of our selfhood become. This clarity, often augmenting itself over time, is, by and large, a one-way street with few channels allowing for redirection or reprogramming.

Although the conditions, features, and events of our lives, transcribed into writing, constitute a text, our selfhood or identity is by its very configuration a brusque dismissal of the incongruities, disruptions, and lapses set into play by writing and thinking alike. Selfhood unthinkingly repeats. It demands the restoration of mastery achieved under earlier circumstances. It calls for a moratorium on contingencies that would otherwise redefine identity and modify patterns of response. The effortlessness for which selfhood militates is akin to the uncanny stasis or repose in whose name Freud posited the death-drive. Selfhood is the mythological—in the Barthesian sense—concretion of thought and the endless negation of the environment comprising an existence.

Our sociological fate is tantamount to the clarity with which we precipitate a self out of the flow of our lives, the definition that the self achieves over and against preexistent values, norms, and rules. To "be someone" is to achieve a high specificity in the ongoing performance of identity. Indeed, for Goffman, the dramaturgy of selves in their current state of finality defines sociological interaction. "Being someone" specific inevitably comes at the expense of the turmoil and flux with which we customarily interact with the environment through a decoding and output of signs.

To the extent that our selves comprise violent stabilizations of our ongoing semiological deliberations, we live in constant exile from ourselves. We live "outside" ourselves. Only the thoughtful exegesis of artifacts and the thoughtful composition of writing spare us from unrelenting cooption by our social roles and performances. We are fated to be outsiders to ourselves because selfhood congeals in response to social contingencies, while the signs continue to dance. As we think the posture of selfhood as it peers into the "play of signs" from which it derives and is wistfully removed, we are reminded of the *stilles Abbild* or "inert image" that Hegel prescribed for each successive stage of abstraction in the vertiginous rise of scientific reasoning in "Force and the Understanding."[64] The dance of the elements of meaning and social interaction thwarts the momentum of selfhood toward closure.

It is in this sense that, on occasion, philosophy and linguistically astute criticism, seeming fundamentally inimical to the tranquillity, harmony, unity, and transcendence ascribed to "Eastern thought" or "religion," nonetheless "do commerce" with a certain tempering, if not abolition, of selfhood and its exigencies. Certainly, we do not emerge from Plato's extended tropes and theaters of intelligibility, from Nietzsche's dialectical/rhetorical stagings of the antagonism between normativity and singularity, or from Derrida's writerly skeins of the detours,[65] ruminations, and accidents that attend and derail Western purisms and pieties in a state of Enlightenment or revelation. But the ultimate radiance and flight from triviality celebrated by Buddhism may be as much a violent stabilization and mystification of its processes as the selfhood crystallizing in the course of Western experience and education. We need to ask, in both instances, Eastern and Western, "What is the process involved in the precipitation of selfhood and in its subsequent abatement?" Not "What is the endpoint of an experience whose finality is never attained?"

★

What is it that one discovers, then, during an act of writing? It may perhaps dawn as something fresh and unanticipated "from the outside," but this is at best "spacetalk,"[66] a spatialized metaphor, for something we didn't have before. It seems "natural" that, in the spatial figures in which we wrap or embellish thinking, what we didn't have before, what we did not yet possess, issues from some hinterland, some beyond extrinsic to the "present" situation. The philosophy of writing has taught us that the inscription of thinking may also be figured as a thread, one meandering compulsively between familiar, that is, "internal," and unanticipated elements. With obsessive force, with gradations and involutions so precipitous that they can't be fully registered, the thread of writing wanders, switches, and veers off between what we never possessed and what was only too obvious.

We learn, we happen upon the knownness, the familiarity, and even the banality—so well staged in Beckett's fictions and dramas—of the outside posited by cultural programming only as advanced students in the philosophy of writing. Until then, we are taken in by this illusion, by the presumption that, at the end of a session of reading or writing, a transaction temporized—that is, something with a certain sequence if not progression took place, leaving us in possession, or perhaps possessed, by something that was not in our "sights" (our discernment, ken, reach, capacity) before. But what a run, what a pageant of costumes and disguises the construct of an outside, one elicited by cultural convention and inscription, assumes in its inevitable trajectory toward debunking by linguistically acute philosophy! I want to dwell a bit—does this betoken a moment, or perhaps a span or stretch of my writing as a literal thread?—on the panoply of appearances assumed by the purported outside of cultural inscription.

We have encountered them all. From dense, primeval forests to lands of discovery and conquest, to the techno-future that has, for recognition's sake, to hold to contemporary mores even more than other literatures. We access the outside in the genetic hybrids and mutants first thinkable in mythology, in the bizarre dialects encountered on literary journeys, in robotic and animal incursions into the standard human division of labor. This "twilight zone" announces itself, as the uncanny, in both the bastions of convention and in the ambiguities broached in the trespass of current mores, by characters as exceptional as Gregor and as exemplary as Emma Bovary. We encounter it under the singular conditions of the 1755 Lisbon earthquake or of the maritime slave revolt aboard the *San Dominick*,[67] but it is ready to declare itself amid the banality of Meursault's everyday walk on the beach.[68] Repeatedly, in literature, the private and most intimate musings of protagonists become so idiosyncratic and constitutive of a world apart that they reify the conditions of a bizarre counteruniverse on the margin.

The question for literature is not the variety and multiplicity of the guises that the intractable and incommensurable dimension has assumed but the compulsiveness with which linguistic programming returns to this very plot, the synthesis of distance out of proximity, of strangeness out of intimacy. When we take up this inquiry we abut less on the arbitrariness of cultural convention than on the dynamics of linguistic composition. The outside is a spacing that this process opens up in the interests of its own possibility and persistence, allowing for its variance and difference from itself.

Each outside that textual invention opens as its precondition and occasion can only be engaged within the architectural setting and settlement of a home. Just as it would be hopeless, according to Kant, to encounter the sublimity of nature from the perspective of being out in the storm, the outsideness that art demands as the setting and bearing of creativity always announces itself from the position of a fixed abode. Inscription requires the specificity of a home address, even a peripatetic or chimerical one, in the same sense and to the same degree that it requires the opening of an outside.

To speak of an outside from which the phrases constituting our ontological singularity as well as our cultural output dawn upon us is to survey the boundaries and internal compartments of a home, a home in language. Nothing could be more sublime and uncanny than the notion of such a home, one emerging from the dynamics of the family, but migrating early in human development well beyond that sphere. Not only does the home in language that each of us fashions around ourselves in our interactions with culture illustrate the Freudian phenomenon of the same name: it defines the general condition of uncanniness, the wavering between the familiar and the horrific, the lucid and the impenetrable, the defined and the indeterminate that is the limit experience of certainty and certitude.

In the parlance of Emmanuel Levinas, the home is the foyer in which we encounter the other, whom he names "the Stranger":

> The way of the I against the "other" of the world consists in *sojourning*, in *identifying oneself* by existing here *at home with oneself* [*chez soi*]. In a world which is from the first other the I is nonetheless autochthonous. It is the very reversion of this alteration. It finds in the world a site and a home. Dwelling is the very mode of *maintaining oneself*, not as the famous serpent grasping itself by biting on to its own tail, but as the body that, on the earth exterior to it, holds *itself* up and *can*. The at home is not a container but a site where I *can*, where, depending on a reality that is other, I am, despite this dependence or thanks to it, free.... The site, a medium, affords means. Everything is here; everything belongs to me; everything is caught up in advance with the primordial occupying of a site, everything is com-prehended. The possibility of possessing, that is, of suspending the alterity of what is only at first other, and other relative to me, is the *way of the same*.[69]

Levinas, characterizing home as an element in the encounter with the other and alterity in general, chooses to couch it in terms of its supportive, sustaining, and facilitating functions. The home undergirds the subject so that he is able to encounter the other. It is also the site in which the subject is able to encounter his own definition of the other, at least at the outset of the encounter, on his own terms. The home, in other words, is the site of the tug-of-war of alterity, the struggle between engaging the other on its own terms and slipping back into the sovereignty of our own perspective.

The outsider can only be measured against the home he has violated or left behind. Let us dwell for a moment on the synergy and complex interaction between two kinds of home indispensable to our cultural experience: the home as the "safe house" affording us pause and leisure to think, and the linguistic home, always an artificial and constructed matter, defining the neighborhood and conceptual underpinnings of our processing of the world.

In its most telling sense, a home is not so much a house or other architectural structure, a community defined by various possible affiliations or an institutional or work setting, it is an environment under whose aegis we can with impunity *laugh*. The stability and protection against dislocation and immanent threat and fundamental deprivation that allows us to laugh, in other words, are the authentic architectural supports of a home, not walls, beams, cantilevers, and other structural appurtenances. My home is by no means rooted in a plot of real estate. I can be at home laughing at something that occurs to me as I wander in the street; my residence can be and often is the setting of my most unsettling anxiety. My laughter, as Freud pointed out a century ago,[70] is the spontaneous expression of my status as a linguistic and hermeneutic being.

My home is not a preexistent address, structure, or series of venues that I enter and leave. My home does not exist or pre-exist; periodically, it happens around me, it comes into being. It happens, whenever, with leave, with impunity, with freedom as Nietzsche, in *Human, All Too Human* and elsewhere elaborates it, I enter the condition of thinking, which is at the same time the process of writing. I lose my freedom in the most significant sense, in other words, when my living conditions no longer afford me the impunity to laugh, to think, or to write.[71] Indeed, political regimes are engaged in the most devastating and longest-lasting repression when they set their sights on communications, the media, and education. This is even more pernicious than bans on behaviors and attacks along the spectrum of sociopolitical organization. Constraints upon the public spheres of expression, informational dissemination, and interpretation debilitate the very process through which criticism of and resistance to public policy and implementation make themselves known. The only way in which we are ever at home, in which we belong to any meaningful homeland, is being at home in generative and productive senses with our laughter, our thinking, and our writing. There are indeed far-reaching and tangible impacts to the quality of thinking encouraged or tolerated in the public sphere. Among the multiple tasks of the critic is the tracking of current conditions in the climate of thinking. Cultural critique of this situation by intellectuals rarely results in screaming headlines.

If it is healthy, a conceptual paradigm bears within it the coherence of the furnishings in a carefully assembled home. The philosophers who inspire us and advance our observations and articulations have in effect welcomed us into a linguistic home. The idiom or dialect we have absorbed there not only names the phenomena within our current domain of attentiveness and questioning, it composes the terms in the language at our disposal in the process of inscribing, debriefing, or embellishing the event, the exorbitant cultural encounter. It is with relief and a sense of empowerment that we accept the invitation, or provocation, of the thinkers who influence us and the teachers who most inspire us into the home of a more-or-less coherent discourse. We accept the invitation into this linguistic home under the obligation and practical requirement of deploying the terms we master there as consistently and rigorously as we can. Our formulations otherwise lose their outline or contour as they aimlessly and unpredictably force themselves out of context.

No thinker explores the broader philosophical implications of dwelling with greater persistence than Martin Heidegger, who comprehends the close tie between homelessness and the paradoxical meanderings of the wanderer:

> The *real plight of dwelling* does not lie merely in a lack of houses. The real plight of dwelling is indeed older than the world wars with their destruction, older also than the increase in the world's population and the condition of the industrial workers. The real dwelling plight lies in this, that mortals ever search anew for the nature of dwelling, that they *must ever learn to dwell*. What if man's homelessness consisted in this, that man still does not even think of the *real* plight of dwelling as *the* plight? Yet as soon as man *gives thought* to his homelessness, it is a misery no longer. Rightly considered and kept well in mind, it is the sole summons that *calls* mortals into their dwelling.[72]

For Heidegger, the plight of dwelling is inseparable from the plight of thinking and writing. The wanderings of thinking and writing can be gauged only against the backdrop of dwelling.

Not only have our inspiring and effective teachers invited us into the expressive cohesion of a linguistic home, they have dramatically upgraded the power and outreach of what we have to say. The Derridean term *logocentrism* not only betokens certain expectations of transcendental purity, spirituality, and immanence applied to language, it crystallizes a broad tradition of sublimated language in thought, non-Western as well as Western, placing a vast array of artifacts in communication with each other. To have metabolized the "lingo" of logocentrism to one degree or another is, therefore, tantamount to witnessing a struggle within the economy and ideology of signification that would not have emerged in the absence of this idiom. The scope of the fluctuations between spirituality and distortion in language, between ideation and materiality, between scripture and aesthetic play, is monumentally vast. The windows in the linguistic home where I first absorbed "logocentrism" give onto the panorama of an ongoing cultural, social, and psychological drama I could not have perceived, let alone to some degree have processed, were it not for the accepted invitation into my teacher's linguistic home.

What message does the outsider bear with him in his wanderings if not the secret? The secret is philosophy's nomenclature for the systemic dimension of the singularly private language that the artist disguises and delivers. The wanderer furnishes the secret at the very limits of comprehensibility and public reception and acknowledgment with a message and delivery service. The ultimate secret that the wanderer conveys is the mystery of language: the aporetic backdrop of mutually disqualifying propositions against which language nonetheless takes effect and happens.

> The autobiographical is the locus of the secret, but not in the sense—as some would have it—that it holds the key to a secret, be it conscious or unconscious. Yes, there is a secret of that sort, but it is not the secret that I attempt to think, i.e., to put into a formalizable, expressible relation with everything that it is not. What is the place of this *unconditional* and *absolute* secret in a space where either there is no secret or secrets are negotiable—secrets that can be hidden, things that are preserved, that are placed in reserve.
>
> Clearly, the most tempting figure for this absolute/secret is death, that which has a relation to death, that which is carried off by death—that which is thus life itself.[73]

So fundamental is the nexus of personal nuances and associations that each language user brings to the field of communication and that the artist inveigles into the artifact with the effect of its strangeness, freshness, and surprise—so irreducible is the secret, as Derrida in his interview with Ferraris characterizes it—that it is inseparable from the experience of life itself. Each programmer in the field of language bears the weight and onus of his own secret idiom; each has been traumatized by a secret heritage only crudely translatable into terms of social or public negotiation or concern. Each, then, is marked by the singularity, in Derrida's parlance, characteristic of the signature. By dint of this stigma, each of us has always been set on the path of the wanderer. It's a wonder that we're as civil as we are.

TWO

On the Butcher Block: A Panorama of Social Marking

The Butcher Boy, directed by Neil Jordan, a 1998 production of the currently daring and inventive Irish film industry, provides a fortuitous occasion for setting out some of the textual, sociological, and theoretical parameters that need to be taken into account in contemporary cultural criticism. Based on a 1992 novel by Patrick McCabe,[1] the film graphically raises questions of social branding, progressive alienation, exclusion, outsideness, community, social oversight and sanction, and the interplay between public and private discourses pivotal at once to narrative, semiotics, critical theory, and the "human science" known as sociology.

The poignancy of the story of a charming and fundamentally sound boy who is, through ostracism, *méconnaissance*, and the misapplication of social resources transformed first into a pariah and then into a homicidal deviant is relevant to our understanding of several interrelated phenomena: of how narratives, especially ones with characters, and indeed all texts, function; of the social sciences as the epistemological and discursive arbiters of human behavior and institutions; and. of the kind of ethics we can begin to imagine for a multicultural, essentially interactive, and philosophically explicit contemporary world. It is crucial for us to understand from the outset that textual complexity and indeterminacy, which have, throughout the twentieth century, initiated fundamental revisions within the field of knowledge and its configuration and in the practices of the learned discourses, could go hand in hand with conceptions of society, community, and ethics. The twentieth century began with a breathless apprehension of the priority of language to reality, knowledge, and even personal experience itself; it took the entire century for the contracts of art and the discourses of culture to integrate this insight; and it shows no sign of waning. Yet just as discord and ambivalence are "hard-wired" into the ideologies and institutions of society, an audience, a proto-community, is implicit in linguistic artifacts that allegorize their own arbitrariness, contrivance, and confusion. *The Butcher Boy*, both the film and the text, is situated on the dynamic border, or borderline, between a critical theory pursuing the impact of linguistic processes and phenomena upon the artifacts and media of ideological reassurance, and a social theory extrapolating designs for modes of social interaction and institutionality in a rapidly changing world. In full appreciation of the inventive demonstrations by modernist and postmodern authors from Kafka, Joyce, and Stein to Borges and Calvino, of language's intractable stance toward easy moral and institutional payoffs, I hold nonetheless to a fundamental complementarity between the linguistic and sociological components of a viable theory of culture.

The present essay sets out on the trajectory of a *parcours*, a generative return to the operational language of sociology from the perspective of the philosophy of writing, a term I broached in the theoretical sections of my *The Aesthetic Contract*.[2] The concern that led me into this project is the current dissonance between the subtlety of contemporary critical theory and the sluggishness of social institutions in advanced technological and capitalist societies in responding to the divergences and proliferation of alternatives that this theory has underscored. Already embedded in the discourse of critical theory are models of difference, alterity, and ethics of potentially enormous consequence for reformulating social responsibility and justice in contemporary societies, in which the nature of socioeconomic relations, including the very concept of work, have undergone rapid and steady change. The rhetoric of marginality, by the same token, has much to engender in the emergence of a countereconomy that might well counter, were its terms and tropes to become explicit, the increasingly stark rift between economic citizenship and statelessness in heavily technological economies.

The quandary here is not so much the remoteness of highly speculative theoretical allegories from "real world" problems as a relative dearth of articulations bridging the two discursive registers; the relative overlooking of what Kant situated in the realm of *practical* reason. The risks of rushing into this particular intellectual space are as multitudinous as the reductions and simplifications to which it is, a priori, prone. To look completely past the *décalage* between theoretical scenarios of deterritorialization, marginality, and destabilization and the increasingly entrenched rigors of doing business in our late-capitalistic economies would be, however, to accept complicity with this new world order. The middle ground, a recalibration of the operative terms and constructs in this pervasive set of socioeconomic conditions in terms of their critical-theoretical nuances, must yield the ambivalence and measure inherently embedded in its domain—of qualification, compromise, and negotiation. Yet precisely this act of retooling, of rewriting sociological relations in terms of the linguistic features and dynamics undergirding and qualifying them, may ameliorate the always treacherous rift between thinking and being in the world.

The Butcher Boy, in keeping with Deleuze and Guattari's trenchant formulation "Our society produces schizos the same way it produces Prell shampoo or Ford cars, the only difference being that schizos are not salable,"[3] pursues the progressive marking, distanciation, criminalization, and subsequent discipline of one Francis ("Francie") Brady by the fictive community of Carn, Republic of Ireland, during the early 1960s, a moment corresponding to the child's puberty years. The relation between the parents of this only child is contentious, to say the least. In the film version of McCabe's novel, the boy's father, Benny Brady, is a gifted horn player, whose aspirations and vitality have been thwarted for reasons left largely unspecified. (Alcohol clearly plays a role here, and we know that he and his brother spent part of their early years "in a home.") Annie, Francie's mother, vacillates between suicidal depression, perhaps occasioned by the grim conditions in the household, and a manic craving for company, family, and celebration. Francie interrupts her once in the act of suicide early in the film. After he has taken a joy-ride to Dublin, in part to escape the endless domestic strife, he is too late to preempt her second, successful attempt. On one occasion, though, having returned from the mental hospitalization precipitated by her initial attempt on her life, Mrs. Brady outdoes herself in producing batch after batch of baked goods in preparation for a Christmas party. (Her obvious delight in a visit by Benny's brother Alo, from London, where he seems to have attained a certain success in middle management—in the novel, he turns out to be a security foreman—precipitates the row that sends Francie off to Dublin and may reflect a longstanding tension in the marriage. The film adaptation goes to special lengths to exploit the dramatic and visual potential in Annie's baking spree.) The party occasioned by Alo's visit ends, predictably, with Benny venting his jealousy toward his brother and his frustration and rage toward his wife and son, and with his wife experiencing stark constraints on her freedom, enterprise, and happiness. Francie's escape to Dublin and his return in the midst of his mother's funeral follow directly on the bittersweet party scene.

The visit by Alo, a beloved family member, and the idealism that still somehow attaches to him are the only factors that can forestall Annie's rush to death—in Deleuze and Guattari's terms, her becoming-death.[4] With the exception of one brief upswing in Benny Brady's life, when he attempts to make amends for his alcoholism and paternal absence to Francie, the father's presence in the film is as a moribund icon of death-in-the-becoming. In keeping with the family's overall suspicion of the community of Carn and its services, Francie allows medical intervention in the house only after Benny has died; until this transpires, his somnolent, vacant presence has been gathering flies for several scenes.

The mother's self-inflicted death is clearly a consequence of the progressive removal of the possibility of idealization from her life. She cannot idealize her husband or her home; she can barely idealize her son. Originally she was a shopgirl from Londonderry, and her few encounters with Benny clearly outgrew any reasonable scale into marriage. Late in the film, Francie, in a belated effort to restore any remaining shards of his own idealism, visits Bundoran, a resort on the Ulster-Ireland border where his parents had honeymooned.

> There was a coach trip all those years ago, to the seaside town of Bundoran in County Donegal. The war was over and everybody was happy. Every time the bus went down a hill they cheered and clapped and sang. She had fallen against his shoulder by accident. Oh dear God!, they shouted, would you look at this!

A camera clicked. We're the talk of the place!, ma cried but what did da do only put his arm around her.

They held hands along the strand and they talked about the brass band he'd started in the town and a book he was reading, the life and times of Michael Collins the revolutionary hero.[5]

This passage contains a rare instance of positive Brady family narrative in the novel. So inundated is Francie by his father's bitterness and endless carping and his mother's evident depression that the memories of unproblematical intimacy are few and far between. The bus scene appears in the film as a brief, disjointed flashback. Even though the parents remember Bundoran happily in the constructed narrative of their shared life, the actuality of their honeymoon in the town is quite another matter, as Francie learns late in both novel and film. The owner of the now-defunct rooming house where the Bradys once stayed disabuses Francie of this last illusion, recalling Benny's infidelities and the newlyweds' rows. At least in Bundoran, Benny's musical career had been on the upswing.

The main part of the film chronicles the progressive revisiting of this thwarted idealization upon the couple's son. The film brilliantly hovers between the tongue-in-cheek, Huck Finnish monologue by Francie in the role of a child-hero discovering the world's ways and a more detached registration of the expressions and acts of the child's rage. This tension defines the child's character, whether barely maintaining its coherence or disintegrating in destructive, antisocial acts.

> The women were standing over by the cornflakes saying things have got very dear. Its very hard to manage now. . . . One of them moved back and bumped against the display case. There you are ladies I said and they all went back on their heels at the same time. What's this? I says, the woman with three heads? When I said that they weren't so bad. Flick—back come the smiles. Ah Francie, they said, there you are. Here I am I said. They leaned right over to me and in a soft top secret voice said how's your mother Francie? Oh I says she's flying she's above in the garage and it won't be long before she's home. . . . Yup, says I, she has to come home shortly now to get the baking done for Uncle Alo's party. So your Uncle Alo's coming home! they said. Christmas Eve I said, all the way from London. Would you credit that now says Mrs Connolly with a warm little shiver, and will he be staying long? Two weeks says I. . . . He did well in London, Francie, your Uncle Alo, says the other woman.[6]

48   *Idylls of the Wanderer*

This scene juxtaposes the townsladies' discomfort with Annie's incarceration and Francie's characteristic wit and bravado. Not only does the boy attach a humorous face to his mother's suffering, to which he is not inured, he actually assuages his neighbors' regret for Annie's plight and sadness toward him. He nudges the conversation toward Uncle Alo, the single intact (though exaggerated, as Benny clarifies) bright spot in the Brady clan.

At the peak of his early troubles, with his mother institutionalized, Francie displays a brave humor, a mark of the overburdened, to the housewives who frequent the pork grocer's. The sociopathy that develops in this rich and appealing character is in no small measure the residue of unacknowledged, underappreciated heroism. In ingenious ways, the novel chronicles the loss of control in Francie's character, metamorphosing him from a sympathetic child-victim of multiple circumstances to a sociopath and despised outsider. At the beginning of the novel, Francie displays enough composure to limit the display and acting out of his private language. Toward the beginning of the dispute with Mrs. Nugent, he chatters humorously to the housewives who shop in Mary's grocery store about a "toll tax," but not the "pig toll tax," incorporating both his social stigma and his defense against it.[7] Around the same time, he thinks of charging Father Dominic a "Going Home Tax,"[8] but drops the idea. Francie's social downfall, initiated by Mrs. Nugent but eventually involving the complicity of the combined Purcell and Nugent families, may be described as a dual loss of composure and effacement of the boundary separating personal expressions, fantasies, and impulses from socially sanctioned protocols and exchanges.

The ongoing devaluation of Francie's noble traits by the community, which acknowledges but does nothing to remedy his plight, explains why the eventual dissolution of his idealized buddyship with Joe Purcell is so devastating. His deprivations, and his characteristic generosity and bravado in the face of them, make him particularly susceptible to chivalric codes of loyalty. These enter his world via the American mass artifacts that exerted such influence in Ireland and indeed the United Kingdom at the beginning of the 1960s.

> After that we rode out to the river, that was the day we built the hide. . . . We built a campfire too. We blackened our faces and painted equals signs under our eyes. We mingled the blood of our forearms and said from this day on Francie

Brady and Joe Purcell are blood brothers and will be friends to the end of the world. We'll pray to the Manitou Joe said so we did. You can have a name said Joe an injun name. I was Bird Who Soars. Off I went across the sky and over the slated rooftops . . . calling down to Joe far below can you see me Joe I'm up here diving with the wind stroking my eyes as I came in to land beside him but he hadn't moved, sitting there hunched up in a blanket, paring sticks and saying yamma yamma yamma, praying to the Manitou.⁹

Both versions of the artifact, the novelistic narrative and the cinematographic landscape, succeed in conveying the idyllic and intimate friendship that Francie and Joe Purcell share early on. Their partnership and conspiracy is set in a magnificent riverscape reminiscent of *Huckleberry Finn*; it is ritually enacted by the trappings of Native American lore, as popularly constructed. McCabe's narrative of the scene rises to the exuberance with which he invests Francie and Joe's friendship. The boys' oath of undying loyalty and friendship is a speech act with decisive repercussions upon the unraveling of narrative events. By virtue of the Brady family's instability and tenuous rapport with the wider Carn community, the oath and its eventual dissolution are of far greater consequence to Francie, to his senses of his social value and even his identity, than it is to Joe, whose family eventually teams up with those self-proclaimed arbiters of social judgment, the Nugents.

In the same outskirts of Carn where the "hide" is located labor in menial occupations the "bogmen" memorialized in the soundtrack's Irish cuts, contemporary vestiges of medieval European peasantry. The bogmen, to whom even the Nugents are related, are primitive to the point of animalism, hardly distinguishable from the pigs that eventually give Francie an occupation and Carn a name.

Joe and Francie trade comic books; they steal them from Philip Nugent, much to the consternation of his mother. Francie fancies his inseparable bond to Joe Purcell as a version of Tonto's loyalty to the Lone Ranger. Clips from "The Lone Ranger," American-style horror animations, and nuclear-age science fiction incorporated into the film not only display the hegemony of the American popular imagination of the epoch; they stress the utter marginality of Francie's situation. His domestic stability and environment are exploding around him in the small-town setting of a no-man's land in the United Kingdom (between the Irish Republic and Ulster), at a time when exported American images were engrossing the U.K.'s popular imagination wholesale. Even the Brady family name is comprehensible only against the backdrop of a U.S. popular culture already disseminated on a global scale. The Brady family's odyssey into general neglect, maudlin depression, and bestiality constitutes an ironic Irish playback to a soporific Hollywood sitcom, *The Brady Bunch*.

> There was picture houses and everything. Over I went. The Corinthian Cinema written in unlit lights. What's going on here I said. The creatures were coming to take over the planet earth because their own was finished there was nothing left on it. The shaky writing said they came from beyond the stars bringing death and destruction. I'd have to go and see them aliens when it opened up.[10]
>
> Soon as she waddled off I waited for the girl to go back into the kitchen. I was in behind the counter like a bullet and I stuffed any notes I could in my pocket. Then I ran like fuck. All the way down the street I kept thinking: Hunted from town to town for a crime he didn't commit—Francie Brady—The Fugitive!![11]
>
> I went into the Gresham Hotel and ordered a slap-up feed. Who's going to pay for this? says the waiter licking his pencil hmm hmm. I am my man I said, Mr Algernon Carruthers. I seen that in one of Philip's comics. Algernon Carruthers always on these ships going around the world and eating big dinners. Certainly Master Carruthers he says. I knew what he thought I was one of these boy millionaires.
>
> I bought bubblegum cards and spread them all out on a park bench. I had Frankie Avalon, John Wayne, Elvis, and a load of other ones I don't know who they were.[12]

McCabe selects Francie's ill-timed joy-ride to Dublin as an occasion to uncover the thick tapestry of elements from American popular culture that have entered into individual and collective everyday awareness in the U.K. The Fugitive emerges as the perfect pop-culture caption for Francie's illicit escape from Carn; in the film adaptation, postnuclear mutants are compelling insignia for Francie's increasing displacement from the mainstream of social life in his community. The pictures on Francie's bubblegum cards—of "Frankie Avalon, John Wayne, Elvis"—are images from the U.S. emblazoned on a currency relatively new to the U.K., a scrip increasingly vital to the interaction and mutual understanding between British subjects. Francie has attained a historically specific literacy in this lingo, but even this does not overcome his separation from his peers and the community to which they belong.

Within the marginal setting of *The Butcher Boy* as a retrospective if not entirely exuberant coming-of-age movie, Francie volunteers that his downfall, the end of anything idyllic in his childhood, begins with the return of the Nugents to town after a sojourn in England. The Nugents as a clan embody the divided loyalty that is the nemesis of Francie's desperate needs for idealization and steadfastness. Their aspirations are upper-class enough to allow them to pursue advantages in the land of the British colonizers. Philip Nugent is a schoolmate whose excessive wholesomeness makes him a natural target for Francie's prankish cynicism, his testing of social boundaries.

Within the sociological allegory of the film, Mrs. Nugent, Philip's mother, is an aribiter of social taste not unlike Mme Verdurin in Proust's *À la recherche du temps perdu*. In part as the result of his own mischief, Francie is eventually leveraged by Philip Nugent out of the one dimension of his life that he can still hold ideal and dear, his friendship with Joe Purcell. Francie's ultimate rejection by Joe, his blood-brother, with whom he has sworn eternal allegiance, amounts to Joe's departure from this Twainlike, very American buddyship under the sway of the Nugents' alien (British, Protestant, and colonial) social code.

To the extent that this film incorporates the elements of a folktale, Mrs. Nugent is the designated witch. The drama from the demise of Francie's family to the homicide that seals Francie's fate is driven by an escalating battle between the roughshod but in many respects endearing homeboy and the witch who controls public opinion. Mrs. Nugent rules by manners, snobbery, and gossip. Early in the film, when she chastises Francie for extorting some of Philip's comic books, she associates him and his own with pigs.

> She said she knew the kind of us long before she went to England and she might have known not to let her son near the likes of me what else would you expect from a house where the father's never in, lying about the pubs from morning to night, he's no better than a pig. . . . Small wonder the boy is the way he is what chance has he got running around the town at all hours . . . but if he's seen near our Philip again there'll be trouble. There'll be trouble now mark my words!
>
> After that ma took my part and the last thing I heard was Nugent going down the lane and calling back *Pigs—sure the whole town knows that!*[13]

This is an utterly formative passage, to Francie's "experience" and character, as well as to the seam between the sociological and the literary that the artifacts trace. As the result of the action that it frames, Francie and his immediate family are branded as a subset of the human community of Carn, as its human pigs. But this immediate distinction (or differentiation, or denigration, or quarantine) is founded on ongoing rifts between the strata in the bedrock of society. Francie's baseness, according to Mrs. Nugent, is exacerbated by the family's residence in the colonial powerbase of the U.K. Being one of Mrs. Nugent's figurative pigs is tantamount to emanating from the hopeless stratum of Irish society known as "shanty Irish," whose abjection appears even more devastating through English eyes. Pigs, although totemic creatures related to Deleuze and Guattari's notion of "becoming animal,"[14] have a meaning not limited to their evolutionary or agricultural status; they have a powerful significance in preexistent economies of national domination and social stratification.

Francie's initial reception of this insult is good-humored: he playfully proposes a "pig toll tax" for people who cross his path. By the end of the film, as the result of several major reversals, including incarceration in the same reformatory that had housed his father and his uncle, Francie has fulfilled the witch's curse. Its words have "made things happen."[15] By the end of his chronological childhood (one could argue that Francie has never been allowed an emotional one), he has become the butcher boy of the film's title, a term derived in turn from a period folk ballad to which his mother took a liking before her death. He has had to apprentice himself to Mr. Leddy, who operates the local slaughterhouse. And when dispossessed of the last shards of his idealism, after being forcibly removed from the boarding school where Joe Purcell and Philip Nugent are now mates, and after an utterly disheartening sentimental journey to Bundoran, he acts out his carnal profession: first he shoots Mrs. Nugent, then he butchers her by chopping off her head.

The heart of the tale from a sociological perspective is the running battle between Francie as a marginal member of the community and Mrs. Nugent as the chief personification and operator of social codes. Mrs. Nugent's judgments and pronouncements have an uncanny prophetic quality. They complete the trajectory from words to eventuality and even to virtuality.[16] She brands the Bradys as pigs, and Francie ends up a pork butcher. From both a literary and a sociological perspective, Mrs. Nugent is a character (or agent, or surrogate) who brands or marks another. She asserts a measure of social control over Francie by determining or defining him as a signifier, within a text whose signification devolves in part on characters and within a society interrelated as a text. Once he is socially marked, Francie's associations, experience, and career path are fated. He will be ejected from an exclusive public school, but not attend it. He will be tracked, rather, to a reform school, where, in part owing to his own wit and in part to the perverse behavior of Father Sullivan, he will never be reformed.

The branding or marking of one character (or complex signifier) by another in a representational artifact is a pivotal phenomenon worthy of our careful and ongoing vigilance, with special significance in demarcating the interface between the literary and the sociological. For a character such as Mrs. Nugent, one of divided loyalties in terms of the artifact's historical and sociopolitical surrounds, to determine that henceforth Francie Brady and his immediate family will have the added (or supplementary) significance of pigs is, in terms of our immediate discipline, an instance of what Roland Barthes called a metasignifier or second-degree sign.[17] Mrs. Nugent, already "her" self a complex signifier, generates a new, or second-degree signifier within the artifact in which she plays, that of the Brady-pig. This increases her power within the artifact as a generator of meaning, and it marks the function in which operators within artifacts are closest to agents in communities or society. The Mrs. Nugents and Mme Verdurins of literature play a disproportionate role in determining the significance and fates of their fellow characters, much as the gossip-mongers and tabloids of society regulate, again through marking and branding, the power accruing to very real people.[18] One could argue that, at least in the privileged sectors of power, an agent's vicissitudes and influence are in large measure a function of the social significance that becomes attached to him or her over the course of time. Reputation and anecdote play a vital role in the social filter that determines, other factors being equal, who enters the sanctum of authority and influence and who does not.

The question of social branding within an artifact and the rather tight analogy between metasignification in a text and the access to power and privilege in society have been with us for a very long time. In the Judeo-Christian Bible the literal brand that Cain receives in the aftermath of killing Abel is an extension of the events and family drama of Eden.[19] It occurs before God indoctrinates the patriarchs into Israel and before the exodus from Egypt and occupation of Canaan define the Hebrew state. As the grounding text of what Deleuze and Guattari would call a signifying regime,[20] the Bible exhibits special theological and ideological needs to regulate the signifiers that it sets into play. If, in the very first scenes of Genesis, this control lapses, the distinctive flavor of the Israelite community is sure to be lost, and from time immemorial. The double-bind occasioned by this sociopolitical and ideological need to control the radical semes endowing a culture with its pith and flavor is at the heart of Barthes's now legendary redefinition of myth.[21] The mythologizing of the signifier, fetishizing and subjugating it in the same act, cuts across articulate cultures and "full-service" civilizations, from the establishment of Western monotheism—that is, the theological arena of Western idealism—to the crisis of the British colonialization of Ireland, to the Clinton-Lewinsky affair and its effect on the U.S. presidency.

Some semiological violence, the outrage of the foreign, announces the arrival of newcomers, to communities and to the synthetic social fabric of novels alike, and attends their departure. We may think of this crime of semiological strangeness either as an incompletion in the assimilation of private (or familial, or local) meaning or as a violation of existing codes of behavior and meaning.

Mrs. Nugent's branding Francie and his immediate family as pigs determines his sociological fate as a fictive surrogate and his semiological vicissitudes as a signifier in the novel. In this sense, there is a rare agreement between the novel as a document with a sociological dimension and field of reference and as a literary text figured particularly around certain metasignifiers, such as pigs. Porcine imagery is far and away the most prevalent metaphoric uniting the novel. Mrs. Nugent relegates the Brady family to the pigpen of the Carn community. Before taking her own life, Annie Brady introduces Francie and the reader to "The Butcher Boy" ballad, which lends the novel and the film their title. It is a maudlin song in which the faithlessness of a young meatcutter incises wounds into the heart of the betrayed female persona, and induces her to hang herself. The slaughterhouse where Francie will work during his own stint as the butcher boy not only fulfills Mrs. Nugent's curse and the novel's semiological patterning, it serves as the visceral underworld to a town given to religious ecstasies, such as the Traynor girl's sighting of the Holy Mother. As Francie's youthful idealism is shaken by his parents' squabbling and marginal position within the community, and given its coup de grâce by the social branding supplied by Mrs. Nugent and associates, so Francie, by the end of the novel, has become a personified impediment to the community's ability collectively to idealize itself.

A disproportionate amount of the work in the novel and film is devoted to the progressive deflation and disqualification of a basically vibrant boy's idealism, sense of self-esteem, and comfort with himself. The sociopathy on the part of this character, who is rich and complex in spite of his youthfulness, is in no small measure the sign of unacknowledged, underappreciated heroism. This partially explains why the progressive loss of his idealized friendship with Joe Purcell is so devastating to him. His deprivations, and his characteristic generosity and bravado in the face of them, induce him to overvalue idealized scenarios of male bonding from the American popular culture that flooded the British airwaves at this particular cultural moment (this is where the spliced clips from TV's "The Lone Ranger" fit into the film's semiological texture). Book and film chronicle the loss of social manners and self-restraint, ultimately resulting in Mrs. Nugent's butchering.

"Right today we are going to do pigs," begins Francie's narration of his own most desperate and repugnant acts:

> I want you all to stick out your faces and scrunch up your noses just like snouts. That's very good Philip. I found a lipstick in one of the drawers and I wrote in big letters across the wallpaper PHILIP IS A PIG. Now, I said, isn't that good? Yes Francie said Philip. And now you Mrs. Nugent. I don't think you're putting enough effort into it. Down you get now and no slacking. So Mrs. Nugent got down and she looked every inch the best pig in the farmyard with the pink rump cocked in the air. Mrs. Nugent, I said, astonished, that is absolutely wonderful! Thank you Francie said Mrs. Nugent. So that was the pig school.[22]
>
> What do you think Mrs. Nugent? Isn't Philip a credit? . . .
>
> It really was a big one, shaped like a submarine, tapered at the end so your hole won't close with a bang, studded with currants with a little question mark of steam curling upwards.[23]

The rhetorical structure of this brief scene within the sphere of Francie's idiosyncratic private language is complex. Here Francie, having invaded the Nugent household, imagines that he is the schoolmaster at a school for pigs that numbers Philip Nugent and his mother among its students. The fantasy enables Francie projectively to transform himself from school pariah to schoolmaster; from the Nugents' pawn to their absolute master; from a species below the Nugents to a species above. Thoroughly absorbed in his fantasy, and in the private language that endows it with its substance and figuration, Francie addresses two characters whose presence resides entirely in his imaginary. This activity at the level of the imaginary functions as a discursive and visual (if not musical) accompaniment to the exceptionally concrete acts of breaking and entering and aggressive defecation. The narrative description of the impressive turd that Francie produces for the occasion relates it to submarines deployed in the Bay of Pigs invasion, and therefore to the artifacts' overall sociohistorical and cultural surrounds.

From a slightly more detached perspective, Francie's scrawling "pig" at the Nugents' during both the rug defecation and murder scenes incorporates the 1967 Tate-LaBianca murders into the historical timeframe of the novel and its screen adaptation, even if these acts didn't occur until half a decade or so after the Bay of Pigs invasion and other telling historical markers to which the narrative alludes.[24] McCabe connects Francie's tale to a set of jarring and concurrent social changes: the dissemination of U.S. popular culture; nuclear sublimity within that imagination; the spread of juvenile delinquency; the transformation, if not decline, of the traditional nuclear family (as well as of the pristine, isolated community); drug culture (as indicated by the allusion to the Tate-LaBianca murders); serious challenges to traditional gender roles. (In the film, the feminization imposed on Francie by his various caretaking roles is more obvious than in the novel. On several occasions, he dons an apron. His name can be applied to individuals of both genders. His ambiguous gender identity links *The Butcher Boy* to another Neil Jordan film that also deals with imperialistic struggle within the U.K., *The Crying Game*.) Thus Francie's story, while revolving around one of the most unique and memorable characters in recent popular culture, is both a product of and a commentary upon a complex of the most significant sociological changes characterizing industrialized societies at the end of the twentieth century. A single, carefully wrought story both sums up a series of sociological changes and suggests the private, imaginary language they might generate in a character placed directly in their path.

A signifier, an epithet, a social label, a marker, determines Francie's place, or rather absence, in society, and, as suggested above, it seals his fate. Society, in *The Butcher Boy*, is an amalgam in which the semiological and communicative functions of people, or rather fictive surrogates, are as essential as their roles as agents or subjects. There are a textual dimension and quality to cultural representations of society to which students of literature and the arts can hardly be insensible. For a vast if not complete portion of their apprehension, society, the community, the stock markets of power and reputation, the phenomena of class and social stratification, and the institutions and organizations that marshal collective social endeavor depend on being read and decoded as textually configured networks. The facility that students of literature and other literacies (e.g., the visual) gain in "handling" and decoding texts places them at a distinct advantage in analyzing social phenomena.

To argue for an inherent sociological dimension to artifacts, however implicit or explicit this social setting may be, will surely be contested more intensely than the inverse position, particularly at a moment when the predominant theoretical models undergirding intellectual work have argued convincingly for the autonomy of textual networks from the influences of subjectivity and other extratextual determinants (e.g., nationality, race, ethnicity). If the torques exerted by textuality and the sociological setting are reciprocal, in exactly what might the latter consist?

If *The Butcher Boy*, not to mention Proust's *Recherche*, *The Tale of Genji*, and the novels of Austen, Dickens, Eliot, and James—as artifacts encompassing a deliberate sociological setting—are any indication, image-driven artifacts are prone to trace out the sociological ramifications of telling metaphors, say, "pig" in *The Butcher Boy*. The implicit society installed in an artifact is not the microcosm of an actual society but of the sociological—referential, communicative, evaluative, and critical—functions with which telling images take effect. To read artifacts sensitively is to trace out these sociological coordinates, among others.

Those telling images bridging between the textual economy of an artifact and its sociological coordinates exist both in and out of time, both derive from and violate a particular moment of history. Particular historical factors explain the selection of certain textually rich images—say, "pig" in *The Butcher Boy* or certain musical compositions in the *Recherche*—yet neither textual allegory nor the text's sociological dimension is reducible to these historically motivated conditions. In *The Butcher Boy*, pigs are at the core of an agrarian Irish economy, still defined in the artifacts' period of historical reference by its subservience to British interests. As an insult and internal social marker, "pig" derives from a vision of the Irish community that, although instrumented by Mrs. Nugent, is ultimately British in origin, one starkly divided between acceptable, socialized Irish and shanty Irish, or pigs.

Yet the historical rationales for the resonance of key images with sociological dimensions are counterbalanced by justifications or compulsions arising from the artifact itself. If Francie's suffering at least partially emanates from a community insensible to his predicament at the same time as being prone to the most frivolous theological fancies and extravagances, the materiality and even bestiality associated with pigs plays a crucial role in debunking this facile blindness. As the artifact spins itself out to greater depth and extension as a text, potential deployments of the pig metaphor within the aesthetics of tone, mood, and moral valuation proliferate.

While "pig" as a metasignifier can work untold effects on Francie and his fellow characters within the novel's sociological allegory, within the textual fabric of the novel Francie (and all characters) are signifiers alongside the term *pig*. Sociological referents thus exert a torque on certain signifiers that they do not on others. The figure *pig* is free to function as the novel's overarching theme, a performative in a speech act that can only be described as a curse, and the trigger in the considerable potential for "becoming animal" that the artifacts contain. In the film, burnt-out pigs figure predominantly in some of the apocalyptic, sci-fi flashes in Francie's "private language." Francie is a complex signifier, but he must also conform to conventions of characterization. He is shown thinking as well as behaving. Even when his mind is deranged and his behavior execrable in the full sense of the word, the artifacts are constrained to posit some correlation between his past, his conditioning, and his attitudes, acts, and even "thoughts."

Even as Francie is progressively marginalized and degraded by the Nugents' insults, his incarceration in a reformatory, Father Sullivan's pedophilic attentions, and his work as a pork butcher, the glimmers of idealism return to him in the recurrent image of his mother, now the Holy Mother, who beatifically smiles and beckons to him from inside the kitsch souvenir he brought with him during his belated return from Dublin. During these flashes, not properly flashbacks, the sanctified Annie in the film is played by Sinead O'Connor. It is not difficult to understand how the overwrought and underappreciated Annie metamorphoses into a Mary who radioactively glows in the uncanny hues of early color TV. The life and adventures of Francie make sense only in an imagery culled from the prevailing religious ideology of Ireland, from Irish Catholicism. Even pigs harbor a distorted theological significance. They are both at the heart of the very practical economy and, in Irish terms, the sacrificial lambs making the Christian agony possible. Catholicism is the driving force behind the educational system that cannot accommodate Francie, the benign local interventions of Father Dominic, and the institutions of juvenile reform and "correction." But the film and the novel on which it is based lose all depth if they do not encompass both the official religion, which is a primary sociological context, and backdrop for Francie's actions and the shadow religion—whose elements include nuclear annihilation and heroes from American popular culture, whether the Lone Ranger or the Fugitive—which have begun to invade and colonize his "inner" life, such as we can infer it.[25]

As a character, Francie belongs to the surrogate society and community contained in the novel. Pigs are also signifiers in the novel, but are constrained less, if at all, by social convention. What we have here, then, is a situation in which the "purer" signifier, *pigs*, the one with greater license to metamorphose within the artifacts' semiological texture, is also the one that would be associated with a greater degree of literary and poetic autonomy and work. Within the framework of *The Butcher Boy*, as has already been suggested, this image predicates sociological features to many of the conditions surrounding signifiers belonging to the surrogate community.

But as a poetic figment of the text, pigs really have little to tell us about how the artifacts comprise poignant commentaries on their fictive time frame, or why they are compelling now. The artifacts' commentary on Ireland's facile religious ideology, its vehement ethnic and class conflicts, its dearth of social backup systems, the emergence of global popular culture within its local traditions, and the pressure on gender identification by volatile and unstable families depends on an internalized societal framework rather than on the semiological dissemination of key images, such as pigs.

The image of pigs is crucial to the artifacts' demarcation of a poetic as well as a sociological outside. There is a close affinity between Francie's social alienation as a neglected and misunderstood child and the aesthetic distance making him the surrogate artist in both versions of *The Butcher Boy*. Francie's charm, his misdeeds, and his metamorphosis into a talisman of social critique or commentary are all extensions of an outsideness that the artifacts take great pains to establish. As a creature of this outsideness, Francie, albeit charming and poignant, joins a long list of compelling characters in the history of literature, extending from Gilgamesh and Odysseus to Joseph K., Joe Christmas, and Dostoyevsky's and Wright's Underground Men. The gravitation of texts to an outside, however phantasmatic or contrived, sutures the arbitrariness of the linguistic medium to a sociological dimension haunting, in the sense of occupying as well as structuring, the cultural artifact.[26] It is not always possible to delineate where the arbitrariness of language ends and the stigmata of social alienation and marginalization begin. The uneasy but inevitable tension between linguistic intransigence and sociological demarcation still warrants study and elucidation, even though contemporary critical theory has definitively demonstrated the extreme tenuousness of "inside" and "outside" markers. Outsideness, even where patently contrived and questionable, is, in multifaceted ways, a precondition for the disbelief that aesthetic programming suspends. The outside is at once the site of transgression, the native land of the artist, and the location for the unsanctioned, nonrepresentational language (e.g., Derridean writing) comprising the literal stuff out of which the artwork is made. The artwork's sociological dimension has no more critical task than the always provisional demarcation of the outside that allows it to test prevailing codes and render its social and aesthetic critique.

Francie's predetermined externality is what makes him interesting as a youthful protagonist in the first place. As his sociological alienation increases, so too does his power as a speaker, as a poetic figure and operator of poetic devises, and as a talisman of the sociocultural issues of his age. Personal suffering and travesty, in Francie's case, correspond to aesthetic quality and interest. In this respect, Francie joins the ever-growing list of literature's demented villains, its inventive heroes, and its staged artists, who may be, from an ideological point of view, less distinct than they seem.

Joe Purcell's attestation to the pugnacious priests of St. Vincent's College that he has severed all ties to Francie is the crushing blow that removes any motivation for Francie to maintain even the pretenses of subscribing to communal aspirations and conventions. From the perspective of the constructed exteriority that defines Francie's interest and the range of his activity, this moment demarcates a crossroads. Joe, in league with Philip and the Nugents, "comes in from the cold" of the mythical and boyish outside to the community that he has playfully shared with Francie. Of course, the writing has been on the wall for some time. While Francie is being sexually harassed by Father Sullivan at reform school, Joe gives the goldfish he wins at carnival games to Philip. Before being sent up to the exclusive public school, the latter two boys, whose families have become close, share music lessons, which embody the preexistent, unmotivated conventions of community life. While Joe makes a sharp turn toward the normative center of the community, Francie veers outward toward a borderland sharing the features of the postnuclear holocaust figured in the film.

Let us make no mistake about it: this growing and changing exteriority is what makes Francie the only plausible candidate for the "internalized" figure of the Western artist in these artifacts. The drama is carried along by Francie's efforts to cope with his mother's depression and his father's drunken absence, by the imagery of fugitives, aliens, and nuclear explosions that he configures in understanding and expressing his predicament. The story, its drama, and its ethical and cultural critiques are couched in his diction and his imaginary. Even defecating on the Nugents' parquet and hiding Mrs. Nugent's corpse in the slaughterhouse brock are, while morally objectionable, also poetic acts defining Francie's aesthetic interest.

The artifact becomes a crossroads for centrifugal and centripetal counterforces pirouetting around the illusion of the outside. To the degree that all narrative artifacts, in whatever medium, establish a trajectory—even where they devote considerable work to exposing the tenuousness of continuity and completion, they establish an economy in which strangeness and outsideness are eventually referenced, if not entirely mitigated and domesticated, by the measures and settings of familiarity. By the same token, it is the very thrust of aesthetic programming to endow the routine with strangeness, in keeping with Benjamin's notion of translation, where the mother tongue may be worked to fullest nuance and effect when it is apprehended in a foreign language. Benjamin's essay "The Task of the Translator" impresses not only translation but aesthetic innovation in general into the service of uncanniness, a vertigo of strangeness experienced semiotically and symbolically rather than as a Freudian symptom.[27] I have no interest in resuscitating the dimension of outsideness, however definitive or porous it might be, as a location for art, social deviance, or writing. But this certainty, the capitulation of the agents and perspectives of exteriority to the systems lending them their significance, in no way denies the multifaceted appeal that mythologies, Western aesthetics and epistemology, and social codes make to the outside as a domain of possible release, freedom, and redefinition. Sociology, aesthetics, and the philosophy of writing join in the foyer leading to this putative outside.

Sociology formulates the parameters of belief and behavior within which communities reside. Among many activities, aesthetics tests, on conceptual and thematic levels, the moral, theological, and metaphysical conventions that communities establish. The philosophy of writing is the aesthetically structured critique bridging between art's transgression and testing of social codes and the established discourses of culture (philosophy proper, history, psychology, literary criticism). The philosophy of writing is an interstitial discursive zone inhabited by artists, philosophers, and critics alike: Plato, Poe, Baudelaire, Nietzsche, Wittgenstein, Benjamin, Borges, Blanchot, and Derrida surely number among its preeminent practitioners.

The Butcher Boy is one of many possible contemporary entries into a study of the allure, inevitability, and illusion of the outside in art and culture, because its social lesson is as touching and compelling as its recourse to the external dimension is systematic. Of recent vintage, it is a work in which a powerful sociological fable merges significantly and indistinguishably into allegories of reading and writing. It is not alone in this regard. Murasaki's *Tale of Genji,* Dickens's *Great Expectations,* Eliot's *Middlemarch,* Nietzsche's *Thus Spake Zarathustra,* Zola's *Nana,* Proust's *À la recherche du temps perdu,* Kafka's *The Castle,* Benjamin's *The Origin of German Tragic Drama,* and Blanchot's *The Infinite Conversation* are among its strange bedfellows.

The appeal that these and similar works make to the outside at once attests to a highly individualized, even singular freedom and forms the basis of the only meaningful compacts that can found societies and communities. I am arguing for a privileged, even fatal affinity between the extreme case of social alienation, or asociality, in the invention that defines the artwork and the very ground or possibility for social communities and other organizations. Individuated language pushed toward a borderline, which is what inventive art offers us, is on a continuum with the contractual arrangements that define communities and establish organizations.[28] Individuated discourse recognized as art is not as unprecedented and singular as social conventions might seem efficacious, predictable, and staid. The appreciation of the full connection and follow-through between culture's most outrageous confections and society's most unglamorous footing requires an investigation on the threshold between the linguistic and the sociological, on the verge of the outside that beckons to the experimental artist and the established citizen alike, even while society's codes aim ceaselessly to disqualify it.

THREE

Exiles in Writing: Joyce and Benjamin

Outside. As we have already begun to discern, what a deluded concept, an untenable, even impossible position. Derrida's encomium to the coincidence of the outside and the inside crystallized almost at the outset of his writings, as he warned us not to expect the emergence of a marginal, differential reprogramming of traditional conceptualization from one outside or another, as so many have done before. Deconstruction intervened apace, but did so as immanently within the systems and economies of language and of life as it seemed to arrive from some frontier or no-man's land. That indeterminate continuum, the inside/outside of writing and interpretation, resituates and redefines the spheres of cultural and literate work.

The establishment of a working, if involuted, corridor between outmoded sections of interiority and exteriority was every bit as important to Paul de Man as he set out to orchestrate the insights accrued in focused studies into elaborate allegories of figuration and reading. We can read his 1979 *Allegories of Reading* as a position paper situating what beforehand were individual critical studies within a rhetorical theater founded on a coherent and evolving theory.[1] As de Man worked the abyss between metaphor and metonymy throughout the studies of Rousseau, Nietzsche, Rilke, and Proust comprising this book—attaining a position at which "the key to this critique of metaphysics . . . is the rhetorical model of the trope or, if one prefers to call it that, literature"[2]—the corridor between a putative inside and outside to signification becomes a decisive location at which the stakes of truth and lie, literality and figurality, are put on the table, if not definitively settled.

From the outset, any recourse we have to an outside—of convention, systematicity, law, the social contract—is subject to stringent statutes of limitation. However powerful and recurrent our intuition that the impetus to an act of inscription relies on the presumption of an opening for that writing experiment, a page, a facet of cultural stone yet blank to that legend, the ongoing transcript of conceptual and cultural transactions is sublime and vast, reaching toward the dimensions that Kafka ascribed to the Great Wall of China. Under what presumptions are we going to access a "true" outside, a "magnetic north" of exteriority?

And yet, just as literal meaning and even thematic strands are often recalled into the convocation of de Man's reading—having been dismissed from that assembly at a point when too much weight had been placed on them—on a higher level, higher not through conceptual revocation or *Aufhebung*, but in the ironic intimacy of rhetorical knowing, one not so remote from its sexual counterpart as it might seem, so the *outside* may still play a role in our compulsive inscriptions, however rigorously it has been called into question, however labored a construct it has been.

Indeed, it is in the act of inscription that the necessity of an *outside* declares itself. This may be as the range of innovation or invention, the presumption of prior cultural obtuseness, or as the writer's delusion of the *demand* for her scribed commodity. The writing act, project, occasion, or experiment fabricates the outside that it thereafter embroiders. The outside so crucial to the occasion of writing is thus fabricated by the "inside," the internal economy of its production. The meditation on this putative outside to writing—a highly ephemeral one, for its invariable fate is to be *filled in*—thus peels the process, phenomenon, experience of writing off from its philosophy, as adumbrated, say, in deconstruction or rhetorical reading, where this outside is, at best, highly suspect. The alternatives available to the writer on the verge of producing an artifact—and the moment when the first line of a production is inscribed on the screen or page is one of the elusive mysteries of culture—are, then, either dances in and out of delusion, truth and lie, literality and something more forced, on the occasion of the outside and other textual transcendentals, orchestrated so well by de Man, or a meticulous, ongoing adherence to the constraints of the philosophy of language, that is, a writing of this philosophy itself. Either "the way is to the destructive element submit yourself," as Stein counsels Marlowe in *Lord Jim*,[3] so that you open yourself, in the guise of a "self-motivated operator," to the random progression of crazinesses programmed into the processes of writing and composition, or you seek higher ground, you rise above the fray, having disciplined yourself beyond it, knowing in advance the specifications you will follow until the termination of your project. And yet this opposition between the fanciful or deluded and obdurate philosophical rigor—to which my own project of writing has led me by the nose, so to speak—immediately founders: the philosophy of writing has more than surpassed expectation in the tangles and accidents of language it has deconcealed, say, surrounding the French syllable *glas*,[4] though the archive of culture is replete with more renditions than it can handle of novels, poems, and artifacts of "creative writing" stamped out with a cookie-cutter.

The outside, like so many of the writerly constructs presenting themselves in the unresolvable fluctuations of aporia, is nothing, or rather less than nothing, a bowl of oatmeal, a kettle of fish. Upon its gelatinous texture we initiate projects of writing that do, occasionally, really go somewhere, like Melville's *Moby Dick*, whose memorable first chapter, "Loomings," is a hymn to the outside. It may be no accident that the frontispiece tale of Calvino's *Cosmicomics* is "The Distance of the Moon,"[5] a love story framed within a scenario in which the moon, whose consistency is akin to Velveeta cheese, begins to dribble down to earth. But no sooner do we turn outside in a direct address, by explicitly invoking the wishes with which its dimension has been invested, than the construct, not to mention the critical allegories we intend to found upon it, founders.

The outside crumbles, however powerfully it has served us as an inspiration, a heuristic device on the order of the ladder that falls away at the end of Wittgenstein's *Tractatus Logico-Philosophicus*,[6] in part because it is an amalgam, a composite film never fully bonded together. It assumes many forms and guises, none exclusive. It morphs between diverse appearances and registers without a trace, like an unmarked car. Yet for all this indecisiveness and anomaly, it is, consistently, highly efficacious in the performance of its job: to create the opening through which the writer or cultural programmer manages to slip her intervention before it is too late, before its plausible and efficacious opportunity, occasion, or moment, closes and vanishes.

By dint of the outside's composite nature, its composition as compost for writing, we cannot demand any firm characterization or scenario of what it *is*. Yet it is not unreasonable to suppose that we might pursue this protean horizon of writerly possibility along the trajectory of its customary bases, its common stopping points or stations on its (utterly nonlinear) route. We might well begin, though not necessarily, with the blank page, whose opening and solicitation is nowhere more provocative than in relation to lines and blocks of poetry. We live in an age when the unruly elements of language and the theorization that insists upon their decisive role in generating cultural cant and deviance have caught up with lyricism, in developments that include "language poetry."[7] This is, politically as well as intellectually, as it should be. Yet if that long-standing and currently bracketed poetic tradition has anything to hold it together, it is its status, however lurid, heretic, or disconcerting its contents, as hymn or prayer. And the addressee of lyricism's unending hymn is more the blankness of the page, openness itself, than it is God, love, the beloved, or what have you. Lyricism is a prayer to the opening that makes it possible, which it shortly obliterates by filling it with specific articulations, whose figurality and accidents of language initiate a second, less poignant opening. The illusion of the outside in literature is a vacuum that becomes voided by scribble, not by some absolute form of emptiness. It arises at the moment when a culture, or its particular cultural programs, has the gall or courage to lift the current scribed membrane of the Mystic Notepad and initiate a contrived innocence, a forgetting. This programmed moment of opening works wonders for shopworn aesthetic contracts and their subprojects; yet the sociopolitical aftereffects of these orchestrated caesuras in cultural composition may not always be optimal.

Then, of course, there is the built-in perspectival outsideness of the narrator, even when the direction in which she gazes is inward. The narrator observes from somewhere. She has a perch. The call to our attentiveness demands a stage, a balcony, the pulpit from which the priest delivers his picturesque sermon midway in Joyce's *A Portrait of the Artist as a Young Man*.[8] The location of this enunciative Holy of Holies is *elsewhere*, if not explicitly outside. The narrator is an outsider, at least while she speaks. She may subside, like the characters in Thornton Wilder's "Our Town," into a silent background before and after her speech, but at the moment of her utterance she is outside. In this sense, enunciation *is* outsideness. Each utterance grafted into the transcript of literature announces a new beginning by henceforth voiding it, by utterly disqualifying it. A narrator, or in certain situations a speaker, an interlocutor, can be, and often is, an outsider: an alien, a member of a social minority, an agent marked in terms of the sociological fetters operative under the prevailing political configuration. The narrator's or protagonists' Otherness not only fulfills literature's ongoing mission of voicing the perspectives of the dispossessed, the muted, the spoken for (sometimes at the cost of *speaking for* Others). It corresponds to a perspectival distanciation within the artifact itself, one crucial to its attentiveness, to the circuit of its intrinsic communication.

It is thus only too easy for the enunciative outsideness of lyricism and the perspectival externalizations of narrative to slip, to morph into thematic and generic expressions. Adventures, escape, the fantastic, unknown worlds: all these comprise the most tangible manifestations of an outsideness figuring prominently in the very motive for writing. Of course, timeframe provides a platform for externality just as much as does putative spatial distanciation. Crusoe's adventure is as much a repository of techno-communicative possibilities at a certain moment as it is an adventure story, an eventuality Defoe could count on, even knowing that for him the story was a more or less contemporary account. Outsideness is a vital promise for the detective story, the romance novel, or the science fiction narrative, one demanding some degree of strategic undermining, lest the depicted world err into the outside of utter incomprehensibility. The law of genre itself,[9] then, makes accommodations, through the appropriation of its own categories, to writing's project of explicitly staging and representing its gestures toward its own outside.

On a more subliminal level than the explicit hypothesis of distanciation and displacement, which can stamp so decisive an imprint upon plot, narrative structure, characterization, timeframe, setting, and related features, some works challenge the integrity of the *tongue* (*parole*) in which they were written, veer toward the frontiers of their historically and/or rationally accrued *language* (*langue*). Indeed, for Walter Benjamin, in his justly notorious essay, "The Task of the Translator," for the most productive deployment of words there are *only* interfaces, interlinguistic interstices, and interlinear gaps. In an art form he perfected in *The Arcades Project*, Benjamin eloquently cites Rudolf Pannwitz: "The basic error of the translator is that he preserves the state in which his own language happens to be instead of allowing his language to be powerfully affected by the foreign tongue. Particularly when translating from a language very remote from his own, he must go back to the primal elements of language itself and penetrate to the point where work, image, and tone converge. He must expand and deepen his language by means of the foreign language."[10] The highest achievement of a translation is not the faithful transfer of meaning from one language to another but the importation of strangeness, the literal signification of the foreign in French, into the "home" language, where its irreducible uncanniness becomes an inexhaustible source of improvisation on the part of its operators. In contradistinction to the Bible, Benjamin would take the figure of the Tower of Babel in Genesis not as a violation of the tenets of an emergent monotheism to be leveled and cleared away but as the very foundation of creative, that is to say, detached work in language. It is in this sense that Babelian experiments in literature over the broader modernity, from *Tristram Shandy* to *Finnegans Wake*, appeal to a different outside than the more obvious ones. They seek a volatile no-person's land where one traditional national or ethnic language seamlessly merges into another, unsettling the senses of identity and integrity that have accrued to the language and highlighting instead the arbitrariness, tenuousness, and fragility of any one language's claims and specifications. Derrida's own Babelian adventure, in "Des Tours de Babel," not only serves as an occasion for his meditations on translation and for his gloss on Benjamin's "The Task of the Translator," it continues his extrapolation of the conceptual and ideological underpinnings common to, but differently deployed by, the three Abrahamic religions.

> Babel: today we take it as a proper name. Indeed, but the proper name of what and of whom? At times that of a narrative text recounting a story (mythical, symbolic, allegorical; it matters little for the moment). . . . This story recounts, among other things, the origin of the confusion of tongues, the irreducible multiplicity of idioms, the necessary and impossible task of translation, its necessity *as*

impossibility. Now, in general one pays little attention to this fact: it is in translation that we most often read this narrative. . . . And yet "Babel," an event in a single tongue, the one in which it appears so often as to form a "text," also has a common meaning, a conceptual generality: That it be by way of a pun or a confused association matters little: "Babel" could be understood in one language as meaning "confusion."[11]

Concentrated in the proper name *Babel* is a tangle of the frustrations and complexities endemic to translation itself, as Benjamin theorized the process. In Derrida's development and problematization of Benjamin's catalytic contribution, the term *Babel* proves ultimately untranslatable, for it is at once the putative name of a location, of the myth or story that presumably took place there, and of the confusion of tongues that was left over from the narrative. The confusion that is Babel's metaphorical meaning, with the overarching or transcendental signification that metaphor transfers, is a limit experience, a phenomenon of tongues pushed, at their boundaries, up against other tongues, where their exclusivity and integrity break down. It is no accident that *Finnegans Wake*, the most sustained text in a language we only *might* be able to call English, impels word after word toward the brink where it belongs to another tongue, where it joins in interlinguistic confusion, makes ample reference to its Babelian pretext. Its author, James Joyce, spent his entire adult life in exile from his native land, as well as his Hiberno-English tongue. It is no accident that Derrida unearths exile as well as messianic redemption in Benjamin's theory of translation. In Derrida's terms:

> The translator must redeem (*erlösen*), absolve, resolve, in trying to absolve himself of his own debt, which is at bottom the same—and bottomless. "To redeem in his own tongue that pure language exiled in the foreign tongue, to liberate by transposing this pure language captive in the work, such is the task of the translator." Translation is a poetic transcription (*Umdichtung*). We will have to examine the essence of the "pure language" that it liberates. But let us note for the moment that this liberation itself presupposes a freedom of the translator . . . and the liberation that it operates, eventually . . . must extend, enlarge, and make language grow.[12]

The messianic scenario and aspiration for translation, which Benjamin inscribes in a sentence that may be taken as the "punch line" of "The Task of the Translator," does not go unnoticed by Derrida. However problematical this linguistic purism may be for a deconstructive view of translation, and to some degree because of that, theoretically mindful translation necessarily marshals originality of a sort that can only in part be recognized by intellectual property law. Deconstructive exegesis invests the translator, in Levinas's terms, with a "difficult freedom," one at the limits of national cultures, archival service, and fidelity to an "original." It is in this sense that language, according to Derrida, in the practice of Benjaminian translation, and in a rhetoric reminiscent of Borges, must expand, extend, and grow. Intellectual property law, in fact, does recognize translation as intellectual property. For translations of work under copyright, however, the translation is usually a "Word Made for Hire," whereby the translator explicitly renounces claim to copyright. As intimately as the translator works with the "original" and knows it, this provision allows the publisher to correct the translation if it is not judged to be faithful, if it has not, in effect, fulfiilled its promise.[13]

Language, as translation underscores, is both the substrate and very substance of systems and the medium that constantly evades and gives the lie to systematic claims. Literature's simulation and questioning of systems is yet another arena in which the prospects for exteriority figure prominently. Indeed, this overview of the power that the mere possibility of and wish for outsideness exerts upon the writer began with Derrida's quintessentially systematic observation "The Outside Is the Inside": there will be no decisive departures from the coherent, persistent configurations of ideology and metaphysics that modulate and temper so many cultural affiliations; theoretically astute reading and decoding of culture will, rather, assume the form of digressive forays and feedback loops. We have ourselves circled back to this seminal moment in Derrida's project. Derrida's notion of cultural empowerment, one presupposing a practice of close exegesis driven by rhetorico-etymological awareness, evokes the architectural figure of the hinge, whose pin facilitates opening and closure at once.

The outside of systems, as of Western philosophy as an encompassing, interrelated project, glimmers; it beckons, but only for an instant. This is not the moment to rehash deconstruction's immense and enormously persuasive project of measuring, delimiting, denoting, and staging systematicity within the spectral surroundings of its metaphysical abyss. This is a mainstay of deconstruction's intervention, and the body of its critical and scholarly elucidation exceeds in scale even Derrida's considerable demonstrations in this regard Within literature one notes a gravitation toward a systematic outside that animates, in very different ways, Zola's *Ladies' Paradise*, Joyce's *Ulysses* (I think particularly of the waterworks and tram network incorporated so suggestively into the novel), Kafka's *The Trial* and *The Castle*, Borges's "Tlön, Uqbar, Orbis Tertius," "The Library of Babel," and "The Babylon Lottery," Calvino's "The Chase," and Pynchon's *Gravity's Rainbow*.

The critic in large measure evolves as a creature of the outsideness to which literature, above all fictive narrative, recurs. The question of the writer's exteriority to a large measure coincides with the one of how it was possible for Walter Benjamin, who spent a sizeable portion of his life in exile, to produce such a wildly divergent body of writings, extending from highly structured studies, with full scholarly apparatus, to, in effect, radio talks and cryptic personal notes to himself, by way of autobiographical reminiscences, whether assuming the form of memories, diaries, or "sequences." In setting out with the critic's protean or polymorphic quality, I underscore the considerable degree to which the critical vocation is invested in the critic's "wrapping" herself "around" a moment, a development, a wrinkle in how things are done, at whatever cost. This openness to the occasion of inscription, whatever its torsion upon the critic, however it may twist and "leverage" her, distinctively imprints a critic's outsideness—a mark that registers her times, her "subject matter," and, especially, everything else she has ever thought or written. From the critic's perspective, outsideness is a matter less of location or position than of openness, susceptibility, being constantly on the alert to integrate culture's ongoing surprises and epiphenomena—not only to register culture's flotsam and jetsam, its ebb and flow, but to adapt each swathe of text to the demands of a writerly situation. This extreme susceptibility comes at certain costs, to be sure: in conceptual consistency, in measures of linear development, in disciplinary contribution, to name a few. The authentic critic extracts every nuance from the auratic artifacts in his collection before looking back to survey the impact of his intervention.

Benjamin thus imports into criticism the perspective that Dziga Vertov improvised for the movie camera in "I Am a Camera": the willingness to go anywhere at any time and to adapt to the particular needs of the situation, however it may imprint the elements of the performance: concepts and key terms, narrative structure, style, syntax, vocabulary. The ability to project, or subordinate oneself to the role of a "kaleidoscope equipped with consciousness,"[14] may seem to confine itself to one particular modernist aesthetic subcontract, akin to Cubist fragmentation. But as a modality of attentiveness or sensibility, this capability embraces far more. The same radical adaptability has been noted with regard to the episodic development in a work of fiction by another lifelong exile, James Joyce's *Ulysses*. The critic's radical exteriority is a nomadic mobility, even away from herself. It is a suspended imbalance more difficult to maintain than an acrobat's tenacious equilibrium. In the subordinate role the evolution and maintenance of a culture-wide conceptual and ethical operating system occupies in the succession of her encounters, the critic bids farewell to the philosopher. To the degree that the composite of her fleeting and even more substantial encounters, in Benjamin's words, "love at last sight,"[15] coincides with no particular academic discipline, the critic is not exactly a professor. Constantly effaced in nomadic wandering, measured only by the volatility of a projective empathy for culture's ongoing articulations, the critic's illumination extinguishes itself at the horizon to which he has been content to remove herself—and pay the price.

Exiles: the standard dictionaries derived from the Latin would have it that they—*exilium* or *exsilium*, terms based on the Old Latin *exul*—are individuals banished or proscribed. But we know better. They are ex-ile: they have left the island, the bounded, protected territory, of familiarity, inborn affinity, intimacy. Their relationship to this homeland is one of superannuation, since they *formerly* were of the place. *Anciens compatriots*. Ex-neighbors. It would take a separate study to begin to imagine why Paris becomes such a magnet for exiles, a second island and refuge.[16] A large portion of this study would have to take into account the marvels, resources, and particular complexities of French public spaces, a unique social environment that has been in continuous evolution since the Enlightenment and the French Revolution. These momentous events may be said to have *decided* a public space with specific features and guarantees in all Departments of France, one in which all people are entitled to certain standards of acknowledgment, civility, and politeness; one offering certain protections against willful aggression, whether in the form of physical assault, public humiliation, or unwanted intrusiveness, what we would nowadays call harassment. This element of natural ideology is no doubt replete with wrinkles and incongruities. But a significant national-historical investment in public space is a remarkable feature of French nationality—and in a public space in which anyone not perceived to be a threat to public security (which opens, of course, exasperating questions), is safe, protected, and welcome so long as he remains within its designated bounds.

This may have contributed to Paris's "draw" for three major twentieth-century writers in exile, whose ex-patriotism happened to coincide with adeptness in several modes of writing and who deployed this writerly "polymorphous perversity" in reaction to the structures of the law of genre. I think of: James Joyce, who experienced his native Ireland as a bog of theological poetry, political reaction, and stifling moral and sexual repression, all damping aesthetic creativity and its full expression; Walter Benjamin, whose messianic project of social redemption through cultural dissemination dwindled rapidly and decisively during and after the fateful year of 1933; and James Baldwin, who recounts in *Notes of a Native Son* that it was not entrenched U.S. prejudices' assault on his person that made continued residence there untenable, but rather their deleterious effect upon his writing, in which his primary allegiance was invested. Joyce spent the years from 1920 to 1939, pivotal to *Ulysses* and *Finnegans Wake*, in Paris. Benjamin's residence there was bound up with the production of *The Arcades Project*, in many senses a new kind of book. James Baldwin forsook his native New York for Paris in 1948, at the age of twenty-four. It was his address for the next eight years, among the most creative and prolific of his career. One product of those years, *Go Tell It on a Mountain*, is the subject of the following chapter.

One can point to many other important literary exiles who turned to Paris for solace and safe haven, so my selection can only be somewhat arbitrary. Yet a telling coincidence in all three cases between nomadic and literary displacement, between geographical exile and a pronounced, memorable gravitation to outsideness, however it may be constituted, brings together this triadic constellation of writers. For none of them can I begin to exhaust the specific manifestations of exteriority that permeated, and tempered, his writing. Each wandered through a distinctive, different labyrinth in search of the outside. But for pivotal stretches of their writings and writerly careers, Paris served as a venue, context, atmosphere, and inspiration for their aesthetic inventions.

It is not difficult to imagine the progression in James Joyce's fiction from the setting of cultural desolation and belatedness in "Araby," one of the stories in *Dubliners*,[17] whose young narrator arrives at a much-anticipated, elaborately imagined bazaar just as it is shutting down, to the bizarre, Babelian, multi-linguistic amalgam of *Finnegans Wake*, which puts virtually all of our understandings of language to an extreme test. The ruined dream of "Araby" derives in part from a family that is oblivious to the strivings of a young boy's imagination. The boy's abortive attempt to enjoy the carnival ends in "anguish and anger." From the outset, the young artist, the James Joyce surrogate in the text, is destined to be thwarted in his inner and creative lives. At whatever tender age he has reached, nine or eleven, he is already a social, that is to say, cultural pariah. He is already fated to cruise Dublin after hours in search of the aesthetic, imaginary sustenance that his stark, unyielding society denies him. In many of the narrative directions in which *Dubliners* turns, the reader comes upon desolation, sterility, and the absence of a future—an intellectual and cultural vacuum.

The ultimate position of exteriority attained by Joyce is, as suggested above, the unique interlinguistic, semantic, syntactic, and orthographic amalgam that he devises for *Finnegans Wake*. Yet any outsideness that he achieves here is predicated by his penetration of writing down to the levels of the syllable and the orthographic as well as postal letter. He penetrates to the level of the "proteiform graph itself . . . a polyhedron of scripture."[18] Yet before Joyce takes off on this last hurrah, this veritable bender of unbounded scriptural *jouissance*, an argosy of escape fueled by language's most technical while most intimate possibilities, he contributes two major novels, each serving to extend aesthetic outsideness in its more conventional aspects. Indeed, looking at the growing tide of sociological alienation, reverie in characters' idiosyncratic "private" languages, and formal, stylistic, and semantic disfiguration is a fecund if not exclusive exegetical approach to *A Portrait of the Artist as a Young Man* and to *Ulysses*, which serves, in a sense, as its continuation. The former pushes the Bildungsroman to the limits of plausibility while pursuing Stephen Dedalus, who bears close affinities to the "Araby" protagonist, to the end of his baccalaureate education, by which time he is at articulate loggerheads with his declining family, Catholicism, his compatriots, and Irish politics, to name a few. The Stephen of *Ulysses*, whom Joyce plays off against the perdurability, earthiness, and everyday artistry of that wandering Jew—or eternal exile—Leopold Bloom, can easily be recognized in his namesake in the *Portrait*. Yet his own cogitations, meanderings, and collisions throughout Dublin are set loose in a novel that does everything in its power—short of the quasi word-salad of *Finnegans Wake*—to achieve an outside to the novel and its entire prior history. Yet this window on the outside to the novel—in Benjamin's words, "every great work dissolves one genre in founding another"—is a monumental task. Joyce breaks *Ulysses* into eighteen distinct chapters. Each comprises a cubist fragment in a concatenation of effacements of narrative traditions, some as old as Homer's *Odyssey*. Whether Joyce parodically rehashes the history of the English language in "The Oxen of the Sun," overruns newsprint conventions in "Aeolus," rewrites the conventions of abyssal drama in "Scylla and Charybdis" and "Hades," or addresses the challenge of a truly musical narrative in "The Sirens," the thrust of his systematic play on established historical aesthetic contracts is clear: toward their outside. And however enigmatic that outside might be, however elusive any tangible or positive characterization of it, the narrative discourse of *Finnegans Wake*, viewed as a certain material, *Stoff*, webwork in its own right— whose overall texture, consistency, or feel *signifies* more than any particular passage or set of formulations[19]—is a logical place to start in the quest to characterize the outside that seems to be one of the major tendencies of Joyce's lifelong project.

The outside demarcated by *Finnegans Wake* is above all a Babelian one, a site *between* tongues, which, however, always remains *of* language, thus enabling it to intimate, in the terms of Benjamin's "The Task of the Translator," "that pure language which is exiled among alien tongues,"[20] a language superseding the specificity of national or ethnic tongues.

> Because Soferim Bebel, if it goes to that, (and dormerwindow gossip will cry it from the housetops no surelier than the writing on the wall will hue it to the mod of men that mote in the main street) every person, place and thing in the chaosmos of Alle anyway connected with the gobblydumped turkey was moving and changing every part of the time: the traveling inkhorn (possibly pot), the hare and turtle pen and paper, the continually more and less intermisunderstanding minds of the anticollaborators, the as time went on as it will variously

inflected, differently pronounced, otherwise spelled, changeably meaning vocable scriptsigns. No, so help me Petault, it is not a miseffectual whyacinthinous riot of blots and blurs and bars and balls and hoops and wriggles and juxtaposed jottings linked by spurts of speed: it only looks as like it as damn it; and, sure, we ought really to rest thankful that at this deleteful hour of dungflies dawning we have even a written on with dried ink scrap of paper at all to show for ourselves, tare it or leaf it.[21]

This passage details the discovery by a hen in a barnyard of the written scrap of paper that, in a key irony, for *Finnegans Wake* is a hyperencyclopedic compendium of World Literature, the closest thing to a canonical text that the novel cites or reproduces. Both in chapter 1.5, from which the citation immediately above derives, and in 1.1, where the episode is glancingly introduced, the discovery of this excuse for and mockery of a primary urtext transpires in an environment of Babelian cacophony, barnyard noise as we might hear it musically transcribed in Saint-Saens's "Carnival of the Animals." The literate superperformance of *Finnegans Wake* is both oral and scriptural, public and private, transpiring simultaneously on the outside and the inside, aspiring, in Joyce's formulation, "to make soundsense and sensesound kin again."[22] As idiosyncratic, open to distortion, as the barnyard of *Finnegans Wake* is, no secrets flourish in its domain; there is no utterly private language. There is an easy transition and fluid interface, in the citation immediately above, from "dormerwindow gossip" and cries from the housetops to the blots, blurs, hoops, wriggles, joltings, and spurts of writing. The questionable note discovered by Belinda of the Dorans,[23] like the entire text of *Finnegans Wake*, is composed of "changeably meaning vocable scriptsigns."[24] Thus, in both of the novel's facile efforts to invoke or introduce a canonical foundation, both at the beginning and in the pivotal Chapter 1.5, the biblical scene of Babel, Western culture's explicit scene dramatizing the arbitrariness and violence of linguistic particularization, instigates a penetration into writing's innermost workings, its guts and minutest internal features. Yet the end result of this penetration into writing's equivalent of Alice's rabbit hole is an overriding, pervasive sense of writing's strangeness, its foreign accent, in every tongue or language.

Writing's outsideness—where sense was to dominate Joyce's life, from his flight from Dublin at age twenty-four to his fascinated, if not exactly loving exile in Trieste, Zurich, and Paris, to the writing practice that he

Exiles in Writing   77

evolved for *Finnegans Wake*, that of synthesizing a novel from keywords culled, as in a barnyard, from newspaper clippings and scripted scraps, reveals itself only through writing's innermost penetration. Hence the gravitation toward the insides of individual *Buchstaben*, or letters.

> The steady monologuy of the interiors; the pardonable confusion for which some blame the cudgel and more blame the soot but unthanks to which the pees with their caps awry are quite often as not taken for kews with their tails in their or are quite as often as not taken for pews with their tails in their mouths, thence your pristopher polombos, thence our Kat Krysbyterians; the curt witty wotty dashes never quite just right at the trim trite truth letter; the sudden spluttered petulance of some capItalllsed mIddle; a word as cunningly hidden in its maze of confused drapery as a fieldmouse in a nest of coloured ribbons; that absurdly bullsfooted bee declaring with an even plainer dummpshow than does the mute commoner with us how hard a thing it is to mpe mporn a gentlerman: and look at this prepronomial *funferal*, engraved and retouched and edgewiped and puddenpadded, very like a whale's egg farced with pemmican.[25]

The highest productions of this splendid Joycean riff are complex semantico-etymological inventions such as the "prepronomial *funferal*" and the "whale's egg farced with pemmican," indicative of a language that has suspended its customary boundaries and constraints. Since the onset of the novel, Joyce has metamorphosed the obsequies common to Finn and HCE into a "*funferal*." In this case, the last rites are also the rites of initiation, for the funferal is "prepronomial." The issues taken up by the passage extend beyond proper names to naming, to the material grounds of substantives. As the initiatory and central social event of the novel, the "funferal" celebrates an unbounded play and substitution of pronouns and prepositions. In order to figure the refinement and civilization imparted to the novelistic community of characters by the "funferal," Joyce trots out a simile: the funeral is as fine as "a whale's egg farced with pemmican," an impossible figure, really, because whales don't produce roe. Yet if we allow that a whale's ovum might be stuffed with pemmican, a dried-meat product of indigenous North American peoples, we are left with a figure bounded on both sides by a certain wildness: on the one side is the whale's unequaled domination of the depths; on the other, the pemmican's rawness. The presumed acculturation brought about by the "funferal," then, doesn't happen at all. Yet it is qualified by a series of adjectives picturesque in their own right: "engraved," "retouched," "edgewiped," and "puddenpadded," the last in the series presumably applying to the whale's egg.

(Terms such as *funferal* and *puddenpadded* are emanations of a language in which volatile "prepronomial" combinations are the rule; one registering the accidents of sound, sense, and orthography comprising its very substance, which I have elsewhere referred to as a "discourse of half-reference."[26] And yet the marvelous image of a farced, or forced whale's egg itself depends on instabilities at an even lower level of generality. At the extreme interior of the monologue—or of its speaker, the "monologuy," the strokes of individual letters, the "bottom line" of orthography, are going astray, producing the semantic distortions, slippages, and simulacra of meaning typically held in check by normative, for example, grammatical, discourse, which Joyce's discursive amalgam quasi-systematically "outs." The above passage deals quite literally with the outlines of the "pees," *I*s, *J*s, *K*s, and "bees" it incorporates. The merest slip of the pen, one confusing a *p* with a *k* and vice versa, results both in "pristopher polumbus" and "Kat Kresbyterians"; *I*s confused with *J*s end up as a "capItallIsed middle."[27] Unvoiced consonants and "bees" literally tipping over into "pees" give rise to the lament of "how hard a thing it is to mpe mporn a gentleman,"[28] especially if "porn" is a birthright. At the same time as Wakean discourse *points out*, as during the tour of the Willingdone Museyroom,[29] the anomalies created by confusions at the literal level, it performs those very difficulties, as the challenge of verbally enunciating "mpe mporn" readily demonstrates. The fluidity of this hybrid, boundary-dissolving fictive texture brings constativity and performativity into unusual rapport with one another. The compulsively auto-performative text thus regularly externalizes itself in the setting of an abyssal theatre.)

Wakean discourse, founded on type characters that cannot be counted on to be themselves, assembled by means of a near-random hen-pecking through scraps of culture, thrusts in the direction of multi-faceted strangeness. This is a compulsively sustained hybridization or pidgenization, comprising semantic distortion, extreme syntactical stretch, diction invented on the spot, and runaway assonance. The relentless strangeness of the patois is achieved through intimacy—and only through intense familiarity—with language's most microscopic epiphenomena. Wakean discourse embodies a strangeness founded on intimacy. It is thus a comprehensive rhetorical performance of uncanniness. Yet its unrelenting fluidity and distortion pushes its script as decisively as possible in the direction of the cultural outside. This outside is often glimpsed through *Finnegans Wake*'s geological setting, "from swerve of shore to bend of bay" and beyond to the farthest-reaching rivers of the world.[30] The rivers spliced and sutured into the "Anna Livia Plurabella" chapter give ample evidence of Wakean discourse's opening, precisely because founded on microscopic undoings and underminings. Rhetorically, the passage is at once a paean, a lament, and a love poem in prose. Anna Livia mourns her husband, HCE, gossips about him, and chronicles his adventures, in the latter function speaking as a loving and faithful wife, yet another resuscitation of Penelope from the *Odyssey*. Among the Liffey washerwomen, Anna Livia Plurabella directs the river of language that is one of the novel's most telling insignia toward the oceanic compendium of culture that precedes it and into which it will drain. "He's an awful old reppe," she declares of HCE. "Look at the shirt of him! Look at the dirt of it! He has all my water black on me."[31] First couching her love in the form of a complaint, Anna Livia reverts to the venerable conventions of rhymed prose, a feature that will be distinctive of her intervention. "O, the roughty old rappe! Minxing marriage and making loof. Reeve Gootch was right and Reeve Drughad was sinistrous! And the cut of him! And the strut of him! How he used to hold his head as high as a howeth."[32]

Yet even in her initial articulations of HCE's earthiness, his concupiscence, "minxing marriage and making loof," his erotically charged style, his cut and his strut, her expressions cannot avoid veering to the extreme referential outsides of rivers and global geography. To her, HCE spans both sides of the Seine, "Reeve Gootch" and "Reeve Drughad." This is merely an early instance of the geographical rivers and streams that Joyce compulsively cuts into Anna Livia's monologue. The effect is both to frame the very intimate and local melodrama of her domestic life in a discourse that is markedly encyclopedic and impersonal, and to "perform" the river, which becomes a talisman for a discourse that Joyce, in his relentless distortions and disfigurations, unmoors from its standard, everyday referential, structural, categorical, logical, syntactical, and semantic functions. The global rivers spliced into this chapter in particular, but also throughout the novel, are both diverse, in the sense of their geographical dispersion, and one, to the degree that they underscore oceanic processes of linguistic association, dissemination, and interconnection. They literally score the globe, the objective world in which the events of *Finnegans Wake* and Joyce's fiction transpire. They catch us short at the moment when we would relegate Joyce's

80 *Idylls of the Wanderer*

hybrid language and bizarre fictive inventions to levels of biography or personal psychology. The rivers have an "objective correlation" on any globe or map of the world, yet Joyce relentlessly splices them into the quasi-systematically odd Wakean discourse. They thus furnish a legend and an index to the depersonalization, alienation, and outsideness effected by any sustained language experiment, however endearingly it may be couched in whimsy and idiosyncrasy.

> In a gaabbard he barqued it, the boat of life, from the harbourless Ivernikean Okean, till he spied the loom of his landfall and he loired two croakers from under his tilt, the gran Phenician rover. By the smell of her kelp they made the pidgeonhouse. Like fun they did! But where was Himself, the timoneer? The marchantman he suivied their scutties right over the wash, his cameleer's burnous breezing up on him, till with his runagate bowmpriss he roade and he roade and borst her bar. Pilcomayo! Suchcaughtawan! And the whale's away with the grayling![33]

> H.C.E. has a codfisck ee. Shyr she'o nearly as badher as him herself. Who? Anna Livia? Ay, Anna Livia. Do you know she was calling bakvandets sals from all around, nyumba noo, chamba choo, to go in till him, her erring cheef, and tickle the pontiff aisy-oisy. She was? Gota pot! Yssel that limmat? As El Negro winced when he wonced in La Plate. O, tell me all I want to hear, how loft she was lift a laddery dextro! A coneywink after the bunting fell. Letting on she didn't care, sina feza, me absantee, him man in passession, the proxenete! Proxenete and phwat is phthat? Emme for your reussischer Honddu jarkon. Tell us in franca langua. And call a spate a spate.[34]

By the banks of the "Phenician rover," HCE, drawn "by the smell of her kelp," playing Ulysses, achieves intimacy with Anna Livia's Circe, in the "pidgeonhouse," not the pigsty. "With his runagate bowmpriss he rode and he roade and burst her bar." "The whale's away with the grayling" just as the lion, in paradise, lays down with the lamb. HCE extends his "codfisck ee," a letter as much as the contents of a codpiece. She, in turn, cries out, "bakvandets sals," "nyumba noo, chamba choo."

This intimacy, of cries, ejaculations, and letters as well as of bodies, is interlaced and embroidered with rivers, mostly without any relevance to the scene, as is the entire chapter: "Yssel that limmat. As El Negro winced when he wonced in La Plate." The river imagery serves to place Dublin, and the intimacy between HCE and ALP, on the map. The chart is both of the world and of the linguistic medium that has been turned inside out. Joyce projects a global scale for his liquid linguistic map of the world, which extends from African languages and idiom ("nyumba noo") to strange places in Canada ("Suchcaughtawan"). The "boat of life" wanders forth on the linguistic ocean of which *Finnegans Wake* furnishes a blueprint, a map, a working plan, even if its operating principles are polymorphously and polysemically perverse. Joyce has been resolute in his pursuit of this voyage. It has taken him as far *outside* as any cultural inventor and programmer is permitted to venture.

It can reasonably be said of the author of such texts as "One-Way Street," "Berlin Chronicle," and "A Berlin Childhood circa 1900,"[35] embodying, among other things, a deep grounding in and commitment to his native Berlin, that by 1926, when his readings, exegeses, and translations of Baudelaire, Proust, and others were in full gear, Paris was rapidly emerging as the true city, the imaginative *polis* of his life. Benjamin first visited the city in 1913, at age twenty; he spent two consequential stays there in 1926 and 1927; and from 1933 to 1940 it was his city in exile, his base of operations, from which he managed, on occasion, to travel. Over the years it became increasingly inhospitable and dangerous; being there nonetheless connected one of the overriding endeavors of his last two decades—a quest for and retracing of the dominant cultural, conceptual, and sociopolitical forces that in complex involution set the stage for the latest major epoch of modernization—with the experience of his quotidian life. Paris epitomized and intensified the seminal moment of modernization, if I may use the phrase, for Benjamin. It was also a treasure trove for documenting it. The Bibliothèque Nationale served him as an archival simulacrum of this history: replete with the literature, primary historical sources, and social scientific analyses, contemporary and "of the epoch," through which it could be traced. Almost until the end of Benjamin's stay in Paris, the BN was both the primary repository of the materials that he incorporated into his mammoth collation and the site where he accomplished his project. *The Arcades Project* may indeed be read as a strategically organized, edited, and glossed microcosm of the BN's holdings on Paris during the Second Empire, a Web site, albeit in print medium, on this topic and many of its ramifications.

Benjamin's Parisian exile culminates the removal of tangible comforts and reassurances that had been in progress since his early adulthood. Whether support assumed the form of his immediate family's approbation and material underwriting of his literary aspirations and multi-faceted talent, or recognition by the University of Frankfurt philosophers who deliberated on his *Habilitatsionsprojekt*, of the exegetical radicality and astonishing erudition that he had imparted to his study on the baroque German death-pageant;[36] or his acceptance as a full-fledged member of German society in 1933 and thereafter, it would be progressively withdrawn throughout his adult years. The radical displacement of exile was thus not a discrete event late in Benjamin's life; it established itself much earlier as a phenomenon and modality of his experience and was formative in defining his bearing toward the artifact of criticism and toward the future, which always dawned with the despair attending the wish, the nuanced awareness of the wish's unattainability.

Since his early involvement in the Youth Movement, one of educational reform, Benjamin had entertained the inebriating but also potentially dangerous notion that ideas and substantial improvements in the quality of literate life could exert a tangible impact upon German society. The forces of nonviolence needed to assert control over history, through the enhancement of conditions of sensibility and the dissemination both of artifacts embodying dense cultural work and of the exegetical skills necessary for their appreciation and multiplication. This did not mean that nonviolence was an unwavering moral imperative in Benjamin's ethics. In "The Right to Use Force" and "Critique of Violence,"[37] he allowed himself to speculate on the forceful means available to workers when under violent, categorical suppression by the state. The messianic wish for a world made tangibly better through the improvement of literate and cultural conditions came to Benjamin from at least three directions: the rage for educational reform among his by and large well-to-do compatriots; the socialist, and to some degree Communist, understanding that education, training, and acculturation constitute a vital form of capital demanding equitable distribution; and Judaism, since the Second Temple a religion in exile, but one nevertheless maintaining the wish "for correction of the world into the Master's kingdom."[38] Within this highly idealistic program for social reform through cultural acuity—to which Benjamin was exposed from early on and to which he contributed as a leading light of the Youth Movement—the purveyor, tester, and publicist of social and aesthetic developments, in short, the critic, had a decisive role to play. Much depended on his or her preparation, autonomy, and exposure to the generative margin of evolving phenomena and new adaptations. It is understandable how, once this scenario for a sustained, even life-long intervention crystallized for Benjamin, a veritable Chinese encyclopedia of interests, some not obviously compatible, became logical, indeed almost natural, for him to pursue. The polymath demands upon a cultural and social critic at Benjamin's particular moment of political upheaval, developments in the mass media and overall technology, and artistic experimentation made compelling sense of crazily dispersed arenas of cultural life—whose scope and configuration strongly resemble a Joycean map. The global chart of Benjamin's fascinations included children's books, cinema, painting, postcards, nineteenth-century Paris, and mind-altering drugs, such as hashish. As a confirmed bibliophile and critic, he was drawn to them, even where he had not encountered them early in life. It can be stated unabashedly, I think, that Benjamin not only *assumed* the many perspectives, literacies, eruditions, and identities demanded of the engaged cultural critic in a world that greatly anticipated our own; he largely *invented* the role.[39] Hence, as the sum total of his contribution becomes available in different languages, the receptions, analyses, appreciations, and adaptations of his work, emanating from pursuits as far afield as theology, law, and architecture, approach the volume of a Borgesian library.

Benjamin's exiles thus assumed proportions far beyond the circumstances of his personal life and were inextricably linked to a messianic mission of cultural uplifting—itself demanding much in the way of diversity of interest, mobility, and adaptability. Benjamin's senses of purpose and mission were themselves in an ongoing process of evolution, and they motivated him to engage a bewilderingly broad range of artifacts, media, aesthetic understandings, and cultural moods. Not only were the phenomena to which Benjamin addressed himself in his self-appointed task as critic amazingly diverse, but he was willing to assume any perspective or rhetorical posture that a particular critical intervention demanded. Moreover, he never sacrificed the acuity of his sensibility or commentary to this protean adaptability. As he ambled, in emulation of the *flâneur*, through the modern panorama, the imaginary Paris that was constantly placing new phenomena before his critical scrutiny, he maintained his openness to the new occasion, his willingness to project himself into it, even at the cost of breaking with his own past formulations. The Benjamin who embroiders Goethe's *The Elective Affinities* with a philosophically rigorous commentary pivoting around German idealist notions of semblance and reconciliation is thus different from the one who writes a children's radio presentation about the 1755 earthquake in Lisbon, or from the one who introduced a literary review entitled *Angelus Novus*, which was fated never to see the light of day.[40] The fascinated reader who approaches the complete transcript of Benjamin's commentary may well come away with a sense of this openness and commitment to each emerging context of inscription, at whatever the cost, as the preponderant thrust of his work.

FOUR

James Baldwin's Exile: Theory, Circumstance, and the Real of Language

It would be so invitingly easy to explore the exiles of James Baldwin. Words would simply cascade forth. The real work would consist in editing out the wrong ones, the ones coming too readily, the ones in formulaic packages. Baldwin was, after all, exiled in his own skin, exiled in a country not accustomed to lending credence to serious writers of his race. His presumed gay sexual preference added to the foregone verdict of alienation. It further reduced the degree of affirmation and support that mainstream U.S. culture would afford his cultural projects, and it drove a wedge between him and the black establishment of his day. It would not be far-fetched in the least to assert that—with notable exceptions, including W. E. B. Dubois and Richard Wright—the writerly drive, calling, and vision of James Baldwin occurred at a moment of sustained national paucity in the constructive mirroring that, according to the psychoanalytical theory of object relations, is essential to mentoring, parenting, and education. Overwhelmingly, the evidence suggests that mainstream U.S. culture, in its multifarious negative reinforcements, had less than nothing to offer him.

By Baldwin's own account, in the "Autobiographical Notes" to *Notes of a Native Son*, reading was his earliest and abiding interest, writing his only aspiration:

> I began plotting words at about the time I learned to read. The story of my childhood is the usual bleak fantasy, and we can dismiss it with the restrained observation that I certainly would not consider living it again. In those days my mother was given to the exasperating and mysterious habit of having babies. As they were born, I took them over with one hand and held a book with the other.[1]

At this particular form of what we now call multi-tasking, the young James Baldwin proves more successful than his obvious fictional counterpart, the governess/lover Ottilie in Goethe's *The Elective Affinities*. Reading, writing, nurturing, being nurtured: Baldwin is marked by these fundamental socio-cultural transactions, all capable of extending into socially defined "deviance" if taken too far. These are strikingly evident in the postures assumed by the narrators and protagonists of Kafka's artist parables. I think particularly of the young narrator of "A Crossbreed [A Sport]," whose sole patrimony consists in a biological mutant, a kitten/lamb. This creature, doubled from the start, belligerent yet touchingly fragile, relating to the narrator as both adversary and confidant, primarily occupies itself by disqualifying and otherwise nullifying all of the categories that the narrator's family, as a microcosm of society, compulsively applies to it.[2] From the outset of his recollections and career, Baldwin is soberly aware that he too has been marked as an anomaly, a category violator, a pariah. He has been summarily banished to a state of exile, always already, according to a phrase Derrida appropriates from Heidegger, before the fact. His 1948 move to Paris—whatever he gained from inhabiting a social space engineered by principles at variance with the ones prevailing in the urban northern U.S.—was by the testimony of the "Autobiographical Notes" already predicated by the basic facts of his life. This story of a priori banishment and alienation is crucial to elucidating Baldwin's considerable achievement. It is a narrative indispensable to understanding the emergence of fictive inventions and modalities with limited precedent or positive reinforcement, but also to an account of the wider pattern of American cultural graftings and dispersion supplemented and modified by Baldwin's contribution.

Baldwin is by no means shy or muted about the impact growing up African American had in the mid-century cultural milieu. He intimates some broad relevance of the Lacanian Real for his writing, not that he's the one on trial here or, for that matter in a clinical setting: "The most difficult (and most rewarding) thing in my life has been the fact that I was born a Negro and was forced, therefore, to effect some kind of truce with reality. (Truce, by the way, is the best one can hope for.)"[3]

Baldwin knows, and we know with him, that the stigmas and anomalies that attend his adapting the conventions of realistic American popular fiction to the realities of contemporary African American life impart to his writing a great deal of its referential singularity and its sociological torque or body-English. Yet a recognition that his particular position, as gauged by the global positioning system of society and his moment, infuse his script with an implicit sociological gloss or annotation (as if penned with milk or lemon juice in the margins of his text) is counterbalanced by his impulse, certainly strong by mid-career, to distinguish his writing, as something with a force and autonomy of its own, from his various social coordinates. "Of traditional attitudes" toward African American writers in the U.S., he writes, again in the "Autobiographical Notes," "there are only two—For or Against—and I, personally, find it difficult to say which attitude has caused me the most pain. I am speaking as a writer; from a social point of view, I am aware that the change from ill-will to good-will, however motivated, however imperfect, however expressed, is better than no change at all."[4]

In reserving for his interventions a distinction between the process or dynamic of his writing and his perspective, experience, and status as both an individual and a phenomenon, Baldwin takes the liberty of saying that the stigma of his blackness and the linguistico-cultural markers and impasses that it set off have wounded him—while ineradicably contouring his writing—independently of any status quo in U.S. race relations, whether collective or individual. Socially, he is saying, in his status as an African American and a cultural programmer he may take cheer as individuals and trends indicate progress away from racial bigotry. But his writing arises independently of this scenario. The degree to which his writing has been scored by the social reality of racism transpires in a different register, in a different zone, from this give-and-take between social repression and progress. In brief, like so many writers of the century, from Yeats to Faulkner and Pynchon, Baldwin scribes a boundary between social reality and writing, despite healthy skepticism toward theorization: "I think that all theories are suspect, that the final principles may have to be modified."[5]

> It is quite possible to say that the price a Negro pays for becoming articulate is to find himself, at length, with nothing to be articulate about. ("You taught me language," says Caliban to Prospero, "and my profit on't is I know to curse.") Consider: the tremendous social activity that this problem generates imposes on whites and Negroes alike the necessity of looking forward, of working to bring about a better day. This is fine, it keeps the waters troubled. . . . Nevertheless, social affairs are not generally speaking the writer's primary concern, whether they ought to be or not; it is absolutely necessary that he establish between himself and these affairs a distance which will allow, at least, for clarity, so that before he can look forward in any meaningful sense, he must first be allowed to take a long look back.[6]

This striking passage begins with a bemused, ironic projection of the anomaly and impropriety surrounding the articulateness of one who belongs to a downwardly mobile social category, a situation expressed poignantly by a range of writers, from whom postcolonial theory, since its outset, has taken important cues, and ends with a second drawing of the boundary between inscription and its sociological parameters, this time in the interest of what we might call "historical objectivity." Being articulate, suggests Baldwin, a fate he inherited with the inevitability surrounding the Kafkan narrator's kitten/lamb, makes him feel like a Caliban, a domestic freak or curiosity with no obvious outlet or outcome for his odd linguistic predilections. Indeed, so odd is this exception that its fate is unlikely to arise beyond deleted expletives, the picturesque and off-target salvos released in the speech act of cursing. And yet, argues Baldwin, and his position is quite familiar to any of us who have generated or even contemplated language calibrated to institutional purposes, "social affairs are not generally speaking the writer's prime concern."[7] If writing's circuits and negotiations eventually have an impact on tangible social conditions, this will be by dint of something endemic to its own processes, not through explicit reference or direct intervention. The justification for the writer's establishing "between himself and these affairs a distance which will allow, at least, for clarity" is above all historical—any incisive predications regarding the future will hinge on "a long look back."[8] But this sometimes exasperating lag between writing and the world that infuses it, not to mention the social injustices and existential importunities it might address and possibly ameliorate, is also intrinsic to the worlds of literature and theoretical discourse that Baldwin's *Notes of a Native Son*, in 1955, join. It is not only in the interest of consolidating his historical stance that Baldwin insists on a distinction, a separation, and a deferral between his writing and his intense social sensibility.

The interface between the social, the human order or ecology within which inscription arises, and the text itself constitutes a problem that has plagued many of Baldwin's forerunners and inspirations, and that continues to daunt, if not actively torment, the present writer. By his own account in the "Autobiographical Notes," Baldwin is a close comrade to so many of us who find in writing a redress and counter to conditions in the human environment. Writing demarcates a sphere of intervention in which we who write afford ourselves the opportunity to formulate the insufficiencies to which we respond, to unpack our often complex reactions to them, to draw a blueprint of possibility beyond the status quo as we formulate it, and to infuse the written simulacrum with a performance of the world in which the text arises and of our own interpretation, response, and feedback to that world. Yet for all that the writerly performance augments—in deconstructive terms, supplements—a world whose deficiencies are both comprehensive and biased (and the account of Baldwin's early years furnishes a compelling instance of proliferating limitations) the act of writing is both constituted and besieged on all sides by dissatisfaction.

The insufficiencies both addressed by and consummated in scribed intervention form an intricate network of their own. As Baldwin recognized, when he was approaching sixty and introducing a second edition of *Notes of a Native Son*, social realities are extremely resistant to change, even in the face of suggestively imaginative artifacts and brilliant conceptual work. First the parlance of culture and then matters of atmosphere, style, even social expectation are affected by major artistic and philosophical interventions, but Baldwin isn't holding his breath to await any transformations his works, or anyone else's, might effect in the world.

Writerly intervention is flanked, on two complementary sides, by a sociological Real that has elicited such characterizations as "the iron law of oligarchy"[9] and by a commitment to deconceal *in language* the infrastructure of all significant social institutions, conventions, and artifacts. Of course, the latter attitude, positionality, and commitment characterizes the shared project of contemporary critical theory, as epitomized by deconstruction, itself the culmination of a century of cultural work in the West dedicated to exploring the premise that language constitutes ultimate being and reality. Very much the citizen of his age, Baldwin knows that it is through the resources of language, a medium that does not neatly translate into and directly address social realities, that his interventions may gain a force, vividness, and impact that can effect an *indirect* transformation of prevailing perceptions and formulations. It is in this sense that "social affairs are not generally speaking the writer's prime concern."[10]

Yet by the same token, linguistically inspired and driven theoretical models, such as deconstruction, for all the richness and suggestiveness of the long-standing conventions and institutions that they retrospectively reconstitute out of Greek, Latin, Hebrew, and German languages and traditions, may well arrive at a "hard bottom"[11] at which the operations of transaction derive more from sociability or from the social parameters of the situation than from linguistic "deep roots." This is not to suggest that the exchanges, negotiations, disagreements, and compromises in the sociological field ever achieve a definitive "outside" of language or an exemption from its processes. According to Derrida's extended project, "sociability" and its "historical" precedents are as much figments of language and its processes as any other situation of mediation, obligation, exchange, and negotiation. This comprises a significant thrust behind many of his late essays on core concepts of the Abrahamic religions.[12] Yet in any given context it is difficult, to say the least, to determine to what degree a sociological outcome or state of affairs, such as the conditions under which Baldwin grew up, is the product of a particular confluence of industrial, technological, socioeconomic, political, and technological factors, as well as the attitudes generated by them and perpetuating them, and to what degree it is nuanced, leveraged, by the deep-seated conceptual-ideological configurations at whose disclosure and elaboration Derrida was a master. (Needless to say, Derrida's embroideries on purity, whiteness, genre, and gender are of the greatest relevance to the material conditions Baldwin had to contend with, even before he had the wherewithal to interpret and respond aesthetically to them. But it is in Baldwin's text, and in our own experiences of late-capitalist and contemporary cultural worlds, that the mutual bracketing of textual domains and relatively harder-core sociological situations and codes becomes explicit. Entire disciplines—much of cultural studies, for example—

have declared themselves into being by virtue of presumed receptivity to the more material conditions under which cultural work transpires. The issue here is not to determine whether the truth resides in the situational experience of social conventions, some of which acquire the force of law, or at the level of infrastructural, conceptual-ideological reprogramming, but to acknowledge the sustained tension and complementarity between the two, the placement of interventions in writing within the framework of this interaction, as Baldwin did and many of us continue to do.)

Under the sway of this meditation, we can formulate the most compelling mega-intervention that could be commissioned under present conditions from the conceptually informed social sciences:[13] a multifaceted testing of the transmission or translation transpiring between, on the one hand, infrastructural reprogrammings of the sort performed upon cultural core-artifacts, in different ways, by Derrida, Lacan, and Deleuze and Guattari, and, on the other, the field conditions under which these phenomena are experienced. Contemporary critical theory has excavated out of the archive of long-standing Western philosophy, religion, and art, as well as the institutions they inflect, an astonishingly rich, wide-ranging, and still-growing network of what might be termed the enabling figures underlying organized, that is, institutional Western life. Yet we cannot gauge the impact of this operating system or network of cultural "deep roots," upon any particular situation, or local neighborhood, whether Italian, Jewish, or black, because contemporary critical theory has, in keeping with its long-standing and declared mission, with cues it has taken from modern phenomenology, among other inspirations, generally eschewed behavioral study.

Yet language is no less real, no less pervasive and influential, than seemingly more tangible conditions, whether socially, industrially, or technologically constituted. Indeed, the philosopher, as Derrida has redirected his or her discipline, mediates the Real of language for the public. In a fashion analogous to the psychoanalyst's public service as the access point to the Reals of death and the drive, the philosopher addresses the deep-seated, impersonal, non-negotiable epiphenomena of the linguistic preprogramming of culture. We could say as well that the poet also orchestrates the Real of language for the public, but in an occasional, performative, rather than sustained discursive and explicative mode. It would be disastrous to miscast Derrida as a philosophically minded archivist of etymological arcana. The linguistic dynamics and features that he accessed in order to deploy concepts and figures to elucidate artifacts, institutions, and the ideologies legitimating them are so deeply entrenched as to be endowed with the sublime wonder—and intractability—of the Lacanian Real. The Lacanian psychoanalyst appeals to the Real, inures the patient to it, to facilitate the mobilization and coordination of psychic agencies and an ensuing enhanced mindfulness. Derrida conjures up the inherently spectral Real of language in order to wean us from the cultural-ideological delusions that have arisen from our inability to gaze upon it directly. Within the parameters of his long-standing project, Derrida is as much of a "Realist"—in linguistic terms, as a thinker who releases and assesses the linguistic play within conceptual constructions whose currency normally depends on its foreclosure—as realism, understood as an aesthetic subcontract, may be associated with a specific novelistic literature.[14] That body of work encompassed, among others, Crane, Zola, Dreiser, Hemingway, and Wright, and comprised a significant cultural precedent and resource for Baldwin's project.

As Baldwin intuits clearly, along with the rest of us who, on occasion, have despaired of the limited social outreach or follow-through of our most edifying critical glosses, the writing project, the material writing desk, as it were, hangs suspended between the Reals of social circumstance and language. Each of these parameters is, in Lacan's insight, sublime, a priori, inconceivable, and virtually unconditional. Any productive negotiation or transaction between the cultural programmer and these two Reals will transpire only by dint of hard work and sustained, disciplined thinking. The Real of social circumstance will simply not account for or exhaust the rich palette of linguistic and rhetorical resources that are indistinguishable from our thought. While the Real of language may claim encyclopedic oversight of our social tools and interactions, it is inaccessible to any bounded and particular social situation. It cannot address our inherited placement and conditions within the social agglomeration (if not "order"). It cannot negotiate or suspend our obligations, according to our roles, or the sanctions meted out to us for failing to meet them.

I am suggesting that one needed way to marshal Lacanian psychoanalysis and deconstruction in an ongoing rapport—to elucidate artifacts that seem to stage a standoff between social reality and writerly intervention—would consist in retrofitting the Lacanian Real, a pivotal construct. It arises as part of Lacan's highly canny and invariably specific supplanting of the triadic division of labor between the three Freudian "intrapsychic agencies," the Id, Ego, and Superego, which are, when all is said and done, specialized psychological homunculi, with explicitly linguistically constituted *registers of articulation*: respectively, the Real, the Symbolic, and the Imaginary. In Lacan's functional characterization of mental life, elements carrying facets of subjectivity (e.g., appetite, understanding, restraint) are replaced by representational and semiological wavelengths or bands of activity: a putative awe peaking short of articulation, resulting in an overload and breakdown of rational deliberation; symbolic conceptualization; and imagistic projection and decoding.[15] Under the aura of deconstruction, it behooves criticism to disengage the Lacanian Real from an inherently subject-predicated and inter-subjective psychoanalytical field and to cast its distinctive illumination on the "object" (as Lacan appropriates the term from Hegel) of language itself. This deconstructive intervention, whether evidenced in Derrida's own Lacan commentaries or in the work of astute critics such as Samuel Weber,[16] has the effect of redirecting insights that Lacan extracted from the Real in a clinical setting back toward the linguistic network that served as the initial breeder for Lacan's overall project. Derrida and Lacan appear in this light as close collaborators in the access and elucidation of the Real of language and in tracking its play, albeit from different perspectives, in cultural artifacts and sociopolitical formations and transactions.

In keeping with the very nature of the Real, Lacan's references to it, especially in his *Seminars 2* and *11*, are glancing, oblique, and haphazard.[17] It is within this aura, in this particular *style*, that Lacan encounters the Real. A telling site for this monster hunt is Freud's own dream of Irma's injection, as recounted in *The Interpretation of Dreams*. In "*Tuché* and Automaton," a section of *Seminar 11*, also known as *The Four Fundamental Concepts of Psychoanalysis*, in which Lacan defines "the *tuché*, of the real as encounter,"[18] he reminds us, in this dream, of the

> unfortunate father who went to rest in the room next to the one in which his dead child lay—leaving the child in the care, we are told, of another old man—and who is awoken by something. By what? It is not only the reality, the shock, the knocking, a noise made to recall him to the real, but this expresses, in his dream, the quasi-identity of what is happening, the very reality of an overturned candle setting light to the bed in which his child lies.[19]

The particular dream that Lacan chooses to orchestrate and recast follows a rhythm alternating between the dream-work's open-ended invention and abrupt incursions of the Real. A knock, a random noise, awakes the old man of the dream, a surrogate for the dreamer, who has suffered the same inconceivable loss. Yet a highly contingent and tangible interruption inside the dream, one announcing the most unwanted eventuality to a father, could also telegraph an immanent threat in the framework (or "reality") around the dream, an impending house fire. The phenomenon of dreaming opens a vertiginous panorama vacillating between the interior and exterior of dream imaging, between unrestrained invention and abrupt incursion. The apparition is a visual phenomenon, to be sure, an image, but an utterly shocking and destabilizing one.

The Real, even as the dream-work displaces it, is irreducible and non-negotiable. It is stark. It speaks to us only indirectly and enigmatically, if at all. "Why don't the planets speak?" inquires Lacan in *Seminar 2*, invoking an image of intersubjectivity as the void or night in which ships and other uncommunicative bodies pass each other by. "The planets don't speak," writes Lacan in answer to his own question, "firstly, because they have nothing to say—secondly, because they don't have the time—thirdly, because they have been silenced."[20] It is a pivotal matter, in Lacan's conjuring up the "big Other" as a significant feature of psychological life in this segment, whether or not we anticipate speech from stars or planets. We shouldn't really expect to hear from the stars: "stars are real, integrally real, in principle, there is absolutely nothing about them pertaining to an alterity with respect to themselves, they are purely and simply what they are. The fact that we always find them in the same place is one of the reasons why they don't speak."[21] But we might expect something more edifying, not to mention more illuminating, from planets, which circulate—their motion is itself a venture into difference—and in symbolically richer networks than the stars. "Why don't the planets speak?" insistently asks Lacan. "That is the real question."[22] It is a Real question because of the inarticulate vividness that the Lacanian Real assumes in its touches on and encounters with understanding, also because it reaches toward the phenomenon of individuals reduced to noncommunication through their encounters with Otherness. As Lacan suggests in these enigmatic passages, planets sharing a sun and a gravitational system may well have more in common with individuals compartmentalized from one another through narcissistic self-absorption than stars do. In their parallel but skewed orbits, they may be fated to "talk" as well as move "past" each other.

The Lacanian Real can best be appreciated as an element in a signifying system emerging in conjunction with Lacan's overall reconfiguration of subjectivity from a model of systematic identity to one of communication or feedback loops. At certain junctures—crucial ones, to be sure, such as the consummation of the seminal "Function and Field of Language"— Lacan closes the loop between conceptual elements of psychological experience, including the Real, and their linguistic embodiment; that is, he accesses the *linguistic* features with which he predicates the Real. At the very end of "Function and Field," for example, he concatenates *da*-syllables and the words built upon them (e.g., *Datta, Damyata, Dayadham*) in a passage from the Bhrad-âranyaka Upanishad.[23] In such an instance he brings "to full termination" the intelligibility (or "encounter") of the Real as a phenomenon or element of experience that emerges only from processes of representation and signification. When Lacan stages the proliferation of *da*'s in the Upanishads, for example, he is making a subtle shift from the Real as a linguistically "updated" intrapsychic agency to the Real of language, language as the only idiom in which reality speaks, the irreducible and unavoidable shards of language broken into its materiality. (This message got through to Benjamin as well when he pursued the trajectories of imaging and figuration in the German baroque death-pageant.)[24] It is not the fact of Lacan's making linguistically acute revisions to long-standing traditions of subjectivity still operative in Freud's major works that would come up on the screen of so rigorous a philosopher as Derrida, but rather the double-dealing, which psychotherapy might well recognize as the mark of a healthy ego, between Lacan's mobilization of the Real as an intrapsychic domain and his encounter with it in language, in the form of linguistic epiphenomena and aberrations.

The Derrida who tracks the reverberations of one French subsyllable, *gl*, in *Glas*, as it inflects both Hegelian ideology formation and Genet's sociocultural margin of deviance, is close indeed to the Lacan who accesses the Real in the unbridled assonances of the Upanishads. The same Derrida "plays" for us grammophonically the buzzes and murmurs pervading Plato's pharmacy,[25] that is, the systemic noise that prefigures the metaphysics embedded in the *Phaedrus* and is oblivious to its rhetoric.[26] Derrida joins

Lacan in serving as an ethnomusicologist of the Real of language, a prominent feature of culture, as of psychological experience, regularly accessed by poets, novelists, dramatists, and songwriters, among others, as well as in dreams, jokes, and parataxes.

In spite of disclaimers to the contrary, elements of the Real can always be assumed to have a linguistic manifestation. The famous Lacanian *point de capiton*, or upholstery button, to the unconscious is more a stutter-syllable, a rhyme, or some other linguistic accident than an idea or even an image. One possible definition of literature is as the sanctioned release and play of the Real of language. Indeed, the only rigorous "psychoanalysis of literature" or "psychology of literature" is one that pursues the Real of language back and forth between psychic and linguistico-cultural arenas.

The only way in which I can approach the Real of social circumstance and the Real of language is by means of linguistic transactions. As an empowered user of language, a writer, with a healthy training and practice as a linguistic programmer, I am more or less constantly renegotiating my stance and my positions in relation to the raw system of language, the Real. But I am limited in my ability to leverage the circumstances under which I was born and raised, as well as the expectations accruing to and the obligations binding the person I have become, through the combination of circumstance, my own connivance, and the process of social marking or branding.

My various roles—this term is common to sociology and to drama—constitute arenas of work or function in which I have, deliberately or not, subsumed myself under broad menus or formats, stereotypes if you will, registered on the map of the subcultures to which I belong. The assumption of a role—getting married, declaring myself straight or gay, achieving a certain level of education, joining a profession—is a collusive act of marking between an individual or a subgroup and a wider collectivity. This process of social marking is to some degree collusive because it is not clear, in the difference between an individual and a social signifier, in the movement from a discrete entity to a site of meaning and expectation, how much of the imprint is self-proclaimed and to what degree it is socially imposed. Needless to say, to the degree to which each member of a community may be characterized as a complex signifier subdivided into many roles, which she fulfills with relative degrees of consistency, it does us no good to foreclose linguistic processes of signification, representation, displacement, metonymy, and so on from the Real of social circumstance.

And yet, I insist, our individual negotiations, transactions, games, inventions, and aberrations with the Real of language are characterized by relatively more give, play, whimsy, and impunity than our parallel dealings with the Real of social circumstance. This is because when we write, which is also when we joke, blather, converse, sing, what have you, we can often suspend or even bypass the various roles and semicontractual arrangements we have either made or had imposed upon us. By contrast, our roles don't change so easily. Indeed, over the course of a lifetime in contemporary civil society, we devote a significant portion of our waking activity, money, and resources to renegotiating these roles, regardless of the degree to which, at an earlier juncture, we either militated for them or they were thrust upon us.

In relation to the Real of social circumstance, some of the roles that we to varying degrees maintain, espouse, secretly wriggle out of, repudiate, or deny are easier to renegotiate or reformat than others. Many individuals under the current configuration of postindustrial, late-capitalist society thrive under the terms of the multi-clause social contract providing for the confluence between monogamous marriage and professional tenure, intertwined bulwarks of stability. This is, indeed, an umbrella term for happiness in this culture. For many others, however, it has become increasingly viable to renegotiate marital status and domestic arrangements, despite the necessity of then encountering the Real in the forms of attorney-mediated transactions with the legal system, hefty costs, sometimes including penalties, and social censure. A similar breadth of options now characterizes such "fundaments" of identity as one's sex and sexual preference. Contemporary surgical procedures make the full or partial modification of one's sex widely available. Role modifications in the arena of gender surely offer a double pleasure: not only the "primary gain" of changing modalities of sexual expression and behavior, but also a recalibration of one's imprint as a social signifier, a revision of established roles and expectations. In an increasingly secular Western social context, religious affiliation has long been the most protean facet of social identity. This is no doubt the result of multiple factors, including improved education and the dispersion of the values and functions traditionally assigned to the "Abrahamic" religions to other sociocultural spheres: notably to professional associations, the "consumer society," entertainment, and professional sports.

But other features of social identity, pertaining to roles that have been predetermined as much as self-professed, are more difficult, if not impossible, to recalibrate. Surely the outgrowths of hegemonic thought, whether these determine tangible degrees of economic and educational opportunity or extend into codes and strictures of racism and ethnic profiling, impose intractable limitations, become ponderously resistant to modification. Matters of economic wealth, related to multiple factors so arbitrary as starkly to belie the foundational U.S. Horatio Alger myth, belong at the more intractable extreme of social circumstance. Both the material abjection of his family that Stephen Dedalus is forced to acknowledge from the moment of his appearance in *Ulysses* and the early misery, rooted in the crudest societal understandings and arrangements, to which James Baldwin can allude only indirectly in his "Autobiographical Notes" are ultimately linguistic and semiological in their provenance, as deconstruction would justly argue.[27] That is, they issue from a sequence of concepts, understandings, definitions, arrangements, foundations, and agreements whose dynamics are linguistic, both in their articulation and their institutionality. But as James Baldwin, the real James Baldwin, that is, and Stephen Dedalus experience these conditions of insufficiency, they attain a material weight, arbitrariness, and vividness prompting us to imagine their provenance "outside of language," in some "Real." The belligerence of this material abjection recalls the hegemonic thought that has resulted in such conditions, but it obliterates the semiological and contractual arrangements that are their source. Hence Baldwin can precipitate his writing, which is his creative margin in renegotiating the hand he's been dealt, out of "this reality,"[28] or "social affairs."[29] Social circumstance embodies the arbitrariness, categorical difference, and inflexibility of cultural misunderstandings and arrangements that have petrified either into misery or privilege.

When Calibans of color, writers like James Baldwin and Richard Wright, with whom Baldwin shared so much in terms of generational and creative challenges, had the cheek to act on their articulateness, devise literary responses to their experience in the U.S., and augment its literature, they faced immense problems: a dearth of kindred spirits, encouragement, and resources chief among them. And when they released the full range of the voices they'd heard in the community into the novel, language ranging from prophetic eloquence in *Go Tell It on the Mountain* to truncated speech and picturesque ejaculations in the same novel and throughout Wright's fiction, they access the Real of language not only in the disclosure of the Real of social circumstance, but in the dissemination of differential articulation, which is the only hope for a civilized culture.

I do *not* like bohemia, or bohemians, I do not like people whose principle aim is pleasure, and I do not like people who are *earnest* about anything. I don't like people who like me because I'm a Negro; neither do I like people who find in the same accident grounds for contempt. I love America more than any other country in the world, and, exactly for this reason, I insist on the right to criticize her perpetually.[30]

Thus writes James Baldwin, at the end of his "Autobiographical Notes."

At certain memorable junctures in Baldwin's fiction, then, the appeal and release of the Real of language is momentous, keyed to particular cultural moments, in a quite specific way. But the Real of language is a transcultural phenomenon, running the full gamut of artifacts whose articulation is deliberate and nuanced. The Real of language announces itself in linguistic shock, a release of material features that customary usage normally holds in abeyance. A comprehensive census of the linguistic features upon which the Real of language leaves an unmistakable imprint is beyond the scope of the present exposition. Surely, though, acts of inscription involving hyperbolic repetition, assonance, a stark retrofitting of "standard forms," and logical and grammatical discontinuities are prime facilitators of the encounter with the Real, in the present instance, the Real of language that Baldwin, in particular, stages.

There may well be tangible grounds for how, in certain passages of *Go Tell It on the Mountain*, we experience the prefigurations, shocks, and aftershocks of the Real of language. These may well be related to certain historico-cultural happenstances like those glancingly mentioned above, which graft a hitherto muffled collective experience onto a thriving standard literature. In this respect, we can read the historical fact of Baldwin's eight-year exile in Paris as an artifact of the collective exile and diaspora of African Americans. This deterritorialization[31] is, to be sure, recounted in some, but not all, of Baldwin's fiction and essays, but its striking rhetorical figuration there constitutes a more pointed and substantial aesthetic intervention than the quasi-historical recapitulation. Getting down to the Real of a certain experience by staging it in the forms in which language *lets drop* that it constantly presses up against the sublime and the inconceivable may well be a propos of the cultural calling that Baldwin devised for himself.

It is crucial to recall that writers as diverse as Baudelaire, Poe, Melville, Whitman, Mallarmé, Stein, Joyce, Woolf, and Faulkner set the same linguistic resources in play as they went about their aesthetico-linguistic missions. The Real of language is not color-coded, though it may announce itself in different hues (e.g., "The Whiteness of the Whale"). It furnishes the present commentator with a helpful *entrée* into the distinctive script of Baldwin, and Baldwin provides one occasion, albeit a powerful one, for meditating on the Real of language.

In one final consideration, I would dwell, for a moment, on the possibility that a literary artifact could splendidly orchestrate the encounter with the Real of language while heavily drawing upon rhetorical and ideological onto-theological conventions whose torsion, closure, and foreclosure have already been uncovered by philosophically informed critique, like that furnished by deconstruction and rhetorical reading. The literary contribution of a fictive artifact inheres in the vividness of its images, the poetic intensity of its narrative and dialogue, the plausible singularity of its characters, and the allegorical continuity between narrated events and the infrastructural resources of language. Fictional performance, briefly put, reaches a crescendo in those of its registers that access the Real of language. It is not compromised by the degree to which the literary programmer has recourse to or actively draws upon metaphysical, onto-theological, or transcendental imagery, which we know, from deconstruction and other perspectives, exerts heavy ideological torque and imposes statutes of limitation. The literary power and achievement of the family argument over Christmas dinner early in *A Portrait of the Artist as a Young Man* and of the priest's sermon in book 3 thus take place, haunt us, both because of their rootedness in specific and identifiable core images and deep tropes of Western onto-theology and in their independence of, and obliviousness to, those bounded complexes of meaning.[32] The prophetic sermons, biblical readings, and hymns of *Go Tell It on the Mountain* comprise the overarching setting for John Grimes's coming of age at the same time as they foreground and stage the Real of language.

It is no accident that Joyce's *Portrait* and Baldwin's inaugural novel converge in adjacent sentences here. The *Portrait*, in its young protagonist's oscillations between institutional participation and "private life," in its explicit appropriations of the ideologically effective rhetoric and narration (theological, political, aesthetic) prevalent in its represented society, and in its drawing upon the auratic powers of music, rhyme, incantation, and other material epiphenomena of language, constitutes a vibrant and direct pretext to *Go Tell It on the Mountain*. John Grimes is more resigned to and accepting of the sociocultural support and capital that he derives from organized religion—his father's church—than his Joycean counterpart. Yet both characters undergo a parting of the ways with established churches prompted to a significant degree by those churches' initiatives to secure their allegiance and professional commitment.

Being Baldwin's initial novel, *Go Tell It on the Mountain* bears disproportionate weight in configuring its author's overall socioaesthetic intervention, his strategy for grafting his own responses onto the trunk of existing American letters. To the degree that it self-consciously follows in the wake of the *Portrait*, and therefore in the configuration of high European modernism, Baldwin's first novel couldn't be more ambitious, in an aesthetic sense. Yet, in line with the long-standing project retrospectively spelled out in *Notes of a Native Son*, and in keeping with Joycean narrative practices, Baldwin cuts what I have been calling the Real of language a lot of slack in the novel, not only poetically, theoretically, and stylistically, but also as an explicit element in its design and perspective.

The novel begins with the dual temporality of a scene repeated so often in the young protagonist's life that it has attained the continuity of a habit: the scene of the Sunday morning service at the Temple of the Fire Baptized in Harlem. When John ultimately contradicts the collective certainty that he "would be a preacher,"[33] he not only makes an alternate career choice, he disrupts the Proustian temporality of a particular experience, in this case, a particular church service, so paradigmatic of his and his family's social setting, life circumstances, and ethos that it recurs to him as an endlessly sustained scene:

> Then Elisha hit the keys, beginning at once to sing, and everybody joined him, clapping with their hands, and rising, and beating the tambourines.
>
> > The song might be: *Down at the cross where my Saviour died!*
> > Or: *Jesus, I'll never forget how you set me free!*
> > Or: *Lord, hold my hand while I run this race!*
>
> They sang with all the strength that was in them, and clapped their hands for joy. There had never been a time when John had not sat watching the saints rejoice with terror in his heart, and wonder. Their singing caused him to believe

in the presence of the Lord: indeed, it was no longer a question of belief, because they made that presence real. He did not feel it himself, the joy they felt, yet he could not doubt that it was, for them, the very bread of life.[34]

John Grimes assists at this scene as a committed family and church member, one intimate with the multiple registers of the ritual, with the rhetorical, musical, and lyrical resources lending it the combined force of a baptism, an immersion experience, and a total artwork. Yet for all this power, he is already an outsider. "He did not feel it for himself, the joy they felt."[35] Perhaps this very distance makes him a tabula rasa, the ideal observer and scribe of this happening, and a provocative author surrogate.

The narrative photographic plate of this scene in John Grimes's "consciousness" mixes an ideology consistent with the belief system prevailing in a somewhat fundamentalist Protestant denomination with influences and shocks of a very different order. This singing, drumming, and clapping is in certain respects at the service of the prayer-meeting's ideological message: "Their singing caused him to believe in the presence of the Lord."[36] The singing saints arouse sublime awe in John. They fill his heart with "terror" and "wonder." A vivid scene of logocentric inspiration is set before us. Our philosophically driven critical theory would underscore the metaphysics of presence disseminated by this religion; it would warn us of less explicit vestiges of presence subtly infused into conceptual and ideological discourse from many provenances. But deconstruction would have no difficulty apprehending why a scene of intense oral representation of a canonical Word, one buttressed by a sensory overload of singing and percussion, would be the setting of the revelation of Presence to John.

The musical accompaniment that in one respect reinforces the metaphysics of divine omnipotence asserted by biblical readings and sermons runs off in other directions as well. It splices hymn titles that belong, in a very Joycean vein, to a quite alien discursive register onto the "continuous" transcript of the narrative. The narrative of the scene of "fundamentalist" ritual is thus already scored by alien notations and legends. And song, even of a liturgical variety, harbors material effects of language inherently askew the metaphysics of presence, even when impressed into religious service. As Joyce did in the "Sirens" episode of *Ulysses*, Baldwin releases this linguistic musicality as an alternative to strict religion. This alternation between discordant registers of notation and sensibility already embedded in the novel's initial scenes—between narrow religious ideology and the musical throbbings of language—is the highest literary expression of the protagonist's, the author-surrogate's, familial and social alienations. The saints "made their presence real."[37] John Grimes's fascinated but alienated attendance at the scene constitutes a double encounter, with both the metaphysics of presence and the Real's linguistic articulation in rhyme, meter, and other articulate forms of sonority.

The scene goes on to generate a visual caption, one not only comprising another nontranscendental supplement to the metaphysics of presence but also indicating the role of the Father, John's actual clergyman father as well as the divine one, in enunciating his already untenable position:

> Something happened to their faces and their voices, the rhythm of their bodies, and to the air they breathed; it was as though whatever they might be became the upper room, and the Holy Ghost were riding on the air. His father's face, always awful, became more awful now; his father's daily anger was transformed into prophetic wrath. His mother, her eyes raised to heaven, hands arced before her, moving, made real for John that patience, that endurance, that long suffering, which he had read of in the Bible and found so hard to imagine.[38]

This scene rehearses metamorphoses that will prevail throughout the novel. Just as the religious service lends the congregation a dimension of Real-ity absent from their quotidian bearings, his role as deacon metamorphoses John's father, Gabriel, into a sublime, distant, and subliminally menacing presence, whose irrational powers John experiences above all *visually*. Under the aegis of the Lacanian Imaginary, in other words, the Real encompassed by the father, whose *Name*, as absence as well as a name prominently engraved throughout the text, shines darkly through.

The crisis late in the novel that decides John's exodus from the Temple and from organized religion in general is set in an extended Miltonic space fitted out, again, with features of intense Imaginary participation. Not the least of John's significant others, virtually all of whom loom out of the abyssal space configured by this epiphany, is his father:

> In the silence, then, that filled the void, John looked on his father. His father's face was black—like a sad, eternal night; yet in his father's face there burned a fire—a fire eternal in an eternal night. John trembled where he lay, feeling no warmth from this fire, trembled, and could not take his eyes away. A wind blew over him, saying: "Whosoever loveth and maketh a lie." And he knew that he

had been thrust out of the holy, the joyful, the blood-washed community, that his father had thrust him out. His father's will was stronger than John's own. His power was greater because he belonged to God.[39]

John's consummate aesthetico-spiritual experience in the novel transpires in the phantasmatic abyss of majesty,[40] transcendental purity, and spiritual immediacy where Derrida situates the conceptual-ideological matrix, or pre-text, common to all three "Abrahamic" religions. This uncanny scene holds much in common with the Elsinore ramparts where, according to Derrida's reading of the Shakespearean tragedy, Hamlet learns an inconceivable truth and receives an impossible mission, from a ghost or phantom who embodies certain projections of Western onto-theology.[41] The novel's racial issues, figured in the phantasmatic fire of Gabriel's face, fit in well with the overall oxymoronic features of this abyss, complement its image of cold fire. John's struggle with an angel—for Gabriel is also an angel's name—ends in his defeat, but also his release from the church toward language's and art's Real, arbitrary, uncontrollable play.

> Now, John felt no hatred, nothing, only a bitter, unbelieving despair: all prophesies were true, salvation was finished, damnation was real!
> Then death is real, John's soul said, and death will have his moment.
> "Set thine house in order," said his father, "for thou shalt die and not live."
> And then the ironic voice spoke again, saying: "Get up, John. Get up, boy. Don't let him keep you here. You got everything your daddy got."
> John tried to laugh—John thought that he was laughing—but found, instead, that his mouth was filled with salt, his ears were full of burning water. Whatever was happening in his distant body now, he could not change or stop.[42]

At the same time that John, imaginatively, decisively encounters his father, he encounters the Real, a Real of death, as Lacan would aver, of unconditional damnation. But the abyss of the uncanny interface with both the transcendental (in Derrida's terms) and the Real (in Lacan's) is also a scene of irony, a place where language usurps control over matters, runs away with the show. John's reactions, as an internal participant in and observer of the dreamlike shop, are involuntary. The fire of his expected laughter is doused by the flood of his tears. But what is in the context of a spiritual confrontation with the Father a horrific loss of control describes in aesthetic terms the writer's cat-and-mouse game, or on-again, off-again struggle, with language.

It is through and by means of the shattering, life-and-death struggle with the horrific father who embodies the Real, even if it is ultimately futile and culminates in defeat, that the son secures the way toward language. That road, ironically, sets out in the father's speech, onto-theologically charged as it is. Baldwin powerfully demonstrates the morphing of the rhetoric of ideology, through the interference of the son, into the stuff of literature. The son, discerning the play of the Real of language in the speech of his progenitor, takes his father at his word: for Gabriel, in the sermon that establishes him as a preacher, proves to be a mesmerizing and devastating speaker:

> He paused only for a moment and mopped his brow, the heart within him great with fear and trembling, and with power.
> "For let us remember that the wages of sin is death; that it is written, and cannot fail, the soul that sinneth, it shall die. Let us remember that we are born in sin, in sin did our mothers conceive us—sin reigns in all our members, sin is the foul heart's natural issue, sin looks out of the eye, amen, and leads to lust, sin is in the hearing of the ear, and leads to folly, sits on the tongue, and leads to murder. Yes! Sin is the only heritage of natural man, sin bequeathed us by our natural father, that fallen Adam, whose apple sickens and will sicken all generations living, and generations yet unborn! It was sin that drove the son of the morning out of Heaven, sin that drove Adam out of Eden, sin that caused Cain to slay his brother, sin that built the tower of Babel, sin that caused the fire to fall on Sodom—sin, from the very foundations of the world."[43]

This paragraph of a somewhat longer sermon sinuously winds around and through the biblical roots, senses, organs, and outcomes of sin, leaving an indelible impression on the son. Sin is the sermon's overarching theme; it provides the rhythm, cadence, and sound-vocabulary governing, even dominating his speech. Repetition, assonance, concatenation—these rhetorical features of discourse work to two major yet disparate effects, not necessarily synchronized. On the one hand, Gabriel may be said to place these pre- or subcontractual dimensions of language at the service of Western theological ideology, a fairly simplistic rendition of the creed at that, one in which sin trumpets its harsh difference from salutary conditions. Yet John, and through him the reader, luxuriates in the poetic richness and power of language released by means of the same rhetorical gestures. He is thus caught in the same double bind as Stephen, listening to the priest's homily at the heart of the *Portrait*: between ideological closure and poetic fascination. The poetry is carried along by the aural materiality of *sin*, its repetitions, its sympathetic resonances (e.g. "son," "Sodom"), its concatenation through the schemas—of the senses, of biblical narrative—invoked to amplify it. The sounds of *sin* derive from a subliminal Real-ity, reversing the field of expectations with which the preacher's sermon as well as the structure of Baldwin's novel are preinvested.

What may comprise the most powerful instance of Baldwin's uncanny attunement to the Real of language in the novel is situated at a moment before his stakes in certain images and rhetorical and narrative devices have been established. The scene is all the more overwhelming because the novel has not yet quite settled into its drift or "groove." This shocking moment, in a full Benjaminian sense, transpires when John returns home after a birthday in 1935 that surely began inauspiciously. Having managed, through his mother's care, to treat himself to a Times Square movie, he arrives home to discover that his brother Roy has been stabbed in the face, a wound whose shock engages visual and Symbolic processing. This is a dreadful downturn, but it is also a dramatic intensification of the day, which begins with a sober catalogue of the family's poverty, a realistic enumeration of the family's inability to mark the occasion with fanfare. John wakes up that day with the thought, "'Will anyone remember?' For it had happened that his birthday had passed entirely unnoticed."[44] In the absence of such affirmation, John sweeps

> the heavy red and green and purple Oriental-style carpet that had once been that room's glory, but was now so faded that it was all one swimming color, and so frayed in places that it tangled with the broom. John hated sweeping this carpet, for dust rose, clogging his nose and sticking to his sweaty skin, and he felt that should he sweep it forever the clouds of dust would not diminish, the rug would not be clean. It became in his imagination, his impossible, lifelong task, his hard trial.[45]

The routine of cleaning the rug is imposed upon John with the inevitability of a preordained sentence, a tribulation that will presumably outlast him. The rug, which has lost any luster it might once have had, is a harbinger of grim prospects. It is in relation to this scene of resignation to the carpet that John's family name assumes its most pointed significance within the novel's vocabulary. The rug is pedestrian and remorseless, yet it is also uncanny, harboring the possibility of release from encounter with the material conditions and limitations of existence. The carpet furnishes the text with a splendid instance of Lacanian otherness, the everyday otherness of the *objet petit a*, the thing that dawns on us as if from nowhere yet epitomizes the semiological truth (or private language) of our lives.[46] The relation between John, as the progeny of his family, and this rug is intimate, to say the least, for the grime saturating the carpet also penetrates his family name, his very identity as a social signifier.

John is uplifted from the abjection figured in his symbolic bondage to the rug by his mother's recognition that he is her "right-hand man,"[47] and by the money that she gives him, in part so that he can broaden his perspective. But the escape is of a limited scope and duration. He returns from his visit to the city's entertainment district via the length of Central Park, an outing in which he has experienced the freedom and display of cultural resources available to any young New Yorker, to the following:

> Roy had been gashed by a knife, luckily not very sharp, from the center of his forehead where his hair began, downward to the bone just above his left eye: the wound described a kind of crazy half-moon and ended in a violent, fuzzy tail that was the ruin of Roy's eyebrow. Time would darken the half-moon wound into Roy's dark skin, but nothing would bring together again the so violently divided eyebrow. This crazy lift, this question, would remain with him forever.... Certainly the wound was now very ugly, and very red, and must, John felt, with a quickened sympathy toward Roy, who had not cried out, have been very painful. He could imagine the sensation caused when Roy staggered into the house, blinded by his blood; but just the same, he wasn't dead.[48]

Roy's wound functions as an express subway returning John from the fancies of Times Square to the very Real circumstances of home. It is at once a painful incursion into his brother's well-being and sense of self-esteem and a diacritical notation in a system far less personal, understanding, and forgiving. It is both a social and a grammatical marker: the result of pervasive, unbounded violence on the streets of New York and a question mark, carved on a vulnerable point of the visage. The literary character so marked will henceforth constitute a pointed physiognomic riddle about the pervasiveness of violence and self-defeating aggression. Roy's wound is a familial stigma as well as a personal catastrophe. Its sources are the deep roots of the family's deracination, precarious economic condition, and overall instability. Its pre-text is the history scored with such power by Richard Wright in *Native Son* and *Black Boy*. John feels "with a quickened sympathy" his brother's pain, redirecting the empathic attentiveness his mother had earlier devoted to him, reversing the rivalry that had flared up over possible offerings for breakfast.[49]

In a single stroke, by a masterly act of literary condensation, Roy's wound fuses a material reality extenuated by financial and sociological conditions, Baldwin's inscriptive process of registering and negotiating the family's predicament, and the tissues, physiological and psychological, of a single character or subject-simulacrum that has been traumatically disfigured. The wound is a shifter or hinge between the registers of representation and symbolic exchange opened up by the narrative. As such, it derives from the Real, sublime and subliminal as It is, the broader intractable Real embodied in the circumstances, but not constitutionally affected by them.

The novel goes so far as to figure the reception of this horrific deed and symbol by the social microcosm of the Grimes family, specifically, by Gabriel and his estranged sister, Florence. The cruel happenstance of Roy's wound mobilizes yet another emanation of the Real, a violence and directness of speech that will brook no moderation.

> "Yes," said Aunt Florence, "I ain't heard you ask that boy nary a question about how all this happened. Look like you just determined to raise cain any*how* and make everybody in this house suffer because something done happened to the apple of your eye."
>
> "I done asked you," cried his father in a fearful exasperation, "to stop running your *mouth*. Don't none of this concern you. This is *my* family and this is my house. You want me to slap you side of the head?"
>
> "You slap me," she said with a placidity equally fearful, "and I *do* guarantee you you won't do no more slapping in a hurry."
>
> "Hush, now," said his mother, rising, "ain't no need for all this. What's done is done. We ought to be on our knees, thanking the Lord it weren't no worse."
>
> "Amen to that," said Aunt Florence, "*tell* that foolish nigger something."
>
> "You can tell that foolish *son* of yours something," he said to his wife with venom, having decided, it seemed, to ignore his sister, "him standing there with them big buckeyes. You can tell him to take this like a warning from the Lord. *This* is what white folks does to niggers. I been telling you, now you see."[50]

For all that Gabriel endeavors to control the scene by attempting to intimidate the women, he ends up affirming that the contemporary U.S., New York City at least, remains a white man's world. He registers, in other words, the whiteness assumed by the Real, from an African American point of view, lending credence, perhaps, to the glancing reference to Melville's white whale above. He justifies his anger toward Roy, who ran afoul of this imperturbable truth. Yet the Real of white absolutism in the U.S. only scratches the surface of Real play in the interchange, which is one of the most pitched and extended in the novel. The dialogue is suddenly and successively performative. A sequence of speech acts, one after the next, ensues. It includes accusation ("make everybody in the house suffer"), command ("stop running your *mouth*"), threat ("I *do* guarantee you you won't do no more slapping"), plea ("ain't no need for all this"), affirmation ("Amen to all that"), and admonition ("take this like a warning from the Lord"). In the heart of Roy's crisis and the overall domestic friction, some of the distinctive forms of African American English take hold to a degree that will not be evident, for example, in Gabriel's sermons.[51] The exchange between long-time family members concerning how to respond to Roy's disfiguration is powerfully direct, truncated, unceremonious, and action-packed.

Baldwin thus metamorphoses the Real (the hostile surround of U.S. racism, the pervasive and random violence in the streets) into an effective and hard-hitting Real of language whose individual components reinforce and magnify one another. A real (like all incursions of the Real) that could only be partially and indirectly intimated through the medium of narrative description is acted out in dialogue, becomes an intense, abrupt performance. The dialogue, involving Roy and John's parents and aunt, may be thought of as an interpretive scene, pondering the wound that Baldwin incorporates into the text. The transformation of the wound from an uncanny textual object (or *objet petit a*) into an object of pitched exegetical dispute mobilizing many of language's most inexorable features is indicative of the intensity and versatility of Baldwin's pursuit of the Real in its linguistic dimensions. Indeed, as I have suggested, Baldwin's writerly alliance with the Real of language constitutes his most sustained tactic in facing the daunting writerly challenges before him: above all, in certain specific works, to translate into the idiom of state-of-the-art twentieth-century realistic fiction the historical, sociological, and linguistic conditions of a community of people largely excluded from meaningful multicultural exchange in U.S. society. Baldwin's invention and achievement are owing in no small measure to the difficulty, indeed, the impossibility, of these sociocultural impediments. To this day he performs the inestimable service of underscoring aesthetic and poetic inventions devised by contemporaries and kindred spirits facing similar sociocultural impasses in addressing the ongoing resistances to writing.

FIVE

William Faulkner and the Romance of the American Drifter

Her voice would not cease, it would just vanish. There would be the dim coffin-smelling gloom sweet and oversweet with the twice-bloomed wisteria against the outer wall by the savage quiet September sun impacted distilled and hyperdistilled, into which came now and then the loud cloudy flutter of the sparrows like a flat limber stick whipped by an idle boy, and the rank smell of female old flesh long embattled in virginity while the wan haggard face watched him above the faint triangle of lace at wrists and throat from the too tall chair in which she resembled a crucified child, and the voice not ceasing but vanishing into and then out of the long intervals like a stream, a trickle running from patch to patch of dried sand, and the ghost mused with shadowy docility as if it were the voice which he haunted where a more fortunate one would have had a house.[1]

Drowned by the perfume of wisteria, the narrative of *Absalom, Absalom!* begins in a concatenation of mirroring and double sense. It can be argued that the emergence of Thomas Sutpen in the virgin hardwood forests of what will become Yoknapawtapha County constitutes as firm a bottom as exists in Faulkner's branching, self-engendering, mythologically nuanced narrative of the U.S. South. Sutpen's purchase of the antebellum plantation Sutpen's Hundred with Spanish coin, his construction of the property with slave labor, his procreation of dual black and white bloodlines, and the repetition of the incestuous pre-text in his own house through his children's encounter with Charles Bon constitute as clear, that is, locatable, a grounding for the idyll of the American South as can be extracted from the pages of his self-referential (incestuous in this sense) fictive world.

Faulkner's works addressing the mixed and by no means certain origins of the U.S. South, its tenuous, supplemental relationship to that other upstart nation, the U.S., and the bewildering amalgam of hegemonic aristocracy, racism, and democracy prevailing within its domains are, of necessity, marked by excruciating narrative complexity. Whose story, exactly, is being told? Within what coherent sociopolitical framework do the ramifying themes and events unfold? What reasonable outcomes can be distilled from such a matrix of skewed and mutually counteracting fictive premises?

As one of the grounding texts in the Faulkner canon, *Absalom, Absalom!*, along with, as we shall see, the tales collected in *The Hamlet*,[2] does not disappoint in the complexities of genealogy, narration, and development that it entertains. Early in the novel, the passage that begins this chapter already introduces us to the novel's dual narrators, both at the end of their bloodlines' creativity. As the novel begins, Quentin Compson, grandson of perhaps Thomas Sutpen's only friend, General Compson, is summoned to Rosa Coldfield's morbid and gothic-feeling house to take on the burden of hearing and marking a not-quite-finished Southern epic, still connected to the spectral, demonic Sutpen but nevertheless in its final throes. Although once solicited to take her sister Ellen's place as Sutpen's wife, Rosa is a childless spinster. She has written poetry, and she displays a pronounced gift for storytelling. She transmits both her flair for narration and an epic rife with imaginative and permutational possibility to Quentin, a brilliant and idealistic son of the South and no doubt a Faulknerian alter ego or surrogate, during his final preparations for an illustrious student career at Harvard. Quentin will bring his own blood and narrative lines to an end in 1910, when he commits suicide in Cambridge, evidencing the inability of a South still tied to agrarian aristocracy and segregationist doublethink to withstand the modernization of industry and urban life, and to enter the modernism of, among other things, cubism, jazz, cinema, and Faulknerian innovation.

This glimpse of cultural transmission and storytelling highlights the spectral features both of Rosa's person, as a living remnant of the narrated epic, and of the trickling stream of the voice of narration. The voice of storytelling is itself a ghost as it rises and falls, stops and resumes. It betokens the sterile ending of a saga that is nonetheless marked by fits of (above all, Sutpen's) passion, violence, and even creativity. As Quentin's eventual demise will suggest, the gift of this rich and imaginatively fertile heritage is at best a mixed blessing. The beginning of *Absalom, Absalom!* goes on to record the impact the unfolding tale begins to have on Quentin, a literary moment of conjugation, incest, and blending, in which it is equally—and indistinguishably—Rosa's tale and Quentin's tale.

> Then in the long unmaze Quentin seemed to watch them overrun suddenly the hundred square miles of tranquil and astonished earth and drag house and formal gardens violently out of the soundless Nothing and clap them down like cards on a table beneath the up-palm immobile and pontific, creating Sutpen's Hundred, the *Be Sutpen's Hundred* like the oldtime *Be Light.* Then hearing would reconcile and he would seem to listen to two Quentins now—the Quentin Compson preparing for Harvard in the South, the deep South dead since 1865, and peopled with garrulous outraged baffled ghosts, listening, having to listen, to one of the ghosts which had refused to lie still even longer than most had, telling him about old ghost times; and the Quentin Compson who was still too young to deserve yet to be a ghost but nevertheless having to be one for all that, since he was born and bred in the deep South the same as she was—the two Quentins now talking to one another in the long silence of notpeople in notlanguage, like this: *It seems that this demon—his name was Sutpen—(Colonel Sutpen)—Colonel Sutpen. Who came out of nowhere and without warning upon the land with a band of strange niggers and built a plantation—(Tore violently a plantation, Miss Rosa Coldfield says)—tore violently. And married her sister Ellen and begot a son and a daughter which—(Without gentleness begot, Miss Rosa Coldfield says)—without gentleness. Which should have been the jewels of his pride and the shield and comfort of his old age, only—(Only they destroyed him or something or he destroyed them or something. And died)—and died.*[3]

This passage, which displays the pyrotechnics of the cultural transmission of a family saga from one generation to the next, rises to heights of poetic intensity and of technical narrative innovation. The unveiling of a narrative as stark and jarringly complex as this one reveals that all stories are born of ghosts, of presences that have vanished but that have nevertheless marked the communities in which they dwelt and the sensibilities they touched. As Quentin hears the background story of his communal life, he is torn between two ghosts: the "garrulous outraged baffled ghosts" of the past making up the tale and the ghost that he, as the bearer of this dead-end narrative patrimony, is about—prematurely and tragically—to become. The uncertainty as to whose tale this really is, Rosa Coldfield's or Quentin Compson's, quickly morphs into a ghostly abyss in Quentin, between the forward-looking young man who has life ahead of him and the stifled, overburdened graveyard historian.

And these ghosts rustle against one another. With a complicated battery of technical devices, in this passage Faulkner orchestrates a dance between the split specters of Quentin's sensibility and the split strands of the narrative, belonging indeterminately to Quentin and Rosa. By means of parenthetical interjections and italicized script (devices that encapsulate chunks of the text or split it off from itself), Faulkner stages a stutter or infinitesimal delay between what Quentin is hearing and what he takes in. (It is in this sense that *"Who came out of nowhere and without warning upon the land"* almost immediately, but with striking discrepancy, morphs, in Rosa's language, into *"Tore violently a plantation."*) Indeed, by the end of this passage Faulkner has created something like a cinematographic afterimage or tonal concatenation in prose. The narrative records the near-simultaneous dying that first befalls Sutpen's strivings in their violence and vanity, and then, directly afterward, Quentin's sensibility: *"And died.)—and died."* This rhythm of slightly delayed afterbeats underscores the folly and disaster ultimately resulting from Sutpen's grandiose vision and the violence, incest, miscegenation, hypocrisy, and doublethink that dominate and ultimately destroy his house.

Such stunning technical innovation in prose is only partly indicative of the fictive task of establishing origins where there are virtually no traces, of establishing lineages, whether of blood or narrative derivation, when only mixture links the categories. Quentin takes in the silence of "nonpeople in nonlanguage," as, under the tutelage of his elder, he assumes the dual social and narratological burden of his heritage. When it comes to reconstructing the cultural as well as the historical beginnings of the community, Faulkner's vocation as a social novelist of the U.S. South demands that he too speak of "nonpeople in nonlanguage," that he invoke, with poetic intensity and thematic resonance, the ghostly, what is no longer there, what may never have been. Indeed, the citizens of Jefferson never directly witness Sutpen's arrival or his initial efforts. These survive only in legend (or gossip). The earliest dependable reports emanated from General Compson and from the French architect that Sutpen brought in thrall to the site with his slaves. It is from these accounts that we learn that at first the "white client [Sutpen] and the negro crew which he [the architect] was to advise though not direct went stark naked save for a coating of dried mud."[4] The nonexistent (let alone nondescript) clothing is not only indicative of Sutpen's amazing achievement in constructing Sutpen's Hundred out of virtually nothing over a two-year period, it signals the amazement of telling the story at all, the amazing intercourse with ghosts that is the founding premise of fiction. It is the dispossessed and marginalized characters of literature, the Sutpens and, as we'll see, the Snopes, who consistently deliver this brand of amazement:

> They worked from sunup to sundown while parties of horsemen rode up and sat their horses quietly and watched, and the architect in his formal coat and his Paris hat and his expression of grim and embittered amazement lurked about the environs of the scene with his air something between a casual and bitterly disinterested spectator and a condemned and conscientious ghost—amazement, General Compson said, not at the others and what they were doing so much as at himself, at the inexplicable and incredible fact of his own presence. But he was a good architect; Quentin knew the house, twelve miles from Jefferson, in its grove of cedar and oak, seventy-five years after it was finished.[5]

So runs the history of a great southern house if not a lineage. Faulkner labored intensively and inventively to assimilate the complexities engendered by such fictive and social narration. He engendered a narrative practice that would perform if not dissolve the historical, spatial, and temporal anomalies invariably unearthed in such storytelling. It is material to our case that Faulkner's stories are borne on the backs of one of the oddest assortment of drifters and outsiders assembled in the history of literature.

★

The outsider, as we have explored above, is the very emissary of externality. But this figure is no stranger to Faulkner. The outsider is less violent than the criminal or outlaw, less deviant than the pervert, less persecuted than an ethnic, racial, or gendered minority, less insane than a madman, less put upon, traditionally, than a woman. The outsider engenders the figures of the outcast and the outlaw, but needn't be either. The outsider's preeminent characteristic is that he circulates, with impunity. Criminality, perversion, madness, minority, and femininity may be features also traditionally ascribed to the gifted, the inherently endowed. But the artist, beneath all these guises, is ultimately an outsider, someone who does not quite belong, someone who has explored the structures of human settlement beyond the limits of her neighborhood.

Civic stability and domestic tranquility fall prey to the outsider, while the outsider, in the mode of Derrida's *pharmakos*,[6] eventually is sacrificed by the community he or she has inseminated and enriched. The outsider is the final emanation of the barbarians who both destroy mainstream civilizations, in the work of William McNeill and like-minded social historians,[7] and sublate them to higher levels. Devastating nomadic influx both delimits cultural configurations and defines their only possibility for persistence. The theory of social history to be extrapolated from Deleuze and Guattari's Capitalism and Schizophrenia diptych is one in which life within the socius is a palimpsest of outmoded social formations, including "nomadic despotism" and feudalism, always ready to break out, wreak havoc, and belie the veneer of liberal rationality that advanced industrialized societies profess.[8] The repression against which Deleuze and Guattari rail is less the subordination of the drive in the interest of stultifying civilization than the denial of the force, appeal, and possible inevitability of these outmoded, and in many senses horrifying, modalities of social organization. Sociohistorical traces of genocide, mass suicide, and "becoming animal" still persist in contemporary forms of social organization, according to Deleuze and Guattari.[9] In refusing to acknowledge and analyze these mass impulses and gravitations, which do not have the immanence and inevitability of drives, contemporary forms of social organization render themselves incredulous and impotent in the face of their own periodic outcomes.

The outsider is the civil, or not so civil, vestige of the nomad and the barbarian. To the extent that the release of stores of energy held in reserve hinges on the visitations and vicissitudes of the outsider, the uncanny visitor, in the form of a fetish, triggers the return of the repressed.[10] The cultivated public awaits the intrusion of the outsider so that it can experience an orgasm: violently, on the battlefield; culturally, at the carnival; or subliminally, in the artwork. In the wake of this release, the outsider is reduced to a has-been, becomes domesticated.. This is not experienced as a loss, because from the moment his strangeness is expressed, the outsider is no longer an outsider.

The vicissitudes of the outsider format a romance whose dimensions are at once spiritual and erotic. This romance arises in the messianic hope for novelty, if not revolution, and in the need to dispose of the corpse of the previous outsider. The outsider's novelty corresponds to a sexual wish as well, to restore primitivity to a dimension of experience primarily repetitive in nature. The idyll of the outsider terminates in the tired absorption by the socius of the revolution that has been ascribed to the errant outsider. The outsider is both the messiah of the moment and the corpse persisting from some common embarrassment, some stain that must be cleared away. The outsider is the scapegoat of sociocultural redemption: his arrival is always immanent, his impact invariably tentative and indecisive.

In the history of Western culture, the opening of the U.S. is the preeminent example of a planned community for outsiders. Although at certain times, as Fernand Braudel documents, Central Europe and the Balkans served the "advanced" nations of the continent as a Third World, a feudally organized source primarily of raw materials,[11] feudalism and natural resources were in the very groundplan of the South, if not the entire American nation. The U.S. is the home of outsiders as well as the free and the brave; and the outsiders who lend a particular, uncanny flavor to U.S. fiction are the outsiders of the outside. It is no revelation that American fiction pivots around the figure of the outsider. The question is not whether outsiders surface in the drama of American letters, whatever the particular stakes may be, but what variety they belong to and how their marginal behavior and status embroider the writing to which they belong.

There is no community less homey than Faulkner's *Hamlet* in the rawness of its manners, its at times barely suppressed violence, its racism, its miscegenation, and its bestiality. Yet it is Faulkner's writerly gift to familiarize us so intimately with its citizens that the community of deviance and brutality feels like our own home town, even if our relatives hail from Japan or Scandinavia. The modern, which in this case means the industrialized, late-capitalist, history of Frenchman's Bend, Mississippi, begins with an incursion of outsiders, the all but nameless peasants from the countryside around Jefferson. The name of the Snopes surrounds the *nope* of negation with spiraling *s*-curves that turn on themselves, a shape whose broadest literary implications are enunciated throughout Barthes's *S/Z*.[12] *Snopes* is a collective noun; a single Snopes is indistinguishable, semantically, from a collectivity of Snopes. Once Flem Snopes establishes himself as the steward of the new economic order in the South, both building upon and deviating from the enterprises of Will Varner, who may be described as a neo-feudal petit bourgeois, Snopes cousins emerge out of the woods and byways to occupy the various sinecures that Flem has created.

> How many kinfolks has Flem Snopes brought in to date? Is it two more, or just three?
> "Four," Bookwright said shortly, eating.
> "Four?" Ratliff said. "That's that blacksmith—I mean the one that uses the blacksmith's shop for his address until it's time to go back and eat again—what's his name? Eck. And that other one, the contractor, the business executive—"
> "He's going to be the new school professor next year," Tull said mildly. "Or so they claim."[13]

The Snopes are intertwined in nepotistic corruption and self-reference. They look out for themselves, collectively, even if not for each other. Flem Snopes is notoriously stingy to his poorer relatives. Yet as signifiers in the sociological fabric of Yoknapawtapha County, on the symbolic level the Snopes are keenly aware of their vicissitudes in the exchanges of honor and face. Only Mink Snopes's murder of Houston can bring his relatives to repudiate one of their own. The murder arises in the wake of a loss of face, Houston's challenging Eck Snopes's right to pasture a horse on his property and Ike Snopes's right to love, carnally, one of his cows.

In name, Flem Snopes may appear phlegmatic, but as the narrator establishes, he is anything but in his business dealings. Flem is almost Flemish, northern European, just as there are mongrel European roots to Frenchman's Bend, whose original manorial property was owned by De Spain. Through Flem's name and multiple references to a distinctly Protestant religion and bipolar culture fusing sanctity and violence, Faulkner grafts the Protestant ideology of an earlier age onto the emerging new Southern economy. The names of the Snopes cousins, blacksmith Eck (German "corner," village schoolmaster IO, almost IOU, an economic liability), and the rodent Mink (who murders Houston but is also taxonomically linked to busybody and storyteller Ratliff), suggest signifieds belonging to an elemental, relatively uninflected, and hence Protestant semantic order. (Indeed, the linchpin of Protestant theology is its turning away, or voluntary regression from the mediation and ostentation that have presumably proliferated beyond control and meaning in the Church.)[14]

Even though Flem Snopes anticipates a new economic order dawning in the South, he and his cousins are peasant stock (the concluding fourth book of *The Hamlet* is entitled "The Peasants")[15] rather than democratic citizens of an enlightened age. In this sense, the Snopes spearhead the kind of irresistible because inarticulate regression to a prior sociopolitical formation that is the bread and butter of the analyses comprising Deleuze and Guattari's Capitalism and Schizophrenia diptych. What is so exciting about the unaccountable regressions that pervade Faulkner's fictive "country" is their metamorphoses among thematic, allegorical, symbolic, and imaginary levels. In the world of Frenchman's Bend, power and shrewdness are established in the qualitative and theatrical domain of horse trading. A significant portion of the first half of *The Hamlet* pursues the concrete and sometimes even boring details surrounding a range of transactions, not only in horses but in goats, sewing machines, and real estate. No small measure of Faulkner's theoretical scope and punch inheres in his ability to displace these thematic transactions to imaginary and allegorical theaters in the outbreak of the worthless—because untrained, that is, presymbolic—spotted horses, in what Deleuze and Guattari would call a pack.[16] This fictively inebriating displacement from the level of symbolic contract to that of untrammeled image also applies to Ike Snopes's love for one of the most adorable cows in the neighborhood, which, in the manner of Lacanian perversion, finds no metaphoric or sublimated expression. The cow belongs to Houston, it happens, and compounds the fatal feud between Houston and the Snopes, as well as contributing to the association, whose inevitability Faulkner assures through the figure of bags, between this regressive cow love, which Deleuze and Guattari might link to the subliminal cultural compulsion of "becoming-animal," and the stupefying female aura and spell that Eula Varner, the epitome of her gender, casts upon all men within her radius, enfeebling their already feeble attempts at discipline. What distinguishes Faulkner as a social novelist and theorist writing in the discourse of fiction is the facility and vividness with which he ties the transactions in the symbolic order to images defying the frameworks of symbolic context and definition, just as the spotted horses, once sold and purchased in a legal and civic, if not civil, manner, will escape their putative owners and the confines of civil law. The dynamic but phantasmatic hinge between the civil and the allegorical and imaginary is a signature both of Faulkner's style and of his manner of composing social history within the fictive sphere.

This capability of fiction, in Faulkner and others, depends on the figure of the outsider. The arrival of the outsider recalibrates the socioeconomic contracts and other formulas already in play, opening a modus operandi, as well as a community, to subversive change. The Snopes belong to that variety of outsiders who emerge from within, from the bedrock of Protestant ideology and peasant belligerence lying just beneath the surface of modern equanimity and indifference. The escape of the spotted horses that Flem Snopes, with the connivance of Buck Hipps, a stranger from Texas, brings to the community, in a kind of equine end-of-year sales event, takes place in the modality of Deleuze and Guattari's account of the holocaust of the Second World War, a precipitous "becoming-death" always *in potentia* at the roots of social memory. Yet the "country" of Frenchman's Bend and Yoknapawtapha County in general depends upon an outside different from the one implicated by Flem Snopes and his intertwined familial offshoots. Houston, whose name is not accidental, needs an outland where he may, temporarily at least, escape the fate of the of the homegirl who loves him as an adolescent and who, without even asking his permission, does his homework assignments for him at school, simulating his signature. McCarron senior, father of Eula's most prominent suitor, vanishes as a young man for ten days with the woman who will become his bride. The outland to which people from Yoknapawtapha County disappear when they need to regroup or when indigenous strictures leave them no room in which to maneuver has a name, and its name is Texas: home of the renegade horse trader who populates the county with runaway horses, scene of Houston's wanderings and cohabitation with a woman he elects not to marry,[17] setting for Flem and Eula's honeymoon, once either he steps forward as the father of her fetus or steps in for the true father. Although deviance may transpire within its parameters, the social space of Yoknapatawpha County is striated rather than smooth. The emergence of a seemingly endless strand of usurpers, hidden agendas, and perversions from its submerged layers is a pronounced depth-phenomenon. Texas is, by contrast, the "smooth" counterspace[18] to the legal and interpersonal involutions prevailing in the County. It is the void making possible the compromises that prevail on the home front.

The Snopes are crucial to Faulkner's account of corruption and deviance in the South. They are in the tradition of McNeill's barbarians who become mainstream insiders. Yet they are also deeply embedded in the sociology of what is, for all its racism and other forms of violence—indeed, in part by virtue of this violence—a stable and even resilient community. The Snopes pass from destabilizing the "country" of Yoknapatawpha County to stabilizing it, to becoming its bulwarks in a new economic order. Faulkner wonders at how Flem Snopes, in particular, a character lacking in culture and altruism, could be so effective in clan and collective senses, and could contribute to a community that could persist powerfully despite the polymorphous forms of its poverty. This paradox or antinomy strikes us, when we survey the hypothetical border between text-based and sociological theories. The Snopes are exceptionally aware of their status as signs on several registers of semiological and socioeconomic activity. We could argue that their semiological shrewdness is what ensures their sociological success. Yet at the same time, their status as characters in a set of social novels is inimical to the socioeconomic reality of the U.S. and beyond. We need content ourselves with a situation in which, especially in the case of fiction, a sociological dimension and arena open up in a text even if there is no objective correlative. Simply in the structure of narrative and the appeal to surrogates, a dimension of society invades the text in the manner of an unwanted outsider, even though there is no correlation between the fictive setting of the drama and any existing community or society. Fiction's "sociological surround" configures itself as much because it corresponds to certain immanent functions of narrative as because it is an unavoidable referential feature. Frenchman's Bend, Mississippi, then, bears powerful traces of how communities function and persist, even though it has arisen in response to an influx of outsiders, and even though the empirical society that it delineates is impoverished, crude, and, in several senses, bestial. These antinomies are not outside Faulkner's designs or texture.

There is no outsider more pivotal to Faulkner's *Hamlet* and more productive in its scene of writing than the spotted horses, even though they are not properly human. We owe to Deleuze and Guattari, themselves responsive to folklore from around the world and to authors such as Kafka, a sense of dynamic fluidity that allows animals to exemplify the human in a broad range of negotiations. The spotted horses, then, belong to a third wave of immigrants who, in the novel's internal history, flood the region: the first left an elite coterie of European aristocrats, local feudal lords; second, a generation of marginal employees from the already overcrowded backwaters of the East Coast and South.[19] Though we might be inclined to dismiss the horses as animal and inarticulate, their intervention is a very precise, even nuanced response to the socioeconomic contracts and cultural codes prevailing in the community that they join, however briefly.

Our first glimpse of the horses coincides with our first glance at their human leader, Buck Hipps, initially described as: "a stranger. He wore a densely black moustache, a pale wide hat. When he thrust himself through and turned to herd them back from the horses they saw, thrust into the hip pockets of his tight jeans pants, the butt of a pearl-handled pistol and a florid carton such as small cakes come in. 'Keep away from them, boys,' he said. 'They've got kind of skittish, they ain't been rode in so long.'"[20] Buck shoots straight from the hip. In this brief vignette, he herds his fellow humans away from the animals under his care. His sudden fluctuations between affability and violence are figured in his pearl-handled pistol, which he packs in his butt pocket. A man of hips and butts, he is a qualified success, a human operator who has assumed some share of his ponies' animality.

The horses, like the Snopes, function as proper and collective nouns at the same time. One moment, they are a collection of individuals, a pattern of distinct spots or dots on a hide: "when they stood once more looking into the lot, the splotchy bodies of the ponies had a distinctness, almost a brilliance, but without individual shape and without depth—no longer horses, no longer flesh and bone."[21] In *Thus Spake Zarathustra*, Nietzsche reveals his own fascination with piebald patterns as a mechanism for decomposing tabulated knowledge and space: he names the city in which the title character preaches the Spotted Cow.[22] In an instant, and at some signal humans cannot discern, endowing the horses with a collective intuition Kant reserves for artists and mathematicians, they can be galvanized into a seething, composite mass.

As anyone whose fate it has been to stumble into a used-car lot knows, there are two phases to the spotted-horses episode, pre- and post-sale. In the first phase of this cycle, the horses are framed, and barely contained, by a combination of physical barriers—barbed wire and wagon spokes—and Buck Hipps's rhetoric, violence, and taste for ginger snaps.

> For an instant it [the horse] and the man appeared to be inextricable in one violence. Then they became motionless, the stranger's high heels dug into the earth, one hand gripping the animal's nostrils, holding the horse's head wrenched half around while it breathed in hoarse, smothered groans. "See?" the stranger said in a panting voice, the veins standing white and rigid in his neck and along his jaw. "See? All you got to do is handle them a little and work hell out of them for a couple of days."[23]

> When the ponies saw the fence the herd surged backward against the wire which attached it to the wagon, standing on its collective hind legs and then trying to turn within itself, so that the wagon moved backward for a few feet until the Texan, cursing, managed to saw the mules about and so lock the wheels. The men following had fallen rapidly back. . . . The blacksmith got back in the wagon and took the reins. Then they watched the Texan descend, carrying a looped-up blacksnake whip, and go around to the rear of the herd and drive it through the gate, the whip snaking about the harlequin rumps in methodical and pistol-like reports.[24]

In this passage, the Texan stranger figures as a circus-animal trainer. The *s*-curve flagellation of his whip realigns the ponies with the mule wagon and later presses them back into an enclosure. At this point, the narrative is filled with details of the linear barriers erected to contain the animals—wire and fence. With his loud, pistol-like whip, whose sinuous lash asserts sadistic sexual dominance as well as military authority, the Texan is still in control.

Yet the ponies also exist as a pack, in spontaneous communication in a language beyond human comprehension. "The Texan grasped the wire and began to draw the first horse up to the wagon, the animal plunging and surging back against the wire as though trying to hang itself, the contagion passing back through the herd from animal to animal until they were rearing and plunging again against the wire."[25] Instantaneously, the pack is susceptible to violent contagions. At this moment in the text, there is a palpable tension between the herd instinct, which multiplies the ponies' power exponentially, and the available mechanical containers. The first horse "crossed the lot at top speed, on a straight line. It galloped into the fence without any diminution whatever. The wire gave, recovered, and slammed the horse to earth where it lay for a moment, glaring, its legs still galloping in air. It scrambled up without having ceased to gallop and crossed the lot and galloped into the opposite fence and was slammed again to earth. The others were now freed. They whipped and whirled around the lot like dizzy fish in a bowl."[26]

The ponies both exist as a fluid aquatic school and collide with the metaphoric bowl. As a further backdrop and measure to what will become their ultimate bolt for freedom, a growing line of wagons occupied by spectators from the neighborhood assembles alongside the corral.

At the heart of this extended scene is a moment when the Texan and one of the horses wrestle each other into a state of intimate and undecidable reciprocity.

> The ponies, huddled, watched him. Then they broke before him and slid stiffly along the fence. He turned them and they whirled and rushed back along the lot; whereupon, as though he had been waiting his chance when they should have turned their backs on him, the Texan began to run too, so that . . . he was almost upon them. The earth became thunderous; dust arose, out of which the animals began to burst like flushed quail into which, with that unflagging faith in his own invulnerability, the Texan rushed. For an instant the watchers could see them in the dust—the pony backed into the angle of the fence and the stable, the man facing it, reaching into his hip. Then the beast rushed at him in a sort of fatal and hopeless desperation and he struck it between the eyes with the pistol-butt and felled it and leaped onto its prone head. . . . For an instant in the dust the watchers saw the man free of the earth in violent lateral motion like a rag attached to the horse's head. Then the Texan's feet came back to earth and the dust blew aside and revealed them, motionless, the Texan's sharp heels braced into the ground, one hand gripping the pony's forelock and the other its nostrils, the long evil muzzle wrung backward over its scarred shoulder while it breathed in labored and hollow groans.[27]

In this passage, the stalemate between bestial man and untutored beast is both obscured and symbolized by the amorphous dust cloud that rises between them. So turbulent is the encounter that for a moment the Texan loses his control over the situation, even loses his own gravitational force and is held aloft in a whirlwind. The pony spins him around like a top. In this segment of the episode, the linear figures in which the epic man-beast struggle have earlier been couched give way to the encompassing dust cloud, which alternatively reveals and obscures. In the figure of the cloud, the scene of anthropocentric mastery produces its own insignia of the irreducible semiotic as well as historical and logical ambiguity staged by the narrative. Eventually, though, by dint of the violence foundational to the culture of Frenchman's Bend and by applying his pistol butt, Buck Hipps regains his footing.

Any chance of reciprocal collaboration between man and beast is over by the time that Hipps, having sold his horses and asked the directions to New York, is on the road to Jefferson. When it comes time to collect the animals they have purchased, the citizens of Frenchman's Bend approach their chattel with caution.

> "Head them," Freeman said tensely. "Turn them back." They turned them, driving them back upon themselves again; the animals merged and spun in short, huddling rushes, phantom and inextricable. "Hold them now," Freeman said. Dont let them get by us.". . .
>
> The line was still advancing. The ponies milled, clotting, forced gradually backward toward the open door of the barn. Henry was still slightly in front, crouched slightly, his thin figure, even in the mazy moonlight, emanating something of that spent fury. The splotchy huddle of the animals seemed to be moving before the advancing line of men like a snowball which they might have been pushing before them by some invisible means, gradually nearer and nearer to the black yawn of the barn door. Later it was obvious that the ponies were so intent upon the men that they did not realize the barn was even behind them until they backed into the shadow of it. Then an indescribable sound, a movement desperate and despairing, arose among them; for an instant of static horror men and animals faced one another, then the men whirled and ran before a gaudy vomit of long wild faces and splotched chests which overtook and scattered them and flung them sprawling aside and completely obliterated from sight Henry and the little boy . . . the herd sweeping on across the lot, to crash through the gate which the last man through it had neglected to close, leaving it slightly ajar. . . . Then the whole inextricable mass crashed among the wagons and eddied and divided about the one in which the woman sat, and rushed on down the lane and into the road, dividing, one half going one way and one half the other.[28]

The decisive collapse of the ponies' restraint by the citizenry and culture of Frenchman's Bend is told in sound and fury: in the desperate roar of the pack and in the colors and shapes of growing collective force, at first vacillating between physical barriers, then crashing through them. With the departure of the newly enriched Hipps, the horses overthrow all manner and materials of restraint, to merge into an "inextricable mass," to cross the borderline from being discrete entities to an amalgam, a "gaudy vomit." Like another collective noun, water, the mass of now-liberated horses dissolves and overwhelms the line of men. In its vivid color and motion, Faulkner's narrative and descriptive rhetoric rises to the splendid violence unleashed by the horses.

Under the administration of Flem Snopes, an outsider from within, the community loses out, being no match for an outsider of more recent vintage, the wanderer from Texas. The locals cannot hold a candle to this stranger, either when it comes to the physical domination of creatures or to rhetorical games of mastery. The horses, however, in the magnificence of their indomitable collective will, one-up Buck Hipps in their control of the situation, taking on the role of the definitive outsiders, the strangers from elsewhere who redefine the history, aspirations, and collective memory and vocabulary of the community.

A pack of animals is for Deleuze and Guattari a category of the anomalous. The phenomenon they call "becoming-animal" is not merely a folkloric curiosity but an adaptation, occurring on textual as well as sociological levels, on the plane of sociohistorical memory as well as of behavior, to singularity and a compulsion to regress that the authors implicitly posit. "Every Animal Has Its Anomalous," they write,[29] and as examples of the "many possible positions" available to "the exceptional individual," they cite Kafka's singing "of mouse society."[30] "Josephine, the mouse singer, sometimes holds a privileged position in the pack, sometimes holds a position outside the pack, and sometimes slips into and is lost in the anonymity of the collective statements of the pack."[31] Like a spotted hide, the pack absorbs individuality and conveys anonymity. "There may be no such thing as a lone wolf, but there is a leader of the pack, a master of the pack, or else the old deposed head of the pack now living alone."[32] The pack has a leader, as a visual composite has a focal point, even if that is not the individuated subject who may serve as the protagonist of a novel.

The pack of animals projects its own shifting boundary, what Deleuze and Guattari call a borderline. Faulkner's spotted horses exist as a herd, a tenuous frieze, in counterpoint to the fences, barbed wire, and other linear frames by which they are subordinated. The borderline of the band bears an entire countermetaphysics as it intersects, undulates with, and countermands the linear boundaries of fences and laws.

There is a borderline for each multiplicity; it is in no way a center but rather the enveloping line or farthest dimension. . . . That is what Captain Ahab says to his first mate: I have no personal history with Moby-Dick, no revenge to take, any more than I have a myth to play out, but I do have a becoming! Moby-Dick is neither an individual nor a genus; he is the borderline, and I have to strike him to get at the pack as a whole, to reach the pack as a whole and pass beyond it. The elements of the pack are only imaginary "dummies," the characteristics of the pack are only symbolic entities; all that counts is the borderline—the anomalous. . . . The pack has a borderline, and an anomalous position, whenever in a given space an animal is on the line or in the act of drawing the line in relation to which all the other members of the pack will fall into one of two halves, left or right: a peripheral position, such that it is impossible to tell if the anomalous is still in the band, already outside the band, or at the shifting boundary of the band.[33]

The spotted horses are the truest outsiders of *The Hamlet* and indeed of Faulkner's entire fictive social history of the deep South. They are the outside that emerges when the indigenous culture and ideology of a society implode. The border they comprise sets in relief Faulkner's human characters and their deeds. His representations of a culture depend, as all national entities and histories do, on an influx of outsiders. But what is memorable about Faulkner's contribution to the stage of world history is that a very functional and serviceable wave of outsiders, the Snopes and their connections, is displaced by the wave embodied by the pack of wild horses, which dissolves it but also renders its allegorical, phantasmatic message. Faulkner's fiction is a Go-game of varying contours and outlines. The novel stages the animal as well as human constraints upon the figure of the outsider, but only the horses set in full relief the violence marshaled by epic realism.

The denouement of this tale of exteriority and cooptation, of ineluctable, unprompted regression, of impulse and restraint, of communal persistence atop a subtext of violence, partly absorbed, partly expelled, the sequel to this forthcoming if scandalous account of the modern South, transpires far afield. Faulkner's fictive social history of the South arrives at a stalemate, a sociological homeostasis, illuminated by untrammeled images, whether of spotted horses, alluring women, or forbidden eroticism. These images, partly normal, partly violent, arise from the everyday, in strong traditions of figuration, epic, and folk art. The fate of the community is to generate these outbreaks of the allegorical and the imaginary, entrusting them to Faulkner just as Ratliff assumes the role of village info-source and chronicler, and to persist, barely, always on the brink of disintegration. On the far side of this tale of sociological survival and of communities illustrated and sublated by the violent images culled from their depths are other stories of disintegration and non-negotiable marginality not left for the men on the gallery of Will Varner's store to recount. There is the massive northward diaspora of the African Americans, whose fate, during Reconstruction, is negotiated in such Faulknerian works as *Absalom, Absalom!* There is the rolling South African space traversed by J. M. Coetzee's Michael K, who is more the errant product of the St. Petersburg underground or of the Hapsburg bureaucracy than the scion of some native village or homeland.[34]

There is an outside to the romance of the outsider, and it is enunciated by she who is held speechless, but acted upon, and held accountable, during the fictive social history of regional characteristics and particularities, however vividly it is accompanied, in the musical sense, by images and enunciations of underlying deviance.

The true ending to Faulkner's *Hamlet* transpires in the sewers of Chicago, where the title character of Richard Wright's "The Man Who Lived Underground" merges into the city's subterranean flows.[35] Falsely accused of murder, the protagonist assumes a second life, an existence that doubles the workers and guards he spies upon in the Chicago underground. The ingenuity he must demonstrate in order to procure the necessities of life and compose a counterlife is in the tradition of other heroic empiricists in the history of literature, characters such as Robinson Crusoe and Lemuel Gulliver. Yet Wright's "Man Who Lived Underground" is more a literary descendent of Dante, Dostoyevsky, Gogol, and Kafka than are Faulkner's gallery of rogues, who step, rather, out of the pages of Chaucer, Dickens, Melville, and Tolstoy.

Faulkner's microcosm structures itself according to oppositions between inside and outside, citizen and deviant, even between symbol and allegory. But Wright's Underground Man and Coetzee's Michael K have migrated to hinterlands of postmodern condition, whose marginality curtails any degree of social and semiological recuperation.[36] Imprisoned as well as distinguished by his own vivid writerly canvases (Faulkner produced visual as well as literary artifacts), the inventor of Yoknapawtapha County invested his aesthetic resources in a modernist fabulation and play of structures. Wright's Underground Man and Coetzee's Michael K act, and only barely speak, from a postmodern marginal zone in which community has been bereft of its power to nurture and to generate meaning,[37] and historical narrative has encountered serious debilities: in definitively identifying its winners and losers and even in persisting.

The visual tension in Faulkner's fictive world is between degrees of density and porosity: a horse running at full gallop into a wire fence; a dust cloud framing an epic battle between a man and a wild horse; a circling line of wagons and the shifting borderline that Deleuze and Guattari imagine as enclosing the pack. By contrast, Michael K ultimately chokes upon the lack of fluids in his barren topographical and social landscapes.[38] In Wright's fable all the boundaries that lend Faulkner's fiction its tension and its implicit hope dissolve. The fate of the Underground Man, who, a generation before, was a subdued, silent partner in a Southern, Faulknerian social canvas and who in Chicago has become the subliminal outsider of the Underworld, is to drown. Wright specifies very clearly in the novella that the conditions and status of the black protagonist are completely autonomous of his actions. He is an outsider whose semiological and cultural values are conferred completely by the Other. The protagonist has been forced, before the novella begins, to confess to a murder that he did not commit; by happenstance and police inefficiency, his confession to the homicide for which he is responsible is dismissed. The Underground Man is nonrecuperably marginal, terminally deterritorialized, by fiat and foregone conclusion. Once shot by his police captors, he can only drown, and in this way merge with the water, and in his demise rests the fate not only of a community of outcasts but of a metaphysics of fictive epic and historical memory. It is no accident, then, that the eventuality awaiting the partners in U.S. racism, its agents as well as its victims, Faulkner's white peasantry as well as Wright's Underground Men, is to devolve to the status of physical objects. It is in the random and accidental concussion of things that the complementary epics of racism figure devastating reversals in thinking and articulation.

> As though in a deep dream, he heard a metallic clank; they had replaced the manhole cover, shutting out forever the sound of wind and rain. From overhead came the muffled roar of a powerful motor and the swish of a speeding car. He felt the strong tide pushing him slowly into the middle of the sewer, turning him

about. For a split second there hovered before his eyes the glittering cave, the shouting walls, and the laughing floor. . . . Then his mouth was full of thick, bitter water. The current spun him around. He sighed and closed his eyes, a whirling object rushing alone in the darkness, veering, tossing, lost in the heart of the earth.[39]

SIX

The Afterlife of Judaism: The Zohar, Benjamin, Miller

Judaism, so the common myth runs, is the Abrahamic[1] religion devoid of an afterlife. Where first Christianity and then Islam are quite explicit regarding the determination of the life hereafter by the quality of the life lived in this world, luridly picturing the conditions, qualities, and experience of Heaven and Hell (and Purgatory, where applicable), Judaism hedges its bets and is more reticent in the sphere of eschatology.[2] The liturgy of the Days of Awe, the New Year's festivals that stage the collective public acknowledgment of mortal human vices, breaches in morality, and crimes, stresses a judgment before God transpiring from year to year. The afterlife, in this theology, is the ethical imprint that a person deposits in the memory, communal and individual, of the survivors that she or he leaves behind. If this is the Judaic afterlife, its image is as vague as personal impressions of a fellow human being are idiosyncratic. Even Buddhism, whose metaphysics is less individual-oriented and rule-driven than Judaism, envisions a more particular and specific relation between past lives and ones yet to emerge.

This familiar and time-honored cant makes the Christian and Muslim afterworld tantamount to a place and a time apart. But if we divert our gaze to look past this imagistic literality and allow ourselves to conflate the afterlife with the spectral, Jewish theology has not been as eschatologically shorthanded as might at first appear. It is true that Judaism fully realized its own distinctive version of the afterlife only after Christianity and Islam had established and represented theirs. But once the Jewish afterlife was inscribed, for all its vagaries and all the specifics of Christian and Muslim Paradise and Hell that it in many respects evades, it disseminated itself to cultural sites far afield and insinuated itself into artifacts and cultural experiments in which its play and connivance have not been divined even to the present day. I would go so far as to say that the Judaic afterlife, inscribed on the eve of European modernity and revising prior Jewish theology in keeping with the emerging lineaments of epistemic revolution,[3] establishes a spectral setting unmistakable in its particular sublimity, poetics, and rhetoric, leaving its imprint on artifacts as diverse as Kleist's tales, Büchner's prose poems, the Romantic speculations of the Schlegels and Novalis, and Kafka's sublime imagery, as well as on Scholem's lifelong project, Benjamin's always-problematical Judaism, and Celan's poetry.

The specifically Judaic provenance and imaginary surrounding this spectral scene of writing has been occulted over a significant segment of its "run." It is incumbent upon us as students of culture to extract and reconfigure this Jewish revenant or afterlife not in the name of nationalistic celebration or under the imperative of ethnic preservation but in appreciation of the broad thoroughfare on which the three Abrahamic religions penetrated and revitalized each other's scripts and scenarios on the most profound and infrastructural levels. The platform common to the three major Western monotheistic religions, as well as the spectral abyss that haunts them,[4] have received an overdue updating and overhaul, in terms of conceptual depth and rigor, in Jacques Derrida's religious explorations of the last three decades. I lean heavily on the conceptual and architectural support furnished by this work.

The "full-service" Judaic scenario of the afterlife is medieval in its provenance. It achieves its full configuration in the Zohar, the Book of Splendor, a major element of the mystical movement and literature in Judaism known as the Kabbalah. Scholem makes an effort to separate Kabbalah from the

Zohar. The Kabbalah, for one, is older. In its seminal moment, Jewish mysticism, according to Scholem,

> did not aspire to an understanding of the true nature of God, but to a perception of the phenomenon of the Throne on its Chariot as it is described in the first chapter of Ezekiel, traditionally entitled *ma'aseh merkabah*. . . . The 14th chapter of the Book of Enoch, which contains the earliest example of this kind of literary description, was the source of a long visionary tradition of describing the world of the Throne and the visionary ascent to it, which we find portrayed in the books of the Merkabah mystics.[5]

Although the Kabbalah claims direct roots in the Book of Ezekiel and the apocryphal book of Enoch and encompasses such works as the eleventh-century Sepher Yezirah, "a compact discourse on cosmology and cosmogony (a kind of *ma'aseh bereshit*, 'act of creation,' in a speculative form), outstanding for its clearly mystical character,"[6] and the early-twelfth-century Provençal Sefer ha-Bahir, it is in Sefer ha-Zohar, the Book of Splendor, that the Judaic afterlife achieves its full configuration. This multivolume work is a compendium of biblical commentaries, or Midrashim, "written mainly between 1280 and 1286 by Moses b. Shem Tov de Leon in Guadalajara, a small town northeast of Madrid."[7]

The most elementary literary criticism makes obvious a present and compelling need for broad-based literary scholars to return to the canonical texts of a broad band of world religions. From such a perspective, one sees that, in the Zohar, the rabbinical contributors to the difficult and technical argumentation of the Talmud, names memorialized in the Mishna, the Gemara, and the several registers of commentary around the Talmudic page,[8] have been transformed into literary characters who are seen discoursing with each other (most often in pairs) as they wander through earthly landscapes, sometimes furnished with geographical coordinates. In the Talmud, the rabbis who figure in the Zohar are remote and forbidding surrogates, distant in their conceptual and legal genius. In the Zohar, the myth of their genius is extended in the highly speculative thrust and tone of their comments and in their stunning capability to issue forth in metaphysical yet precise imagery. We will explore some examples below.

The metamorphosis, in the Zohar, of rabbis into literary characters is a capital development in the cultural history of Judaism. In it, profound cultural change and interchange are brought about by transformations in narrative. No critic of the past several generations has been more exquisitely

The Afterlife of Judaism   133

attuned to the cultural, metaphysical, and epistemological implications of such transposition than J. Hillis Miller. We cannot overestimate the sociocultural and historical effects of the subtle but far-reaching metamorphosis of rabbis who start out as little more than indices or placeholders for the disputations that they propound into full-blooded characters of European provenance and a somewhat modern disposition.

In a Millerian vein, this literary development is tantamount to a mega speech act, a decisive act of narrative radically reconfiguring certain base positions in Jewish ideology while substantially realigning the Judaic position on the differential platform of the three Abrahamic religions. Miller understands this kind of happening both in terms of translation between cultural registers and agencies and in terms of phenomena that arise along the frontiers, no-person's lands, demilitarized zones, and borderlines of textual sites, constructed topographies of reading and thinking. None of these interstitial zones is more treacherous to Miller than the one falling between the particularity of reading and the impulse to theorize. The experiences of reading and theorizing about the text are so similar, on such intimate terms, that one is tempted to collapse them.

And yet, as Miller specifies:

> A theoretical formulation never quite adequately addresses the insight that comes from reading. That insight is always particular, local, good for this time, place, text, and act of reading only. The theoretical insight is a glimpse out of the corner of the eye of the way language works, a glimpse that is not wholly amenable to conceptualization. Another way to put this is to say that the theoretical formulation in its original language is already a translation or mistranslation of a lost original.[9]

It is more than possible, in the distinctive critical climate configured by Miller, for the segue from the Talmud to the Zohar to perform translation and radical mistranslation.

Miller's exploration of a biblical text, the Book of Ruth, from which this citation derives, in terms of the parameters of reading, conversion, repatriation, and translation that it both establishes and violates uncannily anticipates the transformation of Talmudic figures into Zoharic ones. His reading of the Book of Ruth also accesses the abyssal atmosphere of the landscape through which the rabbis, transformed into characters, stroll. That reading is itself an extension of a topographical understanding and treatment of the dislocations, distortions, displacements, and interchanges performed in the course of, and by, texts. The integrity of Judaism—or of any cultural community, for that matter—is less a matter of genealogical purity or the systematic exclusion of "external" influences than a strategic rhythm of appropriations and consolidations. This enables the character Ruth, under Miller's critical gaze and with his biblical erudition, to function both as an agent of the ideology of Judaic commitment, faith, and continuity ("whither thou goest, I will go; and whither thou lodgest, I will lodge: thy people shall be my people, and thy God my God"; Ruth 1:16) and as a talisman for what the story theorizes, namely, the inevitability and nature of the topographical shifts and intercultural and interlinguistic translations involved in cultural "identity," persistence, or perdurance.

For all that Miller is taken with Ruth's characterological vividness, strength, and integrity, he can assign her at best a limited role as an avatar of cultural survival. This is not by virtue of any flaw or shortcoming in her character or activities but is owing to the limited purview of any theoretical or quasi-theoretical figure or act. To the degree that Ruth, in leaving Moab, in assuming refugee status in Judah, and in marrying Boaz functions as a theoretical icon of the topographical and linguistic transpositions required for cultural persistence, her power and efficacy are limited by her definition by and bracketing within a particular set of conditions, circumstances, and nuances. This is, in a limited sense, the "general" limitation upon all theoretical acts, which blend only too well into the literary/cultural compositions that prompted them.

Both the figure of Ruth and the Book of Ruth occupy, in Miller's reading, the status of the cultural mainstream or epitome that arises only in a condition of marginality and displacement and that is irreconcilably alienated from itself.

> Whatever her original language and culture may have been, she can cross the border into Israel and be assimilated there only by translating herself, so to speak, or being translated, into the idiom of the new culture. She becomes a proper wife and mother among the Israelites. Nevertheless, she brings something of her own, something that resists full translation and assimilation. The decision to follow Naomi was her own. . . . She is someone very much in charge of her own life. Whatever the commentators say, she does not seem simply the passive instrument of a historical or divine purpose that exceeds her and that makes use of her to achieve its own ends. In a similar way, literary theory has its own stubborn

and recalcitrant particularity.... It opens itself to assimilation within other cultures and languages. Like Ruth, it is prepared to say, "whither thou goest, I will go."[10]

Miller's reading transpires at the point where Ruth's role as a literary character and as an ideological paragon fuses with her status as a figure, both rhetorical and allegorical. It is a seamless suture. Thematically, Ruth may be taken, as Miller demonstrates, to be both a figure of fidelity and repatriation and subject to jarring displacements. This dual loyalty, assimilation, and alienation is built into her, for she is a trope for the features of language and culture that she performs. Oddly, it is the invisible seam between her exemplarity and her intransigence as a cipher in language (and specific languages) that marks her with the onus, an extension of Cain's mark, of alienation. Miller does not leave this constitutional marginality and deterritorialization unmarked:

> This book of the Hebrew Bible has been alienated from itself, translated from itself. It has been put to entirely new uses, uses by no means intended by the original authors or scribes.... The original writer or writers of Ruth had no intention of using it as a means of legitimating the claim of Jesus to be the Messiah. That, nevertheless, is its "theoretical" function in the Christian Bible. In coming to perform this function Ruth has been alienated from itself. It has been translated in the strong sense of that word.[11]

Alienated from itself on a number of counts, the Book of Ruth may lose control of its initial ideological thrust or semantic meaning, but it joins the only economy of cultural dissemination to which Miller can subscribe: one configured at the linguistic level and operating through events of translation, grafting, and intercultural as well as intertextual sharing. Indeed, Miller's account of the vicissitudes of Ruth is tempered by the openness that is the basis of his own exegetical ethics: a susceptibility and openness that is to be maintained at all costs, including those of clarity, certainty, and political/social/cultural amenity, self-assurance, and self-congratulation.

Speculating on any enduring lesson to be learned from the displacements and translations embodied by the figure of Ruth, Miller is drawn, again uncannily, in terms of the trajectory pursued by the present essay, to her Romantic emanation as conjured up by Keats in "Ode to a Nightingale."

> The poem speaks of the nightingale's song as something that has sounded the same in many different places and at many different times over the centuries.

> The nightingale's song ties Keats's own place and time to innumerable other places, times, and situations in which the nightingale's song has been heard. Thinking of this expands the poet's attention away from his preoccupations with his own suffering, limitation, and mortality to give him a virtual kinship with people in all those places and times who have heard the nightingale. Hearing the nightingale is a momentary escape from the imminence of death, although also a way to experience the desire for death.[12]

One of the emanations of the nightingale's song, which Keats endows with a broad transhistorical and multicultural range, is heard by Ruth as she gleans barley in Boaz's fields: "Perhaps the self-same song that found a path / Through the sad heart of Ruth, when, sick for home, / She stood in tears among the alien corn" (ll. 65–67). It is amid the general "limit experience"[13] performed by Romanticism upon Enlightenment ideology, itself a codification of long-standing and widespread Western aspirations to rationality and utility, that Miller finds a "natural" correlative to the distinctive landscape of displacement and translation in the Book of Ruth. This is an abyss, a spectral setting of the sort surveyed by Derrida in his engagement with Western theology.

It is not entirely by accident, as we will see in tracing a distinctively Kabbalistic zone of cultural production and imagination from the Zohar into European modernity, that a major Romantic poet and theorist, one who theorized along the lines and within the resources of poetry, chose to deploy the topographical and textual features that Miller unearths in the Book of Ruth. In a parallel fashion, as I hope to demonstrate below, it was a generation of Romantic writers, the likes of Kleist, Büchner, and Hoffmann, that proved most receptive to a Kabbalistic afterlife within the imaginary of German letters.

One way of appreciating Euro-American Romanticism is as a fairly systematic "retake," recalibration, and reprogramming of all prior Western thought. This "reediting" transpired as a trans-European happening or event, whose primary impetus was to accommodate a broad range of indeterminacies infiltrating European ideology on a variety of levels and registers: sociopolitical; epistemological, in Foucault's sense;[14] conceptual (there is a reason why sublimity became a big-ticket item at this moment); and rhetorical. Miller's reading of the Book of Ruth demonstrates a subliminal elective affinity between the topography configured by certain works of ancient Hebrew literature, as it theorizes the positionality of its intrinsic ideological and sociopolitical formations, and Romantic literature and theory, which gravitated toward this landscape and its underlying articulations in setting about the work of quasi-systematic reprogramming or *tikkun*.[15]

The Zohar may itself be read as a limit experience applied to an exegetical procedure and way of thinking, as of living, codified in the Talmud. By the time of its writing, it inhabited a different topography from the Book of Ruth, which had been absorbed into a finalized canon and was thereby invested with sacred or transcendental status. Yet its trajectory into modernity follows very much along the lines that Miller has drawn for the values and dislocations of the Book of Ruth. It is indeed against a backdrop of Romantic updatings and appropriations that Gershom Scholem took on, as his life's work, the dissemination, translation, and exhibition of medieval Jewish mystical literature. Precisely the Romantic receptivity to a Judaic abyss and afterlife afforded Scholem hope for the repatriation of the Kabbalah into the broader sphere of European letters.

According to Scholem, the Merkabah or Chariot literature of the Rabbinic period, the centuries straddling the birth of Christ, already "refers to historical figures, whose connection with the mysteries of the Chariot is attested by Talmud and Midrash. The ascent of its heroes to the Chariot . . . comes after a number of preparatory exercises of an extremely ascetic nature."[16] The Zohar builds upon this tradition of narrativizing the theological paragons of Judaism. The inclusion within the narrative episodes of the Zohar of the Amorim and Tannaim, the Talmudic commentators remembered for the logico-legalistic prose of their discourse, humanizes these rabbis in the sense that Jesus humanizes the principles of Judaism by embodying them, that is, by characterologically condensing them. Ironically, then, the Zohar plays the New Testament to the Talmud's obsessional codification and qualification.

There is something surely otherworldly, spooky, I would say, but in a distinctly Judaic grain, in the proclivity of the Zohar's rabbis for imagery that condenses the magical and the metaphysical. In the course of the Zohar's tales, we are made privy to the rabbis' gift for interweaving the logical and conceptually intriguing with imagery "riddled with light," breathtaking in luminosity. Scholem gathered this tendency and poetics of medieval Jewish script under the rubric of "Jewish mysticism." It may well be that the marginal status of Palestine and Israel since the late nineteenth century, combined with Scholem's urgency in establishing the Hebrew University, forced his hand in imputing a revealed foundation to his chosen literature, for his was surely a sophisticated literary and critical mind. Yet what distinguishes "Jewish mysticism" is more a specific poetics and tonality of imagery, which Scholem locates in such works as the Kabbalah, the Sefer Yezira, and the Zohar, than it is a claim to direct revelation.

It is in the Zohar that the afterlife of Judaism is first fully revealed. The itinerant rabbis of the Zohar deliver up their images of splendor, which Benjamin would term their dialectical images,[17] in the aftermath of the formal commentaries they have delivered in the various registers of the Talmud. The rabbis of the Zohar expended themselves centuries before in the intricate and obscure discursive involutions of the Talmudic compendium, so vast that it is repeatedly described in oceanic terms.[18]

Their "life" in the Zohar is a revenant, a Second Coming. It is not only the rabbis in the Zohar who are dead. At least figuratively, Judaism is dead, as well. It has died. The idyllic landscape the rabbis traverse as they discourse on a more speculative and poetic level than ever before may not be the Heaven of Jewish faith, but it is an afterlife. In figurative death, that is, in exile, and bound up in formalistic legal involution, Judaism is freer and more vibrant than it ever was in life, or as a sovereign nation. Many of the Zohar's folktales take place at night.

For purposes of the present demonstration, I want to focus on the figure of the stars, above all because their figure resurfaces as a multifaceted motif in Benjamin's criticism. There it ranges in resonance from an embodiment of metaphysical naïveté that is indispensable to exegesis and inscription yet cries out for debunking to the constellation of anomalous and dissonant cultural counterforces emerging in the particular archive that every working critic assembles and that becomes indistinguishable from her intellectual imprimatur or signature. Within the framework of the mythopoetic reconfiguration or reformation of biblical and Talmudic sources that is the Zohar, the stars are inscribed within a complex of other figures at once poetically rich and hovering and instrumental to medieval Judaic metaphysics, including nighttime, light, plants, bodies and vessels of water, erotic desire, and clothes. Indeed, the stars form one point in a poetically captivating constellation of images whose interaction lifts the curtain on a modern, literarily full-fledged Judaism, and, as a figure, they become key players in Benjamin's most resilient allegory of criticism.

One could argue, moreover, that the Zohar's spectral, nocturnal narrative space, in which everything is phantasmatically after the fact, gives a premonition of the jarringly concussive space of postmodernity, in which the most disparate and unrelated counterforces, formations, and crystallizations coexist with impunity and in mutual indifference. One of many possible fabulations from twentieth-century literature that could be elicited as an instance of this Kabbalistic space, a phenomenon that could transpire only under the aegis of this specifically Judaic imaginary, is the ironic coda and afterlife at the end of Bruno Schulz's *Sanatorium under the Sign of the Hourglass*. In the sanatorium highlighted by the title, the narrator is afforded one last encounter with his domineering yet vulnerable father. The father has died, yet is not yet gone. His affective and imaginary power over his son remains in effect. Their last interview transpires in an uncanny time warp that is after life and before annihilation, during a temporal slowdown and deferral, one nonetheless very much in the province and provenance of language. In response to the narrator/son's incredulous question, Dr. Gotard, superintendent of the sanatorium, characterizes, in terms to which we will return in the next chapter, the father's uncanny, spectral status. The bizarre time-warp into which the father has eventuated even suggests that there is something "mystical," in the Zoharic sense, in the temporality of Einsteinian physics, so much at home in the twentieth century. The radical deferral that has settled over the sanatorium, itself a version of the afterlife, corresponds to the temporal setting of the particular folktales that riveted Scholem's attention. This offers context for a folktale from the Zohar's commentaries on Exodus:

> Once Rabbi Eleazar and Rabbi Abba were sitting together, and then the dusk came, whereupon they got up and started toward a garden by the Lake of Tiberias. Going, they beheld two stars speed toward each other from different points of the sky, meet, and then vanish. Rabbi Abba observed: in heaven above and on the earth below, how great are the works of the Holy One, be blessed. Who fathoms it, how these stars come from different points, how they meet and disappear? Rabbi Eleazar answered: Nor did we need to see these two stars to reflect on them, for we have pondered on them, as we have on the multitude of great works that the Holy One, be blessed, is ever doing. Then quoting the verse, "Great is the Lord and mighty in power; His understanding is without number" [Ps. 147:5], he went on to discourse: In truth, great and mighty and sublime is the Holy One, be blessed.[19]

In a specific setting and location, indeed, in the specific site of Galilee, which was crucial to the birth of Christianity, two of the seminal Jewish scholars and litigators of the Talmud meditate, in solidarity and intimacy, on the sublime phenomenon of shooting stars, which arise, coincide, and pass each other haphazardly, outside the cadres of meaning or necessity. Indeed, the discussion is explicitly more about the condition of such arbitrariness, such physical chaos, than it is about the most mercurial of the heavenly bodies, the shooting stars. The prerogative of thinking people to meditate on shooting stars takes precedence over their actuality or veracity, just as the onto-theological mandate of Abrahamic religion, faith in a monotheistic divinity, transpires autonomously of facts and of the prevailing sociopolitical formation, whose confirmation or approval it does not require. It is in this sense that the extraordinarily innovative and central Rabbi Eleazar can assure: "Nor did we need to see these two stars to reflect on them." He agrees with Rabbi Abba that it is ultimately unfathomable "how these stars come from different points, how they meet and disappear."

The shooting stars' enigmatic trajectory across the sky becomes a legend for a familiar Judaic outcome. The Lord is "Great . . . and mighty in power. . . . In truth, great and mighty and sublime is the Holy One, be blessed." The pretext and predetermined outcome of Jewish theology is faith in God, endlessly reaffirmed faith and commitment, in spite of the chance, accident, arbitrariness, and sublimity inscribed in the metaphysics and image of the stars. This final conclusion, known in advance, is only strengthened by these circumstances. The Kaddish, the formulaic Judaic response to the arbitrariness of death, the textual talisman whose repetition, thrice daily for a year after bereavement and thereafter at specific intervals, is, above all, a responsive series of attributions of omniscience and omnipotence to God.[20] The Judaic gut reaction to death, in other words, consists largely in a subordination of personal loss, despair, outrage, and related psychological reactions to a public figuration and affirmation of God's majesty.

But on the way to this fatal, if uplifting, outcome, however much it might have been reached in advance, the Zoharic folktale registers a number of key modifications that have taken place in Judaic parlance. Rabbis Abba and Eleazar are not sages or legal authorities, invested with quasi-divine intelligence and authority. By the Sea of Galilee, one of the primal scenes of Christianity, they have been raptured up from the Talmud and reborn as literary characters, and as such they have served as conduits or channels, a key Kabbalistic image, introducing several pivotal traits of modernity into Judaism. Indeed, their rebirth as literary characters, under the enigmatic sign of the shooting stars, coincides with the entry of a Christian and Islamic notion of the afterlife into Judaism. The beloved sages of the Talmud, in other words, as avatars of any future Judaism, have to die in order to be reborn, and their rebirth as literary characters coincides with the entrance of figured, depicted, represented death into the sanctuary of Judaism.

But this is not all that is liberated and activated by Judaism's engagement with certain precepts, modalities, and scenes of representation that had been, previously, strictly other. The folktales of the Zohar may coincide with Judaism's acknowledgment of literary characterization and Western eschatology, of Greek as well as Christo-Islamic provenance, but they are also imprinted with a specifically Judaic poetics, one in which the categories of logic and classification are endowed with a vivid sublimity and then dance across the stage or abyss of representation, not unlike the track of the shooting stars across the vault of heaven. The dance of the divinely inflected creatures or creations of logic across the scene of theological speculation, as across the page anticipates by many centuries what Friedrich Schlegel would characterize as *parabasis*.[21] If the specifically Judaic afterlife and scene of representation announced in the Zohar was embraced by and admitted into any mainstream European national culture, that was the domain of German letters and the German literary imaginary. This explains how Benjamin could have embarked on his life's work as a herald and scribe of German-Jewish literary relations; however, this vocation was ultimately sabotaged by the politico-historical events taking place during his lifetime.

A fine display of the poetics accompanying the rebirth of the rabbis as literary figures appears in our legend of the shooting stars:

> Acting as guardians over this world are all the stars of the firmaments, with each individual object of the world having a specially designated star to care for it. The herbs and the trees, the grass and the wild plants, to bloom and increase must have the power of the stars that stand over them and look directly at them, each in its particular mode. The great number of the plants and stars of all kinds emerge at the beginning of the night and shine until three hours minus a quarter after midnight. Thereafter only a small number are out. It is not without purpose that all the stars shine and serve. Some, being at their duty the whole night through, cause the plant which is their special ward to spring up and flourish.

Others begin their activities at the advent of night and watch over their own objects until the hour of midnight. . . . So it was with the stars which we saw, which appeared briefly for their set task. When their task is accomplished, such stars vanish from this world.[22]

In this vignette, each herb, tree, plant, and variety of grass is the "ward" of a particular star. The sublime multiplication of the stars, and by implication, the vastness of the heavens, is infused into the domestic world of cultivation by means of this dedicated stewardship. In this passage, for instance, each of the elements in the vegetable kingdom is activated at a different moment in the course of the night. Based on this stately progression of nocturnal vegetable awakening, God has scientifically coordinated a succession of stars to oversee the worldly garden.

What is stunning about this image is the juxtaposition between earthly plant life and unreachable stars, impeccable divine planning and spaces and schemes of inconceivable vastness. We are speaking here of "guardian stars," if not guardian angels. The passage builds toward a Foucauldian analogy or similitude between the inconceivable architecture of the heavens and the vegetable biosphere.[23] The poetic effect of this coincidence between two realms, which are, from a human point of view, both inconceivable and uncontrollable, is a specific form of Kabbalistic magic—magical reverie, not magical realism. By means of a figure such as the stars, the Book of Splendor marshals the vastness of the universe in the service and representation of God. The Judaic divinity functions not merely as the transcendental signifier of the work; the *Shekhinah*,[24] or divine presence, manifests itself in a specific poetics. This poetics choreographs a dance, delirious both in its exoneration from the constraints of rationality and in its deployment of logic, between the things of our world and the grandeur, multiplication, and endless extension and proliferation characterizing the holy guardians charged with overseeing them—that is, manifesting unwavering attentiveness and intimate, total understanding. "The book of the higher wisdom of the East tells us of stars with trailing tails, comets, which from the skies hold sway and direct the growth of certain herbs on earth, of the sort known as 'elixirs of life' . . . the growth of these is brought about by the flash of that luminous tail trailing after these stars across the firmament."[25] Not only is the magnificent, ineffable design of the universe scored into the earth, implanted, under the sign of the guardian stars but the heavens, as expressed by the comet's tail, take on a worldly ephemerality within the framework of otherworldly movement and time. Indeed, no figure could intensify fleeting intransience more fully than a comet's meteoric or possibly mercurial traces. The sweep of the comet's tail gives full evidence that the dance that is the exemplary figure for the radiation of divine—that is to say, mystical—insight throughout the universe trips across the heavens, as it does across the earth.

The dance of mystical Judaic poetics, a choreography that traverses a liturgical literature, transpires in a scene or theater that is an afterlife. The dance between the plenitude of this world and the ineffable predestination of the divine plan is rendered all the more vital by the fact that it is staged in a spectral setting in which all telling figures and characters have long been dead. This prior death, the transpiration of Jewish mysticism's most striking figures into an afterlife, infuses all Judaic eschatology with an irreducible "pre-text": this is an irony situated at the threshold between life and death. Indeed, the contemplation by Judaism of final things becomes a life-and-death matter, whose endless potential for humor can be taken in exactly the opposite way. It is one thing for Judaism to suspend certain of its discursive preoccupations and the roles it has assigned to some of its key players in an ironic afterlife, quite another for it to be apprehended as a culture that has prospectively, through some bizarre collective death wish, accommodated its own demise.

If we need any further proof that, when Judaism succumbs to the overall Abrahamic tendency to eschatology, it does so with particular vehemence and intensity, we need only examine certain of the folktale commentaries on Genesis in which the afterlife is explicitly invoked. In one of the "basic readings from the Kabbalah" that Scholem translates and assembles in his thin collection of Zoharic folktales, Rabbi Simeon, who appeals directly to God, manages to fend off Rabbi Isaac's impending death, but only for a while. Scholem furnishes this story with the title "The Great Feast," a "parabolic expression of death." In a dream, Rabbi Isaac's father telegraphs ahead his "portion" in the "world to come." The landscape that Rabbi Isaac is about to inhabit has been fitted out with

> seventy crowned places which are his, and each place has doors which open to seventy worlds, and each world opens to seventy channels and each channel is open to seventy supernal crowns, and thence are ways leading to the Ancient and

Inscrutable One, opening on a view of that celestial delight which gives bliss and illumination to all, as it is stated, "to see the pleasantness of the Lord and to visit His temple."[26]

The kernel of this Zoharic fabulation is once again a biblical verse, Psalm 27:4, a relatively bland celebration of the Lord's temple and of visiting him there. The extract from the psalm is merely a pre-text to a celestial panorama of immense splendor, multiplying itself by a constant factor of seventy. In the approach to the ineffable that Judaic poetics makes through multiplication and illumination (the latter term embodying Benjamin's highest hope for commentary), it opens a channel to the iconography of the Indian religions. The channels of the Zohar, like the *passages* that Kafka conspicuously installs in the various court settings of *The Trial* and in the burrow creature's labyrinthine subterranean refuge, function both as features in an expansive architecture and as rhizomatic nodes of textual convergence and displacement.[27]

We need to remember that this splendiferous abode, whose channels and crowns interconnect the Sefiroth or formal spheres of Kabbalistic cosmology,[28] belongs to an afterlife, a setting whose being and opening is conditional upon prior annihilation, the demise not only of particulars, but of all. The sweep of the comet's tail, the limitless domain of the channels, and, as we will see, the splendiferous garment of the days gain their sense only in the face of this death, which may be negotiable to a point, but whose priority and eventuality are final. The only recompense that Judaism offers for the trials and sufferings of this world is a collective splendor, a state of exegetical as well as cosmological luminosity, and it is conditional upon undergoing not a particular, time-specific death, but an ongoing death, a death inhabiting an ecology and a condition. The Zohar figures both our entry into the domain of life and our departure from it as a display of days, days represented not as invisible units of time but as graphic markers, as signs or posters.

> Rabbi Judah said: Men's ears are shut to the admonitions of the Torah . . . in not realizing that in the day on which a human being appears in the world there appear all the days assigned to him, and these swarm about the world and then each in turn descends to the man to warn him. And if the man, being so warned, yet transgresses against his Master, then that day in which he transgressed ascends in shame and stands isolated outside, bearing witness, and remains thus until the man repents.[29]

The days swarm like falling leaves caught by the wind.[30] They are frail and ephemeral, yet they expand the figural two-dimensionality of paper and other surfaces of inscription into a third dimension. At the outset of life, according to Rabbi Judah, they foreshadow the sequence of life and forewarn of the inscriptive consequences of our deeds. Our actions will be collected in a transcript of days, and these, in turn, will determine whether we will be inscribed in the Book of Life or the Book of Death. The swarm of days is thus the pages of a yet-unbound book, the book of our moral profile. On its basis, we may be well booked by the highest authorities.

But the Zohar also figures our private book of days as a garment, a covering with intense symbolic and sociological significance. The poor quality of an ethical life translates into an inferior mystical garment:

> Woe to the man that has lessened his days before the Almighty, nor left himself days wherewith to crown himself in the other world and draw near to the holy King. For being worthy, he ascends by virtue of those days, and those days in which he did righteously and sinned not become for his soul a garment of splendor. Woe unto him that has lessened his days above, for the days damaged by his sins are lacking when it comes time to be garbed in his days, and his garment is therefore imperfect; worse is it if there are many such, and then he has nothing at all for garb in the other world.[31]

More significant than the moralistic dress code enforced by the seaming together of the days that unfold in splendor at the beginning and end of life are the poetic and figurative leaps making the scenario possible. The days first coalesce out of an otherwise abstract and nonrepresentational dimensionality of time into markers and signboards of human life and spirituality. The metaphor of paper or woven days is then literalized to allow their configuration as clothes or garments, garments with a message more spiritual than experiential. The textual days swirl and dance about in the cosmic motion that the Zohar has established as the tenor of mystical apprehension and revelation. The swirling of the days and the radiance of the garments they form join in a *danse macabre*, for the hypervitality of movement and illumination is possible only in the extended afterlife of Judaism, within the framework of the death that Judaism has, metaphysically and aesthetically, admitted into itself.

In keeping with its economy of closed allegorical reading, the Zohar gives a moral point to the possible outcomes that the garment of days can signal. "The righteous are the happy ones, for their days are in store with the holy King and make a splendid attire for clothing themselves in, in the other world. This is the secret meaning of the verse, 'and they knew that they were naked' [Gen. 3:17], which is to say, glorious vestments composed of those days had been ruined and no day was left to be clothed in."[32]

But poetically the Zohar and the Judaism that it presumes to revise have established a figuration and a topography that they cannot contain. Indeed, no specific religious culture could. Set in an afterlife of extended death, the radiance of comets' tails, the palace of proliferating portals and channels, and the garments of days demarcate a distinctive cultural landscape and poetic idiom, but one that was readily transferable to other cultures, theological spheres, and literary and discursive genres. The diaspora of these figures and the imaginary and metaphysical space they inhabit may illuminate historical outcomes as well as cultural phenomena far afield of Talmudic and Kabbalistic formulation. The figures and their tortuous trajectory are obscured by the general inaccessibility of these sources. Yet the comets' tails of the Zohar sparkle over a widely diverse but intrinsically interconnected trail of cultural artifacts.

The afterlife of interpretation, like the abyss of figuration and performance, is rife with irony.[33] Having entered the terrain of Zoharic interpretation, we now need to broach the possibility, however incredulously, that we are all already dead. All of us, not only our two senior and most eminent rabbis, Rabbi Yose and Rabbi Yaakov, aka Rabbi Eli or Eliyahu,[34] have passed on to that ironically configured domain where, as archivists and protectors of the Law, not the moral law but its script, we synthesize interpretations that are hopelessly after the fact and notoriously beside the point, but that may nonetheless claim a certain effect upon the cultural options of the living, those who continue in a different register, who effectively operate in the domain of action and tangible consequences. All already dead. Rabbi Eli's extrapolation, over the past twenty years, of the spectral dimension pervading and intertwining the Abrahamic religions has been decisive in rendering explicit the distanciation, removal, belatedness, and inchoateness in which our running transcript of cultural commentary, rendered by a rhizomatic community of readers, is sheathed. The trajectory of the shooting stars in *The Book of Splendor* is the dawn of the flight of the Angel of History,[35] who inscribes his markings on the mystical notepad of the sky. Benjamin's fascination with stars and their aurioles, constellations, and messianic angels, angels whose transformative vision of the world consists in criticism, is both the endpoint of the modern Judaic reconfiguration of death and redemption in the Zohar and the taking-off point for issues still captivating us today. The comet's tail invoked by Jewish mysticism sweeps over German literature—Goethe's "Egmont" and *Elective Affinities* and Büchner's "Lenz" are only a few of the pivotal sites of textual production that it grazes—effecting the multifaceted Judeo-German cultural graft and touching down, if only briefly, as a posture of radical exegetical credulity in the work of Benjamin and as a key feature in the abyssal poetic landscape carved out by Celan.[36]

The pivotal irony here is that German Romantic literature could transpire in an abyss ultimately configured by Kabbalistic messianism even where it appeals to the trappings of evangelical theology and, on occasion, anti-Semitic folklore (as is evident, for instance, in Büchner's *Woyzeck*). The "Judaic" feature of this literary space is not explicit. It is the irony inhering in the afterlife that persists after the claims of law and sovereignty, and of the actions taken in their name, have been exhausted. It is in this spirit that Jakob Michael Reinhold Lenz, Goethe's "poetic twin,"[37] can go "through the mountains" on January 20, 1778, in search of Johann Friedrich Oberlin (1740–1826), the well-known spiritualist and healer.

Büchner—in recounting Lenz's ascent to the highlands, where the simplicity of rural life continues unabated, and his quest, amid states of incipient madness, for psychospiritual healing—"fills in" the low road or dark side of mainstream Romanticism, with its polymorphous negotiations of the transcendental so magisterially announced by Goethe. In Lenz's wanderings through the mountains, Frankenstein finally meets his younger brother. The power of Büchner's fragmentary tale (really an extended prose poem) derives from many sources, among them its explicit appropriation of the visual effects of the sublime as it irradiates Romantic imagery, particularly in the paintings of Caspar David Friedrich. One could argue, indeed, in parsing the following description, that one of Büchner's primary motives is to furnish Friedrich's landscapes (or Turner's seascapes, or Courbet's caves) with a textual caption in the medium of Romantic prose:

> Huge masses of light gushing at times from the valley like a golden river, then clouds again, hanging on the highest peak, then climbing down the forest slowly into the valley or sinking and rising in the sunbeams like a flying silvery web; not

a sound, no movement, no birds, nothing but the wailing of the wind, sometimes near, sometimes far. Dots also appeared, skeletons of huts, boards covered in straw, a somber black in color. People, silent and grave, as though not daring to disturb the peace of their valley, greeted them quietly as they rode past.[38]

This is a visual landscape configured by the vastness of its zones and the tensions between them. Its sublimity transpires unabated by "human touches" designed to furnish it with scale, the minuscule human figures in Friedrich's *Morning in the Riesengebirge*, or in this verbal canvas, the trail of snowflakes following on from a bird, or in the wake of Kabbalistic comets: "No movement in the air except for a soft breeze, the rustle of a bird lightly dusting snowflakes from its tail."[39]

Within this setting, Lenz and Oberlin make an ironic, if not comical pair, both dwarfed by the prospect of reining in Lenz's recurrent madness. Their partnership, even if its terms are Christological and the redemption it attempts to effect manifestly Christian in its metaphysics, makes sense only in a context of prior ambulatory rabbinic dialogues hopelessly after the fact, the fact of exile, the fact of madness, the fact of endless wandering. This Judeo-German wedding of resources shimmers though the explicitly Christian settings of "Lenz" like snow crystals glinting in the highland landscape. Oberlin's work is indeed framed by this landscape. Its description continues:

The huts were full of life, people crowded around Oberlin, he instructed, gave advice, consoled; everywhere trusting glances, prayer. People told of dreams, premonitions. Then quickly to practical affairs. . . . Oberlin was tireless. Lenz his constant companion, at times conversing, attending to business, absorbed in nature. It all had a beneficial and soothing effect on him, he often had to look in Oberlin's eyes, and the immense peace that comes upon us in nature at rest, in the deep forest, in moonlit, melting summer nights seemed even nearer to him in these calm eyes, this nobler, serious face. He was shy, but he made remarks, he spoke. Oberlin enjoyed his conversation and Lenz's charming child's face delighted him. But he could bear it only as long as the light remained in the valley; toward evening a strange fear came over him, he felt like chasing the sun . . . he seemed to be going blind; now it grew, the demon of insanity sat at his feet.[40]

In Büchner's cinematography, the engagement between the two men transpires in the flashes of their countenances, rather than in the exegetical conundrums they ponder. But an ineffable and fatal intimacy prevails between them. It, too, is grounded in their having, at least for the moment, entered a mystical engagement with one another, signaled by a loss of boundaries between them. Enigmatically, the text does not specify who was "toward evening" overcome by a "strange fear." It is Lenz whose emotional state is turbulent, but it is Oberlin who may experience limits to the delight exerted by Lenz's "charming child's face." The highlands are a place where, very much in a spirit of Christian compassion, Oberlin assumes the burden of Lenz's madness, yet they are also a Kabbalistic afterlife in which madness and meticulous human reform or *tikkun* are one, in which the shimmering dance of nature is also an allegory of understanding and cultural literacy.

The importance of this text as an interface between Jewish and Christian mystical poetics is not lost on Celan. It is precisely as a Lenz

> that the Jew, the Jew and the son of a Jew, and with him went his name, the inexpressible, sets out on his wanderings through the mountains. He went then, one heard about it, he went one evening, a number had already descended, he went under cloud cover and shadow that were his own and foreign—since the Jew, you know it, whatever he has already, whatever belongs to him, that wasn't borrowed, lent out, and never returned—so he went out and came there, came to the road, of the beautiful, the incomparable, like Lenz, through the mountains, who would have been allowed to reside below, where he belongs, in the lowlands, he, the Jew, came and came.[41]

His name may be this Jew's only possession, everything else having been "borrowed, lent out, and never returned." Celan alludes to a moment when the landscape has been largely emptied of Jews. The mountains remain, but not the Jews of the lowlands. This Jew, the Jew of the prose poem, resides in a spectral afterlife. It is only in this sense that his advent, his arrival, could be multiple and ongoing. He "came and came." Whether belatedly and indirectly or not, this Jew comes bearing his only property, his name, which walks with him and beside him. This figure consists, precisely, in a word, an element of language, the nominative, mystically transformed into a figure, a character, one free to dance and play, like days woven into garments, to dance within a world suffused with mystical meaning, a world defined by its role in a consummate exegesis by God. This Jew doesn't encounter many interlocutors. One is the figure of Büchner's Lenz. And, of course, the remnants of a family, his cousin and his *Geschwisterkind*. With them he will join a chatter haunting the sublime landscape filled with Jews, as absences and memories as well as voices and figurations.

If Celan was free, in his own postdisaster poetics, to resume both a practice and setting for figuration established in the Zohar, it was Benjamin who, in his wanderings on the frontier between Judaic and German letters, elaborated the terms and theory of this grafting, made it historically explicit. Benjamin was long a careful reader of the stars. He had pursued their spectral sway over Paris, in Baudelaire's expletives and in Grandville's cosmic cartoons, since the outset of *The Arcades Project*.[42] He was exquisitely sensitive to the shooting stars' role within the narrative of the Goethean novel in what is arguably his first full-fledged work of literary criticism, his essay on Goethe's *The Elective Affinities*, in which he effects a full crossover between his philosophical readings and his critical ambitions. As late as "On Some Motives in Baudelaire," he still was charting the trajectory as the shooting stars thread the seam between loss and redemption, ritual and industrial time, and poetic inspiration and shock.

Benjamin volunteered himself as the astronomer of the mystical Kabbalistic heavens in the turbulent domain of advanced modernity. He would not allow his readers to overlook Goethe's caption for the last moment in *The Elective Affinities*, when romantic love might win out over social convention, when desire might realize itself instead of capitulating to diversions and dissimulations: "Hope shot across the sky above their heads like a falling star."[43] This burst of hope, set in one of German literature's most resonant and suggestive novels, is all the more poignant for being destined to extinction amid the truisms of *Sittlichkeit* and the economics of bourgeois domesticity. Its short-lived flash reminds us that the broad swath of German letters in Goethe's wake was susceptible to messianic time. The final one of the two afterthoughts that Benjamin appended to his "On the Concept of History" characterizes this openness: "For every second was the strait gate through which the Messiah might enter." Not only does this brief note characterize the hope that briefly flares for the love-crossed modern prisoners of desire in *The Elective Affinities*; it reminds us of Benjamin's explicit desire, one also not realized, to pursue messianic mysticism into the nexus of modern urbanity and shock.

This aspiration, which might seem out of character with his secular sophistication, his commitment, first and foremost, to letters, and his receptivity to social as well as conceptual revolutions of the mind, is spelled out in that text. Given the commitment to fragmentary utterance, to dialectical imagery, and to epigrammatic closure in "On the Concept of History," it is not by chance that here Benjamin signals his meditations on the afterlife of Judaism: "We know that the Jews were prohibited from inquiring into the future: the Torah and the prayers instructed them in remembrance. This disenchanted the future, which holds sway over all those who turn to soothsayers for enlightenment. This does not imply, however, that for the Jews the future became homogeneous, empty time."[44]

The Jewish future here becomes an afterlife of hope, not of projection. Benjamin enlists the words of Joseph Joubert to characterize the messianic hope that still suffuses the modern world. "Time is found even in eternity; but it is not earthly, worldly time. . . . It does not destroy; it merely completes."[45] This time is still accessible in a modernity that has largely degraded the "crowning of experience" consummated by the fulfillment of the wish.[46] This is a modernity in which the folkloric wish embodied in the falling star has been supplanted by "The ivory ball that rolls into the *next* compartment, the *next* card that lies on top," in gambling.[47] In this degraded but captivating time, the wish is served by the one-armed bandit, operated by a spasmodic gesture carried over from the assembly line. "On Some Motifs in Baudelaire" is, after all, a crystallization of the materials gathered in *The Arcades Project* and a starchart to their many convergences, departures, and collisions. The world configured by both works, the former at an extreme of poetic condensation in critical discourse and the latter at an extreme of archival dispersion, is nothing but the complex of late-modern commercial, urban, communicative, and technological forces that first coincided in Paris under the Second Empire. Benjamin makes Joubert the mouthpiece for a radical messianic temporality that persists in this configuration. Yet Benjamin is explicitly, ironically, and morbidly aware of its Kabbalistic provenance.

Many were the dreams that failed to be realized in the twentieth century, a period of unprecedented violence, genocide, and disregard for life. Yet the blueprints for these dreams survive. In the fictive topography configured by a set of obscure medieval rabbis and in certain of the tropes that they tripped into motion, the likes of Benjamin and Scholem accessed a *genizah*, a repository for disrupted dreams, whose crypt then mirrored, reenacted, and extended their life.

SEVEN

Modernist Night: Distortion, Regression, and Oblivion in the Fiction of Bruno Schulz

> At a certain moment, we have entered an illegal time, a night beyond control, liable to all kinds of excesses and crazes.¹

To penetrate the world of Bruno Schulz's fiction is to err into the immensity of the childhood summer night that it invokes, with a poetically marvelous, figurally inventive, and invariably apt diction, a past teeming with chatter, animals, and mutations. This is a night conducive to the flights and pyrotechnics of the childhood imaginary, but also to sublime violence and destruction. Bruno Schulz conjures up this night in part to illustrate the temporal anomalies of narrative art, in part to assemble a catalogue or stamp album of the developments in twentieth-century culture he witnesses from the perspective of Polish "minor literature,"² in part to render an early postmodern commentary upon the modernist experiments in which he is engaged. Indeed, Schulz's discourse as a whole furnishes early-twentieth-century Western culture the retrospect or afterimage that Father Jacob achieves through his incarceration in *Sanatorium under the Sign of the Hourglass*: "'The whole secret of the operation' he [Dr. Gotard] added, ready to demonstrate its mechanism on his fingers, "'is that we have put back the clock. Here we are always late by a certain interval of time of which we cannot define the length. The whole thing is a matter of simple relativity. Here your father's death, the death that has already struck him in your country, has not occurred yet.'"³

In context, this statement furnishes a caption for the bizarre fictive and temporal setting in which the narrator finds himself, but it is also a trenchant formulation of Schulz's critical stance toward the modernist literature his own discourse both devours and dislocates. Indeed, the narrator, who plays Joseph to his father's Jacob, is the central citizen throughout the main part of the novel, in what may be described as a distinctly modernist landscape or universe of nostalgia, loving hindsight, or retrospection under an aura of gratitude and admiration. Until the novel's coda or fictive afterlife in the sanatorium, the narrator has maintained an engaged dialogue with the past, even if the past also plays host to corpses refusing to die, fathers reincarnated as crabs, and other monstrosities. As a faithful and loving son of the past, Joseph has been automatically issued a literary passport gaining him entry into such other modern homelands as "Marcel's" Combray in *À la recherche du temps perdu*, the rural setting in which Kafka's "Children on a Country Road" frolic, and even the Dublin in which the protagonist arrives late to the "Araby" carnival, in which he has invested yearning and hope. However horrific the sanatorium into which Schulz's Joseph has stumbled may be, with its compulsive repetition of the father's most memorable (and hence traumatic) idiosyncrasies (for example, his dyspepsia and his greed) and its uncanny deferral of the inevitable, the sanatorium scenario reposes architecturally upon a highly characteristic European modernist foundation of hope, fascination, and horror invested in the past.

As Dr. Gotard explains to Son Joseph, the deferral and persistent but imperfect repetition of time in the sanatorium opens his fictive existence and the narrative medium of the novel to a distinctive relativity. Schulz's invocation of the traumatic Einsteinian principle here is anything but casual. Like the Kafka of "A Common Confusion,"⁴ Schulz has discovered that the narrative medium of fiction, at least as nuanced by characteristic modernist apprehensions, is a setting for radical and fundamental dislocations along the continua of space and time. The "experiences" and "developments" of *Sanatorium* transpire within a cloud chamber of stunning transformations and mutations. Einstein serves as merely one instance of the radical modernist patrimony that Schulz appropriates, in ironic contrast to the nostalgic rhetoric in which Joseph's appeals to his forthcoming and sensuous past are cast. Freud, Kafka, Proust, Bergson, Joyce, Benjamin: all are fellow inmates in the sanatorium of delayed modernist death and afterlife: these authors all plumb the hidden depths of memory and ponder, with rigor, the ultimately futile efforts to structure experience by means of repetition. Briefly put, with Schulz a full-fledged partner in their inquiry, they all submit to time's unending mystery. So pervasively does Schulz appropriate their imaginations that these key modernists end up as quasi-characters populating the childhood night of twentieth-century invention.

My purpose in the present chapter is to offer a tribute to Schulz's strikingly singular imagination (or imaginary), as evidenced in *Sanatorium under the Sign of the Hourglass*, to elaborate the conditions of this singularity, and to place his work on the map of twentieth-century aesthetic and theoretical experimentation. To map Schulz is to collaborate with, to play into the hands of his own fascination with compendia, whether the book—a dog-eared, prototypical mail-order catalogue—or the stamp album the narrator, Joseph, as a young man appropriates from his friend Rudolph. The narrative of *Sanatorium* mythologizes a certain plenitude of the childhood imaginary in establishing Joseph's overall neighborhoods, whether these be the domains of his family, his psychosexual relationships, or his creativity. Childhood, in this overall map, is a setting for the overvaluation of facts and details emanating from around the globe, for sexual drives so overwhelming they cannot be narrowly placed or identified; for family melodramas cataclysmic in their intensity. Childhood, the retroactively constructed origin of art and artistic activity, is a "blooming, buzzing" garden or system,[5] fecund with outgrowths and associations, in an ongoing state of expansion or intensification. The summer night that Schulz so lovingly and memorably invokes throughout *Sanatorium* is the primordial setting or moment for the expansion, ramification, and intensification that the text identifies as preconditions for art and linguistic facility. Childhood is the garden of the associations that make for art, but the fecundity and expansiveness of this moment do not make for innocence. Indeed, as *Sanatorium* unfolds, aesthetic sensibility becomes epitomized and haunted by monstrosities and mutations interposing themselves within the innocence imputed to childhood's incubator or garden. For Schulz more than for Kafka, Joyce, or

Proust, childhood's exalted nights metamorphose into breeders of the uncanniness nonetheless essential to mature aesthetic creativity (at least in the Western tradition as institutionalized by Kant and the Schlegels and initiated by the ideology and events of eighteenth-century emancipation). In Schulz's fiction, the innocence and ultimately playful horror that are both necessary in an aesthetics calibrated to the vicissitudes of the modern drive achieve a distinctive and unique constellation.

Sanatorium under the Sign of the Hourglass is a setting, a narrative, and a collection of brief vignettes. In its temporal framework, an extended present of childhood reminiscence is juxtaposed with the cycle of a single fictive year, whose seasons extend beyond a spring of discovery and a summer of flowering and ripeness into the allegorical fall and winter of Father Jacob's demise and ironic afterlife. Schulz's temporal framework, in other words, allows both for the extended elaboration of an aesthetic "sensibility" and object-world (as in the Joycean "interior monologue" and Kafka's late animal ruminations) and for episodic introjections and closures.[6] The narrative episodes that structure *Sanatorium* exist on vastly divergent scales. Father Jacob's mastery of his world—as evidenced by the force of his personality in family matters and his business acumen—and the subsequent evidence of his childishness, imagined grandiosity, temper, and senility constitute the major overarching conditions in the novel, which may be said, in a sense, to be unified by his inconsistent and fitful personality. Yet the novel is also free to "play host," once Schulz establishes its characterology, to the customs of its social universe (akin to Proustian "habit"), and its physical and cultural features, to much shorter-lived interventions or appearances by minor characters distinguished by their own irreducible peculiarity. It is within the compass of this supplementary, ephemeral timeframe that we meet, early on, Shloma, during his annual spring recess from jail, as he relieves the sensuously alive housekeeper Adela of her shoes, dress, and beads,[7] and that the novel's denouement (following Joseph's visit to his father at the sanatorium) is punctuated by the appearances of such characters as Dodo, Eddie, and the "old age pensioner." So convincing and captivating is the novel's virtually simulated world that in the end it is open for "bit parts" for all sorts—a hypothetically unlimited set—of minor characters, characterological "odds and ends."

Sanatorium is thus rife with the "cloudy spots" that Walter Benjamin located in Kafka's *The Trial* and identified as an oft-repeated feature of twentieth-century fictive narrative.[8] Treated categorically, these would be defined as special kinds of discontinuities rupturing narrative continuity and making openings for potentially endless sets of new episodes or plot "revisions."

The pivotal "cloudy spot" to which Benjamin refers in Kafka is situated between Joseph K.'s fatal dismissal of his lawyer and the Priest's recitation and elucidation of the Parable of the Doorkeeper, which may also be regarded as K.'s death sentence.[9] During this break, any number of additional meetings with Court officials and legal and quasi-legal machinations could hypothetically take place. (Virtually all the characters in this novel, including the Priest, eventually turn out to be Court officials of one sort or another.) In Schulz's *Sanatorium* there are three discontinuous junctures at which any number of potentially jarring and disorienting novelistic emendations (Bernhard would say corrections[10]) could take place: before and after Joseph's utterly surreal and temporally complex sojourn at the Sanatorium, and any time during the parade of bit characters whose emergence immediately precedes Father Jacob's ultimate demise and transfiguration as a (wholly non-Kosher) crustacean.

Schulz thus institutes the Kafkan cloudy spot as a narrative principle fundamental to a fictive discourse itself hovering between the imaginary wholeness and stability of remembered life and the monstrosities and weirdness of twentieth-century experience, lived and written. Schulz's discourse and illustrations transpire in this temporal interregnum, when time has happened and is about to "take place," when duration, if not eternity, has shown its hand, and yet a host of contingencies are free to enter the picture, deranging all plans and good intentions.

★

In keeping with *Sanatorium*'s temporality of delay and repetition, it is fitting that there are two unforgettable nights in the novel, more precisely, a spring dusk and a "night in July." I can do no better here than to let these moments of linguistic fecundity and uncanniness "speak" for themselves.

> A band is now playing every evening in the city park, and people on their spring outings fill the avenues. They walk up and down, pass one another, and

Modernist Night   157

meet again in symmetrical, continuously repeated patterns. The young men are wearing new spring hats and nonchalantly carrying gloves in their hands.[11]

Then the whole park becomes an enormous, silent orchestra, solemn and composed, waiting under the raised baton of the conductor for its music to ripen and rise; and over that potential, earnest symphony a quick theatrical dusk spreads suddenly as if brought down by the sounds swelling in the instruments. . . .

A hardly perceptible breeze sails through the treetops, from which dry petals of cherry blossom fall in a shower. A tart scent drifts high under the dusky sky and floats like a premonition of death and the first stars shed their tears like lilac blossoms picked from pale, purple bushes. . . .

Wandering blindly in the dark plush of the gardens, the young people meet at last in an empty clearing, under the last purple glow of the setting sun . . . on a rotting balustrade, somewhere at the back gate of the world, they find themselves again in pre-existence, a life long past, in attitudes of a distant age; they sob and plead, rise to promises never to be fulfilled, and, climbing up the steps of exaltation, reach summits and climaxes beyond which there is only death and numbness of nameless delight.[12]

There is a distinctive narrative sequence to Schulz's evening in spring, which proceeds from the exaggerated conventionality of a Victorian bandstand to the discovery of oblivion and primordiality behind the obvious. The designation of music as the vehicle of conventionality is far from accidental; the Spring evening serves as a Proustian overture to the decisive turn in Schulz's fictive event-world and poetry, the explosion of violence, semiological as well as lustful, from within the constraint of the Law. The evening's promenaders are as trite and oblivious as the people "in their Sunday best" viewed from a conspicuous distance at the outset of Kafka's "Description of a Struggle."[13] But beyond the park's civilized precincts, the evening is a clearing or theater of linguistic ferment, the devolution of time and things into a poetic compost, at the heart of the Heideggerian redefinition of Being. It is nothing less than his Being as a visual artist and poet that the narrator of *Sanatorium* first encounters in the spring evening prelude: in hardly perceptible breezes, tart scents like the first premonitions of death, and a shower of cherry blossoms.

The earth, which increasingly preoccupies the narrator on the occasion of *Sanatorium*'s spring evening, a soil with key affinities to the ahistorical, ontological earth in Heidegger's "The Origin of the Work of Art,"[14] almost immediately acquires a cultural as well as a geological status:

It is only now that we realize what the soil is on which spring thrives and why spring is so unspeakably sad and heavy with knowledge. Oh, we would have not believed it had we not seen it with our own eyes! Here are labyrinths of depth, warehouses and silos of things, graves that are still warm, the litter, and the rot. Age-old tales. Seven layers (like in ancient Troy), corridors, chambers, treasure chests. Numerous golden masks—one next to another—flattened smiles, faces eaten out, mummies, empty cocoons.... Here are columbaria, the drawers for the dead, in which they lie dessicated, blackened like roots, awaiting their moment. Here are great apothecary storerooms where they are displayed in lachrymatories, crucibles, and jars. They have been standing on the shelves for years in a long, solemn row.[15]

The depths that emerge on the putatively naïve evening of spring are at least as linguistic—textually configured—as they are psychological or conventionally sublime. The compost of spring—spring as the activation of the imaginary as well as the season of rebirth—is a detritus of involuted narratives and scientific specimens of extinct life forms. Schulz is guilty of a widespread modernist fascination with the exhausted remains of prior cultural formations, evident in Kafka, Joyce, Stein, Pound, Stevens, and others as well. Like them, Schulz luxuriates in the possibilities for recycling and recombining these inherently worthless and supplemental cultural materials. An overpowering death—as the negation of organic metaphysics—becomes the life animating the depths disclosed by a night in spring. The emergence of depths (or pictorially, the crystallization of perspective) is precisely what the young artist discovers at the moment of his imaginary's spring. The netherworld whose apprehension is so closely tied to the emergence of an aesthetic sensibility thus bears striking affinities to the depth/surface phenomena proliferating throughout the early passages of Proust's *Recherche*, which presumably correspond to young "Marcel's" first apprehensions of aesthetic violence and anomaly, as well as textual involution. I think here of the abysses that the magic lantern opens up on the walls and surfaces of "Marcel's" bedroom and of the Ali Baba's cave over which the consistently misapprehended Swann secretly presides.[16]

Inculcation into the labyrinths of language and into the violence and transgression of art is, then, tantamount to plumbing increasing depths. On this fateful Spring evening, the narrator is transformed from the explorer of these depths into their agent. The narrator effects a transference of *his* aesthetic awakening to the readers of the *Sanatorium*.

But we have not finished yet; we can go deeper. There is nothing to fear. Give me your hand, take another step: we are at the roots now, and at once everything becomes dark, spicy, and tangled like in the depth of a forest. There is a smell of turf and tree rot; roots wander about, entwined, full with juices that rise as if sucked up by pumps. We are on the nether side, at the lining of things, in gloom stitched with phosphorescence. There is a lot of movement and traffic, pulp, and rot, tribes and generations, a brood of bibles and iliads multiplied a thousand times! Wanderings and tumult, the tangle and hubbub of history! That road leads no farther. Here we are at the very bottom, in the dark foundations, among the Mothers. Here are the bottomless infernos, the hopeless Ossianic spaces, all those lamentable Niebelungs. Here are the great breeding grounds of history, factories of plots, hazy smoking rooms of fables and tales. Now at last one can understand the great and sad machinery of spring. Ah, how it thrives on stories, on events, on chronicles, on destinies! Everything we have ever read, all the stories we have heard and those we have never heard before but have been dreaming since childhood—here and nowhere else is their home and their motherland. Where would writers find their ideas, how would they muster the courage for invention, had they not been aware of these reserves, this frozen capital, these funds salted away in the underworld? What a buzz of whispers, what persistent purr of the earth.... And spring, helpless and naive, takes them into its slumber, sleeps with them, wakes half-conscious at dawn, and remembers nothing. This is why it is heavy with the sum of all that is forgotten and sorrowful, for it alone must live vicariously on these rejected lives, and must be beautiful to embody all that has been lost....

There are so many unborn tales. Oh, those sad, lamenting choruses among the roots, those stories outbidding one another, those inexhaustible monologues among suddenly exploding improvisations! Have we the patience to listen to them? Before the oldest known legend there were others no one has ever heard; there were nameless forerunners; novels without a title; enormous, pale, and monotonous epics; shapeless bardic tales; formless plots; giants without a face; dark texts written for the drama of evening clouds. And beyond these lays, sagas, unwritten books, books—eternal pretenders, and lost books *in partibus infidelium*.[17]

Through the narrator, the reader of *Sanatorium* metamorphoses into the fully enfranchized citizen of a distinctly modernist oblivion. This oblivion is both the repository of language and the site of artistic composition, visual as well as textual. Yet there is no mistaking this Schulzian oblivion for a void. It is astir with the buzzing of language in its presymbolic, incantatory, introjective, and inarticulate forms. One of Schulz's truly singular fictive signatures is the poetic specificity with which he endows the inarticulate. Schulz's fictive landscape is saturated with a buzz, a murmur, and a groan irreducibly linguistic and semiotic in nature but belonging to the same inchoate domain of half-reference, partial meaning, that one finds throughout the late Joyce.[18] Where Joyce, throughout *Finnegans Wake* and in the "Penelope" episode of *Ulysses*, compulsively introjects the partially referential and presymbolic at the levels of semantics and syntax, Schulz makes the inchoate the predominant feature in *Sanatorium's* spatial landscape, its *locations*. The inarticulate burgeons out of the oblivion Schulz takes such pains to articulate.

In the passage above, language abdicates its significatory and representational imperatives in a variety of ways: it is in a preliminary state of *becoming*; it is formless and indistinct; exhausted and fallen out of context; unmoored from the historical contextualization that would give it meaning. The spring evening that is the aesthetic awakening of Schulz's Joseph is a quasi-systematic disclosure of this language that doesn't quite mean: in its dimensions, sounds, appearances, and locales.

"At the very bottom" of history,[19] the text arrives at the traditional netherworld of Western metaphysics. In Schulz's rendition, as for Wagner and before him Goethe, this netherworld is the repository of an ur-sound (*Urgeräusch*), an inarticulate murmur or resonance indicative of linguistic articulation yet prior to meaning.[20] The wanderers of spring, and with them the readers of Schulz's fiction, confront in these depths "bottomless infernos," "hopeless Ossianic spaces," "lamentable Niebelungs," "factories of plots," and "smoking rooms of fables and tales."[21] Schulz creates in this passage a subliminal location for the fabrication of linguistic artifacts and draws upon Wagnerian goldmines and Ossianic expanses to reinforce the subterranean and dubious foundations of literary composition and imaginary process. Such is "the motherland" of "everything we have read, all the stories we have heard and those we have never heard before but have been dreaming since childhood."[22] "There are so many unborn tales. Oh, those sad, lamenting choruses among the roots."[23] It is amid the germination of spring that the artist in flower encounters the fragmentary literature-before-literature serving as an infrastructural précis to literature and representation in general.

The Spring night is the uniquely generative moment at which oblivion is transmogrified into the compost and humus of art. Schulz grafts the narrative of *Sanatorium* onto an oblivion whose characterization also forms, according to Benjamin, the backdrop for much of Kafka's fiction. For Benjamin, the latter's writing is dominated by "prehistoric forces."[24] The shame whose apotheosis constitutes the end of *The Trial* is a primordial motive emanating from the hearth of the family, which becomes a shifter linking the present to prehistoric times:

> Shame is an intimate human reaction, but at the same time it has social claims. Shame is not only shame in the presence of others, but can also be shame one feels *for* others. Kafka's shame, then, is no more personal than the life and thought which govern it and which he has described thus: ". . . . He feels as though he were living and thinking under the constraint of a family. . . . Because of this unknown family . . . he cannot be released ['*Er*']." We do not know the makeup of this unknown family, which is composed of human beings and animals. But this much is clear: it is this family which forces Kafka to move cosmic ages in his writings. Doing this family's bidding, he moves the mass of historical happenings as Sisyphus moved the stone. . . . His novels are set in a swamp world. In his work, the creature appears at the stage which Bachofen has termed the hetaeric stage. The fact that this stage is now forgotten does not mean that it does not extend into the present. On the contrary: it is present by virtue of this very oblivion. An experience deeper than that of an average person can make contact with it. "I have experience [*Erfahrung*]," we read in one of Kafka's earliest notes, "and I am not joking when I say that it is a seasickness on dry land."[25]

Kafka may experience oblivion as an evolutionary swampland, while Schulz does so as a fecund spring or summer night, but the two modernists share a powerful association between the repository of exhausted cultural remains and oblivion. It is in the voids of time, culture, and memory that fresh writing inscribes itself with the brashness of sin and the intensity of shame. Kafka and Schulz share a studio for the composition of twentieth-century poetics and *écriture*: "What has been forgotten, and with this insight we stand before another threshold to Kafka's work—is never something purely individual. Everything forgotten mingles with what has been forgotten of the prehistoric world, forms countless uncertain and changing compounds, yielding a constant flow of new, strange products. Oblivion is the container from which the inexhaustible intermediate world in Kafka's stories presses toward the light."[26] What distinguishes the projects of both Kafka and

Schulz is the voids out of which linguistic composition emerges and by which it is permeated and engulfed. Kafka's Odradek and the mail-order catalogue and stamp album in *Sanatorium* are all constructions of a culture exhausted of meaning that continues to consume and generate signs in a dim-witted, mechanical way. For Schulz as well as for Kafka, the family is a setting in which the uncanny emptiness of poetic invention opens up. The uncanny familial foyer plays home to pets as well as human relatives. Benjamin is wonderfully acute to the totemic sensibility in Kafka that juxtaposes familial relatives lost in the oblivion of the past with present-day characters, that establishes the continuum joining human and animal Otherness. Schulz may not be as prehistorically oriented as Benjamin would have Kafka. But Father Jacob does devolve into a crustacean at the end of *Sanatorium*, the young artist's village issues forth family relatives, such as Shloma, of dubious lineage and character, and boundaries between family members, servants, employees, and animals are hopelessly blurred in the household.

> To Kafka, the world of his ancestors was as unfathomable as the world of realities was important, and we may be sure that, like the totem poles of primitive peoples, the world of ancestors took him down to the animals. . . .
>
> In Kafka's work, the most singular bastard which the prehistoric world has begotten with guilt is Odradek ["*Die Sorge des Hausvaters*"]. . . . "At first sight it looks like a flat, star-shaped spool for thread, and it really seems to have thread wound around it; to be sure, this is probably just old, broken-off bits of thread that are knotted and tangled together." . . . Odradek "stays alternately in the attic, on the staircase, in the corridors, and in the hall." So it prefers the same places as the court of law which investigates guilt. Attics are places of discarded, forgotten objects. Perhaps having to appear before a court of justice gives rise to a feeling similar to that with which one approaches trunks in the attic which have been locked up for years. One would like to put off this chore till the end of time. . . .
>
> Odradek is the form which things assume in oblivion.[27]

Schulz may choose to situate his version of the oblivion out of which poetics and fiction press forward in nights in spring and July, but his own writing process is as invested as Kafka's in the exhausted remnants of dead culture, the past whose actualities and truths are hopelessly obscured, and a genetic pool in which mutation is at least as much the rule as "normality." Indeed, it is Schulz's distinction to extrapolate and specify the conditions of the modernist night, the oblivion on which modernist script is founded, in a fashion even more consistent and better realized than Kafka's. Only Proustian time may be a generative oblivion as fully composed as Schulz's "buzzing, blooming" nights.

> During every spring night, whatever might happen in it, that story unfolds itself above the croaking of frogs and the endless working of mills. A man walks under the milky stars strewn by the handmills of night; he walks hugging a child in the folds of his cloak; he walks across the sky, constantly on his way, a perpetual wanderer through the endless spaces. Oh, the sadness of loneliness, the pathos of orphanhood in the vastness of night. Oh, glare of distant stars! In that story time can never change anything. The story appears on the starry horizons and will do so forever, always afresh, for once derailed from the tracks of time, it has become unfathomable, never to be exhausted by repetition. There goes that man who hugs the child in his arms—we are repeating on purpose that refrain, that pitiful motto of the night, in order to express the intermittent continuity of walking, sometimes obstructed by the tangle of stars. . . . The distant worlds come within reach, glaring frighteningly, they send violent signals through eternity in an unspoken, mute language—while he walks on and soothes the little girl endlessly, monotonously, and without hope, helpless against the whispers and sweet persuasions of the night, against the only word formed on the lips of silence, when no one is listening to it.[28]

Schulz grafts the underworld of submerged networks of allusion, inchoate half-meanings, and prelogical articulation onto the vastness of the thought and realm of creativity surveyed by Kant in his *Critique of Judgment*.[29] The galaxy of stars "strewn" by a naturalistic night transformed by sanctioned poetic play into a "mill" is an example of the mathematical sublime culled from Kant's pages. Schulz, at the same time as he establishes the foundations for a scene of writing truly singular in its style and its dense, writerly foliation, frames his particular version of textual epigenesis and involution within the sanctioned Kantian framework of artwork in the service of sublimity as the secular art-religion of modernity. The sublimity of the Milky Way and the exorbitant spring night legitimizes the textual involution richly unfolding at ground level. Oddly enough, this combination of sublimity and textuality during the developmental spring of the artist's sensibility reinstates the analogical relation between the transcendental and the worldly that Foucault, in *The Order of Things*, ascribes to the Renaissance.[30] But perhaps it *is* in the order of things for Schulz's singularly sublime setting for a distinctively twentieth-century script to initiate a renaissance, the renaissance of textuality dramatized in its positive manifestations that has been theorized so definitively by Derrida.[31]

By July, summer in the year of our young artist's initiation, the air has thickened with signs and swirls of signification.

> A night in July! What can be likened to it? How can one describe it? Shall I compare it to the core of an enormous black rose, covering us with the dreams of hundreds of velvety petals? The night winds blow open its fluffy center, and in its scented depth we can see the stars looking down on us.
>
> Shall I compare it to the black firmament under our half-closed eyelids, full of scattered speckles, white poppy seeds, stars, rockets, and meteors? Or perhaps to a night train, long as the world, driving through an endless black tunnel; walking through a July night is like passing precariously from one coach to another, between sleeping passengers, along narrow drafty corridors, past stuffy compartments.[32]

The speckles, poppy seeds, and rockets speak again to the expansiveness within which, according to Kant, the transcendental parameters of sublimity can be deduced. Schulz weaves a tapestry here in which the universe, in summer nighttime, serves as a blackboard or tabula rasa for the inscription of writing. In this passage, the firmament figures as an immense, involuted flower; white poppy seeds, stars, rockets, and meteors splash across this background, forming a script that is modern in its partial comprehensibility.[33] It is the inherent quality of this night to expand, to harbor near-incomprehensible shards of obsolete cultures, to juxtapose the vegetable with the purely symbolic. Although Proust, Kafka, and Beckett also furnish glimpses of this twentieth-century horizon of writing, Schulz is surely the most comprehensive of his modernist peers in forming the surreal constellation that incorporates the Kantian sublime, natural fecundation, poetic expansion, and the radicality of writing, viewed in its deconstructive explicitness. These are the elements out of which Schulz fashions his own unique, prosaic poetry.[34] He sets the composition of this poetry during the expansive nights of a natural year proceeding toward its vernal plenitude, a plenitude overwhelmed by voids and anomalies. It is a poetry that, in the end, speaks for itself.

> A night in July! The secret fluid of dusk, the living, watchful, and mobile matter of darkness, ceaselessly shaping something out of chaos and immediately rejecting every shape. Black timber out of which caves, vaults, nooks, and niches along

the path of a sleepy wanderer are constructed. Like an instant talker, the night accompanies a lonely pilgrim, shutting him within the circle of its apparitions, indefatigable in invention and in fantasies, evoking for him starry distances, white milky ways, the labyrinths of successive Coliseums and Forums. The night air, that black Proteus playfully forming velvety densities streaked with the scent of jasmine, cascades of ozone, sudden airless wastes rising like black globes into the infinite, monstrous grapes of darkness flowing with dark juice! I elbow my way along these tight passages, I lower my head to pass under arches and low vaults, and suddenly the ceiling breaks open with a starry sigh, a wide cupola slides away for a moment, and I am led again between narrow walls and passages. In these airless bays, in these nooks of darkness, scraps of conversation left by nightly wanderers hang in the air, fragments of inscriptions stick to posters, lost bars of laughter are heard, and skeins of whispers undispersed by the breeze of night unfold. Sometimes the night closes in around me like a small room without a door. I am overcome by drowsiness and cannot make out whether my legs are still carrying me forward or whether I am already at rest in that small chamber of the night. But then I feel again a velvety hot kiss left floating in space by some scented lips, some shutters open, I take a long step across a windowsill and continue to wander under the parabolas of falling stars.[35]

Then I realized what I had to do; I began to pull from the cupboards old Bibles and my father's half-filled and disintegrating ledgers, throwing them on the floor under that column of fire that glowed and brightened the air. I wanted more and more sheaves of paper. My mother and brother rushed in with ever new handfuls of old newspapers and magazines and threw them in stacks on the floor. And I sat among the piles of paper, blinded by the glare, my eyes full of explosions, rockets, and colors, and I drew wildly, feverishly, across the paper, over the printed or figure-covered pages. My colored pencils rushed in inspiration across columns of illegible text in masterly squiggles, in breakneck zigzags that knotted themselves suddenly into anagrams of vision, into enigmas of bright revelation, and then dissolved into empty, shiny flashes of lightning, following imaginary tracks.

Oh, those luminous drawings, made as if by a foreign hand. Oh, those transparent colors and shadows. How often, now, do I dream about them, then rediscover them after so many years at the bottom of old drawers, glimmering and fresh like dawn—still damp from the first dew of the day: figures, landscapes, faces![36]

It is uncanny how often the exuberant literary art of modernism figures the artist as a child, a little person dancing around the certainties of a revolutionary but transfiguring knowledge. The cast of modernist adult-children is boring in its predictability: "Marcel" witnessing Françoise's chicken executions and Mlle Vinteuil's lesbian love at Montjouvain; the protagonists of the early tales in Joyce's *Dubliners*, who discover a "queer old josser" on a truancy day's jaunt and arrive belated and disheartened, already, to the "Araby" bazaar. In the engravings with which Schulz decorated *Sanatorium*, an already aged and tyrannical father is often paired with a child at a strikingly raw level of personal evolution with a sullenness uncannily beyond his years.

In context, the passage immediately above describes explosions of graphic art that overcome the youthful narrator, Joseph. Joseph's first, intensely memorable artworks are scored upon the pages of ledgers, on scraps of magazines and old newspapers. The ledger pages that Joseph decorates are as out of date as his father's increasingly feeble hold on reality. An art of "breakneck zigzags" and "anagrams of vision" arises out of the scraps of exhausted records and cultural documents. Joseph's youthful work, in its relation to the past, its appropriation of existing materials, its radicality, and its shock, is quite distinctly a modernist creation, to be recognized in conjunction with the aesthetic games and experiments of modernism.

Only Proust is Schulz's peer in exploiting the impact of books upon a child's aesthetic sensibility. Schulz surpasses his French counterpart as an avatar of modernism and postmodernity by exploiting the potential of such publications as stamp albums and mail-order catalogues to engage the child-readers exposed to them in paradigmatic experiences of art. Schulz's graft of Joseph's exposure to the book and the album onto *Sanatorium's* narrative becomes a Benjaminian rendition of the readings of Georges Sand "Marcel" does with his mother early on in the *Recherche* and the vivid impressions made by Catholic ritual and theology upon Joyce's youthful protagonists in *Dubliners* and *A Portrait of the Artist as a Young Man*.

The passage in which Joseph's drawing explodes out of boredom and the ordinariness of a small Polish city belongs to allegories of aesthetic epigenesis. It should be read in the context of similar accounts in Proust, Joyce, and Kafka. Schulz appeals to a childlike world of expansiveness and unrealized potential rendered by these other modernists as they stage the inaugural experiences of a specific modality of art. Yet except for Kafka, whose horde of intrusive girls led by a hunchback torments Joseph K. as he gains Titorelli's aesthetic knowledge of the Court at the end of *The Trial*,[37] Schulz has no equal in exploring a certain corruption, as opposed to demonic possession, that can be situated amid the openness of life's early years. In *Sanatorium*, there is no delineation between childhood as a playground of aesthetic possibility and as a prison of resignation to what is at best moral as well as creative corruption.

The aesthetic contracts of modernism leave their distinctive signature upon the pages of the *Sanatorium* in a multifaceted way.[38] Radical creativity interposes itself within the detritus of exhausted cultural remains embodied by the book and Rudolf's stamp album. The maid Adela functions as a magnet for a sexual yearning common to children, prison convicts, and aged men in decline. Joseph's discovery of Adela is simultaneous with his initiation into the Benjaminian aura of the book: "One day during that winter I surprised Adela tidying up a room. A long-handled brush in her hand, she was leaning against a reading desk, on which lay some papers. I looked over her shoulder, not so much from curiosity as to be close to her and enjoy the smell of her body, whose youthful charms had just revealed themselves to my recently awakened senses."[39] This yearning is plaintive and explicit, inextricable, as the passage makes clear, from the eroticism of inscription and figuration.

As the discussion of the novel's ironic afterlife in the sanatorium and the evenings of spring and summer has made explicit, Schulz appropriates considerable narrative resources to provide a phenomenological account of writing's temporal and spatial settings. "Have you ever heard of parallel streams of time within a two-track time?" the narrator asks us a page before the account of his early graphic apotheosis. "Yes, there are such branch lines of time, somewhat illegal and suspect, but when, like us, one is burdened with contraband of supernumerary events that cannot be registered, one cannot be too fussy."[40] With a singular style and imagination, Schulz densely scored *Sanatorium* with the concerns and invariably stopgap measures of modernism: a celebration of drawing and writing uncoupled from their representational imperatives; the recycling of cultural remains; sexual obsession; a keen historical sensibility coupled with the compulsion to disfigure tradition and the Law; a parallel phenomenological project to chart the spatio-temporal parameters of writing; the inscription, in the pages of the book, of a phantasmatic link between Emperors Franz Joseph of Austria and Maximilian of Mexico illustrative of tangible and imaginary impacts of Europe upon its Others (a nascent postcolonial sensibility, in other words); a fascination with the interstitial foyers *between* art forms—in this case, the verbal and the graphic arts—transforming aesthetics into synaesthetics and expanding the domain of discrete genres into a general economy of signs.

These comprise some of modernism's most characteristic art games;[41] in singular fashion, they pervade the text of *Sanatorium* as they also do, in a different way, the pages of Proust, Kafka, Joyce, and Stein. (In the nighttime of indifference for which Schulz, as we have seen, makes ample room, these contractual clauses of modernism predicate as well the conditions of their *post*modernity.) Yet in an overview of this scope, it behooves us to delve into the singular terrain that Schulz crystallized for twentieth-century fiction rather than attempt a stultifyingly comprehensive catalogue of his modernistic devices.

Sanatorium never exhausts or overcomes its ironic epiphany, that the book of tradition and the paternal Law also encompasses the pages of the argosy and discoveries common to the childhood imagination and the aesthetic contracts of modernism. Father Jacob's ledgers, inscribed with the traces of his economic life, constitute his version of a personal Bible. The youthful narrator, Joseph, will read into those pages adventures grafting Emperor Franz Joseph's Austria onto the Mexico of Archduke Maximilian. These flights of fancy, fueled and reinforced by figures from a Wax Museum,[42] are historically grounded in the adventures of the French Second Empire. Schulz gives them a specifically colonial cast, reminiscent of Joyce's significant and pervasive racial references in *Ulysses*.[43] The overarching irony of *Sanatorium* is that the Bible, site of an unyielding Law in a state of ongoing degeneration parallel to Father Jacob's, is also the architectural foundation for the imaginary play that childhood metamorphoses into narrative and graphic art. While father devolves into a crustacean,[44] endowing the fate of Kafka's Gregor Samsa with a certain twentieth-century inevitability, son metamorphoses paternal degeneration into playful, ironic, and monstrous art. This is the deal between sociology and art, between successive generations of cultural formation, struck by Schulz's *Sanatorium*.

The book, then, that both inspires and overburdens Joseph is in its very constitution a double text, the Bible and its modern/postmodern disfiguration. At the moment of Joseph's sexual/textual awakening, Adela exposes him to the "after" photograph from a journalistic hair remedy advertisement. One Anna Csillag, "born at Karlovice in Moravia . . . struck with a poor growth of hair . . . received signs and portents and concocted a mixture, a miraculous nostrum that restored fertility to her scalp. She began to

Modernist Night 169

grow hair, and what is more, her husband, brothers, even cousins were covered overnight with a tough, healthy black coating of hair growth."[45] The book, which "in the dawn of childhood . . . lay in all its glory on my father's desk" has degenerated:[46] "Not a single page of the real text, nothing but advertisements and personal announcements" remain from the "old Book."[47] Yet the book retains its aura[48] as a spectacle of signifiers and breeder of aesthetic apprehensions. Its "pure poetry" crosses the border into yet another art form, music: "barrel organs, real miracles of technology, full of flutes, stops, and pipes, trilling sweetly like nests of sobbing nightingales. . . . One imagined these barrel organs, beautifully painted, carried on the backs of little gray old men, whose indistinct faces, corroded by life, seemed covered by cobwebs—faces with watery, immobile eyes slowly leaking away, emaciated faces as discolored and innocent as the cracked and weathered bark of trees, and now like bark smelling only of rain and sky."[49] Even where the book opens upon an enchanting, because surprising, music, it bears the stigma of old age and decline. As in many of the engravings with which Schulz illustrated *Sanatorium*, the sensibility of a creative if overburdened boy walks hand in hand with premature, unregenerate old age. The childhood revelations of the modernist night are framed and bounded by paternalistic Law. Yet the baggage and corruption cannot stifle the explosion of art.

The father's book, which also becomes the son's first book, becomes a paradigm for the aesthetic experience available to the artist as a young man in provincial Poland. Its successor is a stamp album capable of reactivating mystified cultural memories of the French Second Empire's colonial exploits and the conquistadors' adventures, also of framing a romance with Bianca, a soulmate whose enchantment of Joseph bespeaks the aura of a romantic icon, reminiscent of the effects of Mercedes, appropriated from Dumas's *Count of Monte Cristo*, upon the young Stephen Dedalus in Joyce's *A Portrait of the Artist as a Young Man* and of the youthful Gilberte Swann upon her contemporary narrator in Proust's *Recherche*.

> Suddenly Rudolf, his mouth still full of cracknel, produced from his pocket a stamp album and spread it before me.
> I realized in a flash why that spring had until then been so empty and dull. Not knowing why, it had been introverted and silent—retreating, melting into space, into an empty azure without meaning or definition—a questioning empty

shell for the admission of an unknown content. Hence that blue (as if just awakened) neutrality, that great and indifferent readiness for everything. That spring was holding itself ready: deserted and gloomy, it was simply awaiting a revelation. Who could see that this would emerge—ready, fully armed, and dazzling—from Rudolf's stamp album?

In it were strange abbreviations and formulae, recipes for civilizations, handy amulets that allowed one to hold his thumb and finger between the essence of climates and provinces. These were bank drafts on empires and republics, on archipelagoes and continents. Emperors and usurpers, conquerors and dictators could not possess anything greater. I suddenly anticipated the sweetness of dominion over lands and peoples, the thorn of that frustration that can only be healed by power. With Alexander of Macedonia, I wanted to conquer the whole world and not a square inch of ground less.[50]

The opening up of an imaginary space occasions in the youthful narrator both a sense of and a quest for power. There is something imperialistic in the enlargement of small-town Poland prompted by the images in the stamp album. The second emanation of the book in *Sanatorium* conjures up foreign expeditions and conquests, ancient and modern. This imaginary expansionism carries economic implications, as well. The glimpses of a vast and romantic world that Joseph steals from the stamp album constitute down payments on a universe even more magnificent. The album, fully realized in Joseph's life, will enable him to duplicate Alexander the Great's conquests, "not a square inch of ground less."[51]

Ah, it is the bird cherry that gives depth to the limitless night. . . .

Ah, all these rapes and pursuits of that night, the treacheries and whispers, Negroes and helmsmen, balcony railings and night-blinds, muslin frocks and veils trailing behind hurried escapes! Until at last, after a sudden blackout, a dull black pause, a moment comes when all the puppets are back in their boxes, all the curtains are drawn, and all the bated breaths are quietly exhaled. . . .

Only now will the nature of that spring become clear and legible to an attentive reader of the Book. All these morning preparations, all the day's early ablutions, all its hesitations, doubts, and difficulties of choice will disclose their meaning to one who is familiar with stamps. Stamps introduce one to the complex game of morning diplomacy, to the prolonged negotiations and atmospheric deceits that precede the final version of any day. From the reddish mists of the ninth hour, the motley and spotted Mexico with a serpent wriggling in a condor's beak is trying to emerge, hot and parched by a bright rash, while in a gap of azure amid the greenery of tall trees, a parrot is stubbornly repeating "Guatemala, Guatemala" at even intervals, with the same intonation, and that green word infects things that suddenly become fresh and leafy. Slowly, among difficulties and conflicts, a voting takes place, the order of ceremonies is established, the list of parades, the diplomatic protocol of the day.[52]

Schulz endows the argosies that Joseph, by means of the stamp album, is able to project with explicitly colonialist and Eurocentric overtones. The Mexican and Central American site of the adventure is colorful to the utmost degree: "motley and spotted," populated by parrots that, "in a gap of azure" repeat "'Guatemala, Guatemala' at even intervals."[53] The dramatic Mexico that Joseph conjures up in this episode in fact derives from a third book, whose citation is left inexplicit, or, rather, from a play, J. M. Barrie's "Peter Pan, the Boy Who Wouldn't Grow Up." The "Negroes" in this and related passages function,[54] as do the Indians in "Peter Pan," as atmospheric accoutrements to the action, but with no volition or dramatic consequence of their own. By means of the expanding fantasy world revealed to Joseph in the pages of a constant but substitutable book, Schulz sets in sharp relief the specificities of the playful imaginary available to the European artist as a young man in the early decades of the twentieth century. This alternative universe is expansionist, exploitative, and heavily racially coded at the same time as it manifests open-ended intellectual play.

Joseph's nascent aesthetic sensibility is not so steeped in Romantic experiments of fragmentation and sublimity as to leave *Sanatorium* devoid of humor. Indeed, the peculiar humor pervading Schulz's fictive world is as singular as the summer nights in which language and the imaginary bifurcate into additional levels of meaning and involution while feeding upon themselves.

Schulz's humor is inextricable from horror. The monsters that err into Joseph's childlike gaze turn out to be quite amusing creatures. The childhood aesthetic sensibility of Joseph keeps breaking thresholds of understanding and discovery. There is a marvelous *jouissance* in the progression of Joseph's apprehensions, yet in every new theater of action monsters invade the field of vision, monsters that turn out to be endearing and downright funny. Schulz is not above borrowing a monster or two, say, from

Kafka. But while the grotesque in Kafka is maudlin, and uncanniness in Gombrowicz has a distinctly alienating or defamiliarized quality, the horrible in Schulz is invariably playful. An intimidating patriarch metamorphoses into a crab-in-aspic; the ingrown atmosphere of a small-town dry goods store produces a breed of mutant killer flies. A facile separation between the playful and the horrific becomes another manifestation of the inscription of the Book of Adventure and Discovery in the margins of the Bible of Patriarchal Law.

> When, at noon, my father, exhausted by the heat, trembling with futile excitement and almost on the verge of madness, retreated upstairs and the ceilings of the floor above cracked here and there under his skulking step, the shop experienced a momentary relaxation: the hour of the afternoon siesta.
>
> The shop assistants turned somersaults on the bales of cloth, pitched tents of fabric on the shelves, made swings from draperies. They unwound the cloth, set free the smooth, tightly rolled ancient darkness. The shopworn, felted dusk, now liberated, filled the spaces under the ceiling with the smell of another time.... Blind moths scattered in the darkened air, fluffs of feathers and wool circled with them all over the shop, and the smell of finishing, deep and autumnal, filled this dark encampment of cloth and velvet. Picnicking in that camp the shop assistants devised practical jokes. They let their colleagues wrap them tightly up to their ears in dark, cool cloth and lay in a row blissfully immobile under the stack of bales.... Or else they let themselves be swung up to the ceiling on enormous, outspread blankets of cloth. The dull thudding of these blankets and the current of air that arose made them mad with joy. It seemed as if the whole shop was taking off in flight.[55]

A constellation of motifs and images emerges here that is decisive to the novel's dénouement. Father Jacob's increasing feebleness occasions the release of his servants' and employee's mirth. The slapstick pranks in which they engage unleash a cloud of cotton fluff serving as an apt figuration of the father's disconnectedness and decline. The father's retreat stirs up the animate and inanimate markers of fragmentation, contingency, and the transformation of agency into physical chance: feathers, wool, "blind moths." The novel ends in a wild poetic festival celebrating the loss of paternal Law and control: shop assistants run amok in games reducing them to physical objects; the fluff collected over a lifetime in the small-town dry goods business scatters through the air; insects fill the air with their buzzing and mindless frenetic activity.

Father Jacob's decline has been sealed, of course, since *Sanatorium's* outset, when Joseph demonstrated his ability to usurp and appropriate the book's restrictive Law to his own purposes, to graft the Books of Play and Argosy onto the Bible of Commerce and Restraint. The emergence of insects and crustaceans at the end of *Sanatorium* not only signals a devolution in Father Jacob's world order and ability to control his affairs but an irrecuperable outbreak of linguistic dispersion and dissemination. Insects are animate beings that behave irrationally and unpredictably. Along with bacteria, they comprise human beings' most prominent partners from the animal world in settings of fecundation and decay. Insects thus link death, mindless activity, and the vacancy or abandonment of the scenario of metaphysical agency and introspection.

It is Father Jacob's fate to devolve into a manic crustacean while Son Joseph experiences an apotheosis into an artist, one whose primordial inspirations have included summer nights in the Polish countryside, a housemaid, an early mail-order catalogue, a stamp album, and the storms of fluff and fibers erupting amid the order of a dry goods store. Father Jacob's decline is tantamount, at the end of the novel, to a field day for a vast and growing throng of insects, whose buzzing is itself an instance of the linguistic dissemination central to the project(s) of modernist art.

> In the summer the back of the shop was dark because of the weeds growing in the courtyard. The storeroom window overlooking it became all green and iridescent like submarine depths from the movement of leaves and their undulating reflections. Flies buzzed there monotonously in their semiobscurity of long afternoons; they were monstrous specimens bred on Father's sweet wine, hairy hermits lamenting their accursed fate day in, day out in long, monotonous sagas. These flies, inclined to wild and unexpected mutations, abounded in unnatural specimens, bred from incestuous unions, degenerated into a super-race of top heavy giants, of veterans emitting a deep melancholy buzz. Toward the end of the summer some specimens were posthumously hatched out with wasted wings—mute and voiceless, the last of their race, resembling large, bluish beetles—and ended their sad lives running up and down the sad windowpanes on busy, futile errands.[56]

As Father Jacob devolves into a manic crustacean and descendent of Kafka's Gregor Samsa, the insects from his shop develop into poetic entities that dramatize the generation of textually articulate language. Antithetical to the master of the house as the insects may seem, the flies and the head of the dry goods firm issue forth in droning tirades.

The political message emanating from this passage is a mixed one. The end of Father Jacob's commercial life and paternal role within his family is accompanied by an invasion of surly and genetically deficient entomological storm troopers. The passage both celebrates the fall of Father Jacob's regime and mourns the passing of a world and a way of life: the playful banter of the fabric shop; the allure of a nubile female servant; the material richness embodied in bolts of fabric, variegated by color and weave. Father Jacob is both tyrant and victim in this passage, which resonates with an uncanny political aura. The bluish beetles surfacing at the end of the extract imply a political reading of the loss of control that seizes Gregor Samsa and the K.s of Kafka's novels. Kafka is often credited with an uncanny anticipation of World War II's authoritarianism and genocide. There may well lurk a political critique in the figure of the belligerent insects swarming at the end of *Sanatorium*.

Father Jacob devolves into the crustacean intensification of an insect, a super-insect, if you will. Yet he is also beset by insects. He victimizes his shop assistants, yet is lionized and parodied by them as well. His assistants function as human literary surrogates, yet on occasion they metamorphose into insects as well, as will be evident in the next extract, a final vignette from the dry goods shop in the season of Jacob's demise. The loss of Father Jacob's world, then, not only gives rise to the apotheosis of an artist as a young man, but eventuates in an unpredictable reversal and fluctuation of the values the fiction has advanced in the enterprise of its own legibility. The equivalencies and values that the text has ventured in its own communicability begin to swarm and reverse like a swarm of heat-maddened flies:

> Once a peasant from the country, barefoot and smock-clad, stopped in the doorway of his shop and looked in shyly. For the bored shop assistants this was a heaven-sent opportunity. They quickly swept down the ladders, like spiders at the sight of a fly; the peasant, surrounded, pulled, and pushed, was asked a hundred questions, which he tried to parry with a bashful smile. He scratched his head, smiled, and looked with suspicion at the assiduous young men. So he wanted tobacco? But what kind? The best, Macedonian, golden as amber? Not that kind? Would ordinary pipe tobacco do? Shag perhaps? Would he care to step in? To come inside? There was nothing to fear. The shop assistants prodded him gently deeper into the shop. . . . Leon went behind the counter and pretended to pull out a nonexistent drawer. Oh, how he worked at it, how he bit his

lip with effort! It was stuck and would not move. One had to thump the top of the counter with one's fists, with all one's might. The peasant, encouraged by the young men, did it with concentration, with proper attention. At last, when there was no result, he climbed, hunched and gray-haired, on the top of the counter and stamped it with his bare feet. He had us all in fits of laughter.[57]

This powerful vignette stages the bedevilment of a simple man (perhaps related to the "Man from the Country" in Kafka's parable "Before the Law") by Father Jacob's playful shop assistants. The peasant is eventually reduced to a Jacoblike rage by a barrage of the assistants' self-contradictory questions. The passage compares his fate to that of an errant fly in the hands of a swarm of voracious spiders. In this instance, the assistant named Leon gets the best of the peasant. In the long run, however, as is made clear in the passage prior to the one just quoted, the entomological storm troopers will win out. The story of the assistants' trickery sets certain aspects of Jacob's commercial life in vivid relief. Yet this very vividness may be symptomatic of the depicted world's evanescence and immanent collapse. Jacob's dying encompasses much of the novel. In its final stages, Jacob comes to resemble the simple-minded peasant at the pinnacle of his pique.

> At that time, my father was definitely dead. He had been dying a number of times, always with some reservations that forced us to revise our attitude toward the fact of his death. This had its advantages. By dividing his death into installments, Father had familiarized us with his demise. We became gradually indifferent to his returns—each one shorter, each one more pitiable. His features were already dispersed throughout the room in which he had lived, and were sprouting in it, creating at some points strange knots of likeness that were most expressive. The wallpaper began in certain places to imitate his habitual nervous tic; the flower designs arranged themselves into the doleful elements of his smile, symmetrical as the fossilized imprint of a trilobite. For a time, we gave a wide berth to his fur coat lined with polecat skins. The coat breathed. . . . Putting one's ear against it, one could hear the melodious purring unison of the animals' sleep. In this well-tanned form . . . my father might have lasted for many years. But he did not last.[58]

Father Jacob is the victim of an extended, redundant, serial death, one that, as we have seen, transpires through a nearly imperceptible time-lag. His external world, as he becomes dehumanized, begins to take on his idiosyncratic quirks and other features. Even before his demise, Father Jacob has impressed an indelible stamp on the people and objects around him. The symmetrical floral designs that crystallize in the wallpaper in imitation of his smile reveal the troglodytic dimensions of his personality. Jacob has one way to grow and reach apotheosis at the end of the novel. It is by evolutionary, intellectual, and interpersonal regression. So prepossessing and rigid is Jacob's impact on the people and things around him that a return to the development of a crustacean is the fullest realization of his manic fixity.

Yet Schulz attaches a peculiar oral fixation to his comic-monstrous devolution. Father Jacob not only "evolves" into a presumably more primitive life form. His metamorphosis transforms him into a dish for consumption, specifically, a seafood delicacy that happens to be prohibited by Jewish dietary law. In keeping with the Freudian calculus of totemism, his dictum of aporetic and self-negating instincts, the domineering patriarch who has ruled by intimidation, who has metaphorically devoured his wife, siblings, children, servants, and employees, metamorphoses himself into a primitive and ultimately inedible delicacy.[59] This transforms his devolution into an oral event, one bespeaking extreme attraction and revulsion. He is inedible not only because Uncle Charles can't eat him but because as a patriarch, a vestige of eternity, he is, in keeping with the inflexible laws of *kashruth*, taboo.

> When Father was brought in on a dish, we came to our senses and understood fully what had happened. He lay large and swollen from the boiling, pale gray and jellified. We sat in silence, dumbfounded. Only Uncle Charles lifted his fork toward the dish, but at once he put it down uncertainly, looking at us askance. Mother ordered it to be taken to the sitting room. It stood there afterward on a table covered with a velvet cloth, next to the album of family photographs and a musical cigarette box. Avoided by us all, it just stood there.
>
> But my father's earthly wanderings were not yet at an end, and the next installment—the extension of the story beyond permissable limits—is the most painful of all. Why didn't he give up, why didn't he admit that he was beaten when there was every reason to do so. . . . After several weeks of immobility in the sitting room, he somehow rallied and seemed to be slowly recovering. One morning we found the plate empty. One leg lay on the side of the dish, in some congealed tomato sauce and aspic that bore the traces of his escape. Although boiled and shedding his legs on the way, with his remaining strength he had dragged himself somewhere to begin a homeless wandering, and we never saw him again.[60]

So hardy is Father Jacob, of such a vigorous constitution is he, that his endless contortions and metamorphoses continue into the terminal stages of death. A wandering Jew to the core, his death is one of migration and continuing vacancy rather than biological termination.

Father Jacob's demise casts a long and comic shadow over the events in *Sanatorium*. Yet his universe also gives rise to Schulz's fictive and graphic art. *Sanatorium* fluctuates between a staggered and periodic demise and a *durée*, set among the good times of spring and summer. Surely the art that the modernist night, the evenings of spring and summer, inspired in Schulz has outlasted a spasmodic death by regression. It is during the extended and uneventful *durée* of the modernist night that the dimension of writing—a state of Being as well as a dimension—opens up for the nascent writer starstruck by the text, made resilient and evanescent in its composition.

I thus end my survey of Schulz's art with one final glimpse of this telling, all-significant modernist night. Many of the characters, tropes, and phenomena responsible for the singularity and touching, inexhaustibly surprising eloquence of Schulz's art are "present" and accounted for:

> Apart from Adela, one or two neighbors sit on these balconies in front of their doors sprawled on chairs or squatting on stools, wilting faintly in the dusk; they rest after the toil of their day, mute as tied-up sacks, waiting for the night to untie them gently.
>
> Down below, the courtyard quickly fills with darkness, but the air above it does not yet relinquish its light and seems to become steadily lighter as everything below gradually turns pitch dark; it shimmers and trembles from the sudden, furtive flight of bats.
>
> Down below, the quick and silent work of night now begins in earnest. Greedy ants swarm everywhere, decomposing into atoms the substance of things, eating them down to their white bones, to their ribs and skeletons, which phosphoresce in the nightmare of this sad battlefield. White papers, in tatters on the rubbish heap, survive longest, like undigested rays of brightness in the worm-ridden darkness, and cannot completely dissolve. . . . Then they emerge again, but in the end it is impossible to say whether one sees anything or whether these are illusions that begin their nightly ravings; in the end people sit in their own aura under stars projected by their own pulsating brains, by the phantoms of hallucinations.[61]

EIGHT

Incarcerated in *Amerika*: Literature Addresses the Political, with the Help of Ernesto Laclau

Kafka's novel *Der Verschollene, The Man Who Disappeared*, also known as *Amerika*,[1] in its attention to the socioeconomic conditions of all its characters, to the phenomenon and underlying motives of Euro-American immigration, which was at its peak during the composition of the novel and its fictive time frame, and to the aggravated class conflict between, on the one hand, such characters as Uncle Jakob and the owners of Montley's department store and, on the other, Karl, the Stoker, Delamarche, Robinson, and the student Josef Mendel—is his most extended artifact with explicitly political themes, events, and considerations. If I endeavor to trace the interface between this most political of projects and something called "the political," as if this entity were able, somehow, to function outside and beyond the parameters of specific texts or documents, I do so in response to the pressure meaningfully, that is, thoughtfully, to address the prevailing sociopolitical forces and influences of our day. Exactly how, and in what senses, is Kafka's arguably most political novel political? What is the set of relations—parallelism, dissonance, mutual confirmation, undermining, or supplementation—between a specific set of affairs prevailing in Kafka's day and the work of literature that embodied his response to multiple and multifaceted factors? Can there be any political commentary or critique emanating from Kafka's novel *Amerika* other than the thoughtfulness that the novel, as an extended hypothesis or elaboration of possibility, fosters and promotes? Does thoughtfulness, whether understood as a Heideggerian engagement with being as the poetico-linguistic format of culture or as the text-based set of cultural addresses improvised by deconstruction, in itself, *an Sich*, constitute a political achievement or end? Is the aggravated thoughtfulness induced by a dense visual, or literary, or cinematographic, or dramatic artifact *enough*? Or does the analysis of an artifact have to mark and present itself as political in some explicit way, thematically, allegorically, or invectively, in order for it to claim participation in the discourse, and theory, of politics?

It can only come as the most intense disappointment—almost, in psychoanalytical terms, a sexual frustration, or the denial of psychosexual needs—that the works of literature we consult for some illumination of the world's absurdities and exasperations answer back—like the oracle—only in riddles and additional questions. For each clarification that we exact from the artifact—What is its meaning? What was the author's intention in composing it? How does it resolve the idiocies coming down from all our noble estates and classes, from the White House to bourgeois mafioso platitudes?—it only throws additional complexities and aesthetic smoke screens in our faces. We are indeed so *pressed*—by our own fatal curiosities, by the crassness of sociopolitical stopgap measures that surpass each other only in their progressive ill advisement, by the logic of our academic careers, for those fortunate enough to have them (which are, according to my analysis, private corporate affairs, with their departments of publicity and merchandizing). We are pressed on many levels to come up with answers. But the artifacts under our cultural and often institutional stewardship—through such activities as archiving and the preparation of authoritative editions—resist more vehemently the more pointed the demands made of them for resolution.

One viable definition of class is as the perch or perspective—whose play is thematized in the modernist canvasses, photographs, and sculptures of cubist fragmentation and kaleidoscopic variation—from which events are taken in, lent a certain significance, rendered an exegesis. Indeed, the balcony on which Karl Rossmann, the childlike protagonist and wanderer of *The Man Who Disappeared*, is incarcerated by oversized ex-opera queen Brunelda and her consort Delamarche toward the end of the novel is the perspectival perch from which he views an American political demonstration that devolves into anomie. In line with the other images of bewildering complexity in the novel and elsewhere in Kafka's writing, figures including the Hotel Occidental information givers and the telephone system between the Castle and the village below it, the chaos is both destructive—it frustrates the desires for crowd control and a clear political message—and indispensably generative: its sensory overload is the basis for further fabulation and exegesis. The position of the balcony furnishes the perspective that we demand from such a construct as class identity, or from the intrapsychic agencies or levels of consciousness in psychoanalysis. But the narrative cinematography that Kafka splices together for the scene and for the novel issues forth, in words used to describe his hybrid thing, or *objet petit a*, Odradek, from "no fixed abode."[2] In its perspective, the scene wanders from balcony to balcony and follows first the increasingly incoherent political candidate and then the mute giant who is his handler.

The tangle, nuance, and gradation of language may well constitute the ultimate emanation of the *Big Other*, even though its workings have been installed in culture and experience forever, always already. The Big Other is less the omnipotence of God, the horrendous arbitrariness of Stalin, or the inconceivable perversity of Hitler than the oracular uncertainty of writing, issuing forth from Western civilization's abyssal scene of representation and offering complexity in place of clear response. Literature arises under uncanny and in certain senses untheorizable conditions of intuition, elective affinity, sympathetic vibration. It is surely possessed of psychological and psychoanalytical pre-texture, formatting, and templating. But psychoanalysis and psychoanalytical programming and dramaturgy no more exhaust the literary than they do sociological stratification or political fragmentation. There is always something unaccounted for in a densely woven text. This reminder belongs no more to liberal bourgeois deconstructionists than it does to the proletariat or California Buddhists.[3] The extent to which language both facilitates and derails systems, schematics, and equivalencies can be read by the bourgeois, the Marxist, the conservative, and the dispossessed. Yes, upper-class education and taste may succeed in showcasing a fuller range of linguistic and, for that matter, technological and scientific options than the alternatives available to the rest of the population. But since the oracular, the auratic, and the undecidable are dimensions of language rather than class appurtenances or properties, the underprivileged and those antagonized by elitist manners are free and able to access these embedded linguistic programmatics, and they regularly do. Such a politically savvy contemporary poet as Charles Bernstein brings the full weight of his formation and practice to bear in his admiration for the poetics of rap and hip-hop.

The political thematics and allegory of *The Man Who Disappeared* are endowed with a full range of psychoanalytical parameters. As a teen-ager Karl Rossmann has already fulfilled one of the imperatives of his petit-bourgeois European heritage—to reproduce—before he is cast out of his family for the shame of it and left to fend for himself in a welcoming/predatory America. Kafka places the discovery of the seamy side of the widespread myth of American assimilation and restitution of disadvantages unfairly distributed under the European ancien régime in the hands of a walking time-contradiction, a living metalepsis, someone whose premature ejaculation and fatherhood render him forever both ahead of and behind his time. Karl's seduction at home by the thirty-five-year-old family maid is couched as an event of brutality and revulsion:

> Then she lay down beside him, and asked to hear some secret or another, but he was unable to tell her any . . . then she listened to the beating of his heart and offered him her breast for him to listen to, but Karl couldn't bring himself to do that, she pressed her naked belly against his, reached her hand down, it felt so disgusting that Karl's head and neck leapt out of the pillows, down between his legs, pushed her belly against his a few times, he felt as though she were part of him, and perhaps for that reason he felt seized by a shocking helplessness.[4]

The setup to Karl's wanderings in America, the foundation for an endless vacillation between allure and disgust, between release and imprisonment, is the seduction, in lurid detail, of a male youth by an adult woman. This prequel to the novel installs an overarching dynamics of gender role reversal and sexual revulsion—in which male characters are abjected by domineering female counterparts—throughout the format of the rags-to-riches American adventure. Indeed, this uncanny twentieth-century adaptation of the Bildungsroman stages not an accommodation and harnessing of the drive in the course of self-fulfillment and realization, but a tyranny of the drive, the sense of the drive as a distraction and fatal diversion from the needs of personal experience and civic well-being. There are one or two sympathetic female characters in the novel, but none are alluring. The sympathetic ones are motherly, like the Head Cook at the Hotel Occidental, or wounded and fragile, like hotel secretary Therese, who as a young girl witnesses the collapse of her destitute and tubercular mother at a construction site. In the aftermath of Karl's initiation into sexuality at the hands of Johanna Brummer, the women he encounters in America are physically domineering, like Clara Pollunder, who wrestles him into submission, or sexually repulsive, like the oversize warden of his life imprisonment, Brunelda. Kafka transforms the epic novel of American release into a sordid decline into abjection.

The instruments of the metamorphosis from aura to revulsion, from release to domination, from comfort to suspended impending menace and threat, installed throughout the novel, are the hands constantly extending from one character to the next, in gestures ranging from supplication and stroking to accusation and corporeal restraint. So prevalent is the image of hands in the novel that this most human of appendages achieves a figural and dynamic autonomy. So important is the notion of hand and handling that the specific hands in the novel become severed from the "characters" to whom they putatively belong. In their uncanny disembodiment and autonomy, they anticipate the motifs and devices of surrealist cinema. They become a superordinate allegorical index in the novel. Wherever they point, liberty has devolved into bondage, sexual desire has metamorphosed into terror, consummation and transcendence have become a worse fate than the abjection that prompted their pursuit. The novel teems with hands, as it might with insects if it were a piece of meat left out in the open. To give a few examples: "So thinking he [Karl] walked slowly over to the stoker, pulled his right hand out of his belt, and held it playfully in his own."[5] "They sat close together, and Mr. Pollunder held Karl's hand in his while he talked."[6] "You, I would say, are strongly suspicious," declares the hotel's Head Porter. "And delighted with that he lifted his hands off Karl and let them fall again, which made a smacking noise and hurt."[7] "On balconies that were occupied by partisans of the candidate, they began chanting his name and clapping their hands mechanically, leaning far over their railings."[8]

The exploitative relations with his putative friends that seem to dog Karl, his recurrent encounters with the Law, invariably culminating in kangaroo proceedings expedited by the paradoxical logic of guilt described so well by Slavoj Žižek, among others, the repeated encounters with scenes of writing or representation run amok, whether Uncle Jakob's telegraph room or the Hotel Occidental information givers: these features of the novel can all be approached via political theory, particularly a theory open both to psychoanalytical structures and to linguistic contingency. It is at the point where the novel becomes encrusted with the hands that have become Kafka's insignia for a constellation of values erratically but continuously morphing into one another, where the hands, as in the famous Escher print, point at each other and become building-blocks in the picture that they form, that the literary, having danced compellingly with the political for a time, peels off and veers in a different direction, one neither more edifying nor more utilitarian than political articulation, but different.

The childlike vividness of Karl's apperceptions is the immediate context in which he can bond with the titanic figure of the Stoker—over and against the symbolically "correct" characters of the ship's captain, the ship's administrator, Schubal, and last but not least, the Chaplinesque apparition of a long-lost uncle from America, Senator Edward Jakob. European *Wunderkind* and capitalist success-story, Uncle Jakob is a living figment of the American dream at the same time as his murky dealings and influence as a captain of industry furnish Karl's nascent adulthood and the novel as a whole with an ethical point of reference as dominant as are the Statue of Liberty and the Woolworth Building within the New York cityscape of the day. Even the two vagabonds, Delamarche and Robinson, French and Irish transplants who trail Karl throughout the novel and who spoil his every initiative at self-advancement, are up-to-date on the ill-gotten gains and exploitative labor practices of Senator Edward Jakob. Robinson references *Crusoe* and with that a system of world literature whose elements include Genesis, Exodus, Cinderella, and the *Manifesto of the Communist Party*. We might say of these and parallel works to which the novel gestures that they claim a global outreach within the framework of *The Man Who Disappeared*. They constitute an overarching imaginary space for Karl's wanderings.

Against the backdrop of these beacons of world literature, Karl's forced march with the vagabonds (Delamarche's name means "on the road") does not lead him toward any high moral ground. The ominous corruption of patriarchal Uncle Jakob, who will disinherit Karl on the basis of his first curfew violation—metamorphosing Karl into a degenerate Cinderella—is a major, but by no means singular element in a psychosocial backdrop against which Karl will vacillate between equanimity and disorientation. America, in other words, is quick to transform Karl into—or *produce* him as—a Deleuzian schizo.[9]

Not unlike the real-life Kafka, who handled workman's compensation cases for two of the multinational insurance corporations of his day, and some of whose accident investigation and reporting procedures are still in use, Karl Rossmann manifests a preternatural empathy for the working men and women he encounters and for their working and living conditions under voracious U.S. capitalism.

> Now her mother had been offered work on a building site the following morning, but as she told Therese all day long, she was afraid she wouldn't able to take up this good opportunity because she was dead tired, that morning to the alarm of passers-by on the pavement she had coughed up a lot of blood, and all she wanted was to get in the warm somewhere and rest. But on this one evening it was proving impossible to find a place. . . . They would hurry through narrow icy passages, climb long flights of stairs, circle the narrow courtyards, knocking randomly on doors, sometimes not daring to speak, at others asking anyone they met.[10]

Therese's traumatic first-hand assistance at her mother's death while still a child is transferred to us via Karl's attentive ear. What colors this death so vividly is the surround of wandering and sublime indifference in which it is couched. Mother and child are early-twentieth-century urban homeless people. Technically speaking, the mother's death is an industrial accident.[11] It transpires at a construction site. The Chaplinesque humor with which Kafka surrounds the maudlin event—as if Charlie had roller-skated over the edge of the unguarded department-store mezzanine in *Modern Times*—only adds to the sense of hopelessness. In this passage, two figures in the parable of American indifference and dislocation wander through an involuted architecture that elsewhere in Kafka, particularly in *The Trial*, radiates an aura of textual wonder and complexity. Amid the heightened political sensibility of *Amerika*, labyrinthine spatial configurations underscore social destitution rather than exegetical possibility. Not even the physical slapstick of architectural collapse and flying bricks and boards can redeem the abjection of the mother's death.

> Up there [in the scaffolding], her mother skillfully went around the masons laying brick on brick, who surprisingly didn't ask what she was doing, she held delicately on to a wooden crate that served as a railing, and Therese in her doze below, marveled at the sure-footedness of her mother, and thought she caught a friendly glance from her. Then her mother came to a little pile of bricks marking the end of the railing and probably the path as well, she walked up to the bricks, her sure-footedness seemed to have deserted her, she kicked over the bricks and fell with them over the edge. Many bricks fell after her, and some time later a heavy board became detached and crashed down on top of her as well. Therese's last memory of her mother was of her lying there with legs apart in the checked skirt she had brought with her from Pomerania, the rough plank on top of her.[12]

In this fictive digression from Karl's progressive woes, Kafka successfully melds a realism in social description that he took over from Dostoyevsky, among others, with a triumphant American humor and faith in the overcoming of adversity that he witnessed in the films of the teens. The political lesson to be gained from the bricks and boards that mark the mother's resting place is a hegemonic one. To be absorbed by class, fully appropriated by it, even at a moment of unusual social flux and mobility, is to be buried—in this case quite literally—under the dictates of the prevailing regime. Kafka deploys the tension between untrammeled movement and its precipitous arrest with particular invention and unpredictability in *The Man Who Disappeared*. One way of understanding the proliferating hands to which I pointed above is as instruments of restraint and arrest, on the one hand, and of release, on the other. The tension between humor and abjection in the mother's death scene may be the direct connection between the vignette and the most explicit depiction of political process anywhere in Kafka's writing, the political rally that Karl witnesses when he has already been enslaved by Brunelda and Delamarche. But in this overview of the American sociopolitical landscape, there is no redeeming humor as the candidate becomes increasingly entrapped and ineffectual.

> In the course of obviously what were preparations for a great round of free drinks the candidate never stopped speaking for a minute. His bearer, the colossal man who seemed to be subordinate exclusively to him, kept making little turns after every few sentences, to distribute the speech equally to all parts of the crowd. The candidate's position was generally hunched over and he tried with jerky movements of his free hand, and with his top hat in the other, to lend emphasis to what he was saying. Sometimes, almost at regular intervals, he went into a

> kind of convulsion, he rose up with outspread arms, he no longer addressed a group but the generality, he spoke to the dwellers of the houses right up to the topmost storeys, and yet it was perfectly obvious that even on the lowest floors no one could hear him, yes, and that even had the possibility existed, no one wanted to hear him, because every window and every balcony was tenanted by at least one shouting speaker of its own.[13]

Back-lit by the harsh illumination of Kafka's literary montage is the contrast between the candidate's colossal carrier and grandiose aspiration to address *all* the spectators in sight and his inability to make himself heard. The inarticulateness of the message reduces his political position to nullity, to an empty gesture choreographed by politics as a distinctly American spectacle. The politician appears to be what Deleuze and Guattari will term a schizo, equipped with a decentralized "body without organs."[14] His body convulses in response to the energies and vibes emitted by the crowd. He is a puppet who might have stepped out of the pages of Kleist's "Marionette Theater," but in the twentieth century his strings are pulled by audience response and live, or possibly "canned," laughter. Yet in his staging of the scene, Kafka is enough of a political theorist to cast the candidate's struggle to be heard in terms of the distribution of his words to the most general possible audience. In this respect, Kafka understands that the airing of political positions is in the interest of forming constituencies that advance their interest in the public sphere. But amid the chaotic spectacle of American politics, nothing much is going to get advanced, at least in a rational way. A subsequent passage from this scene chronicles its degeneration from political debate to chaotic mass entertainment and spectacle.

> The moment he reached the door of the bar, the candidate, in the beam of a tight circle of headlamps, embarked on his next speech. But now everything was much harder than before, the bearer no longer had the slightest freedom of movement, the crush was too great. The closest supporters . . . were now struggling to remain in his proximity, some twenty of them were desperately clinging on to the bearer. But strong as he was, he couldn't take a single step as he pleased, there was no possibility of influencing the crowd by revolving or advancing or retreating at given moments. The crowd was in chaotic flux, each man was leaning against his neighbour, none was standing upright any more, the opponents seemed to have gained strength greatly from the new arrivals, the bearer had stood long in the vicinity of the bar door, but now, apparently unresistingly, he allowed himself to drift up and down the street, the candidate was speaking all

the time, but it wasn't clear any more whether he was laying out his programme or asking for help, and there was every indication a rival candidate had appeared.[15]

It is in these dire straits that we leave our political candidate. The mass demonstration, the shower of electric lighting and attention from every angle, the personal bearer who has been assigned to be the candidate's literal transportation—this is before the age of Lear jets—belong to the appurtenances of hegemony. The progress of the political rally, set among the residential towers of a cosmopolitan city, whether Ramses, Manhattan, or Barcelona is immaterial, is beset with what Ernesto Laclau would call contingency. The candidate cannot make his voice heard; his message therefore belongs to the register of empty signifiers; eventually, by dint of an opposition every bit as incomprehensible as his own cause, the candidate held aloft by a cretin comes to a definitive impasse. Fueled by liquor, political antagonism and counterpositionality degenerate into anomie. In Kafka's staging, this scene, which conveys something of the feel of the apotheosis of Nathanael West's *Day of the Locust*, bears witness to a metamorphosis of grassroots American democracy into a phantasmagoria of malevolent political power, civil society drifting and keeling, on the verge of collapse.

Few instances of political theory are poised to go head to head with the fragmentation, dislocation, anomaly, arbitrariness, absurdity, and inconsequentiality foregrounded by Kafka's writing. Laclau's longstanding and ever-self-refining project is surely one of them. From a conceptual point of view, Laclau's theory is nothing less than revolutionary in its acknowledgment of contingency, indeterminacy, and undecidability within a political arena gravitating only too easily toward the hegemonic and the absolute, as accounted for by the discipline of "political science" as much as by society's deliberative processes. Any universality to which Laclau can subscribe has been preconditioned by contingency and the double-binds, not unfamiliar to students of German idealist philosophy, that emerge when class interest confronts hegemony. As the inscriber of limits to the certainty that political leaders as well as students of culture desperately seek, he belongs more to the camp of the anal fathers than the oedipal ones. He is a most respectful, in the sense of the term delineated in Derrida's "Faith and Knowledge," purveyor of whatever wisdom and illumination have accrued from intellectual work to political phenomena in our time.[16] Specifically, he is explicitly attentive to the manner in which linguistic processes and dynamics, and by implication deliberations on rhetoric coterminous with Western philosophy, may be said to inflect a contingent apprehension of the political, one in which the absolute, the a priori, and the tautological emerge only through a tortuous and never definitive series of negotiations with the transcendental. *The Man Who Disappeared*, then, and a few of Kafka's other explicitly political works, "In the Penal Colony" and "The Great Wall of China" among them, should prove excellent test cases for the relevance of an enlightened discourse of political theory to literary texts bespeaking the full density and aura of Derridean textuality or Heideggerian poetry.[17] It is Laclau's very senses of contingency, dislocation, and constitution not by sameness but by exteriority that we need to infuse into the encounter between the dense literary artifact and any conceptual model that would, even in the best of faith, appropriate and dispatch it.

Bringing the full weight of his philosophical erudition to bear on the political, Laclau is intensely aware of the dynamics by which class interest is both *constituted* and *obliterated* by the forces of political antagonism. He demonstrates an acute sensibility to the aporias, in political process as well as Western metaphysics, enabling the same state of affairs to produce mutually undermining understandings of political constituencies, agency, and self-interest. There is a distinctive rhythm in Laclau's thought between the constitution and negation of agency, and it is not unlike Karl's progressive oscillation between authorities only too lucid and mad in their rigidity, whether Uncle Jakob, the Hotel Occidental Head Waiter, and the policemen outside Brunelda's apartment, and the outbreak of what we would call textual proliferation and undecidability, whether in the bowels of the ship, Uncle Jakob's telegraph room, or the Hotel's elevator and telephone systems.

> Insofar as an antagonism exists between a worker and a capitalist, such antagonism is not inherent to the relations of production themselves, but occurs between the latter and the identity of the agent outside. A fall in a worker's wage, for example, denies his identity as a consumer. There is therefore a "social objectivity"—the logic of profit—which denies another objectivity—the consumer's identity. But the denial of an identity means presenting its constitution as an objectivity. This throws up two alternatives: either the element of negativity is reabsorbed by a positivity of a higher order which reduces it to mere appearance; or the negation is irreducible to any objectivity, which means that it becomes

constitutive and therefore indicates the impossibility of establishing the social as an objective order.

As is known, the philosophies of history were oriented in the first direction. A concept such as the "cunning of reason" in Hegel can only assert the rationality of the real at the expense of reducing antagonism, negativity, to an appearance through which a higher form of rationality and positivity works.[18]

It is exasperating, asserts Laclau, to attempt to pinpoint precise positions of social agency and interest, because antagonisms are mediated by factors outside the particular opposition. Workers experience their underpayment in what they cannot purchase, not directly in their encounters with their bosses. This fundamental state of affairs instantiates a broader tension between the *constitution* or construction of class interest and its treatment as a fait accompli, a known quantity, whether through objectification or denial (within the framework of political semiosis, these contraries amount to the same thing). The very configuration of factors on which we base the formation and action of a political entity derealizes and disqualifies it at the same time. This thinking leads Laclau toward a highly qualified sense of the reality that can be extrapolated from the observation of political process. "Antagonism is the *limit of all objectivity*," underscores Laclau. This is not to say "that antagonism does not have an objective meaning, but is that which prevents the constitution of objectivity itself."[19]

> The Hegelian conception of contradiction subsumed within it both social antagonism and the processes of natural change. This was possible insofar as contradiction was conceived as an internal moment of the concept. . . . In our conception of antagonism, on the other hand, we are faced with a "constitutive outside." It is an "outside" which blocks the identity of the "inside" (and is, nonetheless, the prerequisite for its constitution at the same time). With antagonism, denial does not originate from the "inside" of identity itself, but, in its most radical sense, *from outside*; it is thus pure facticity which cannot be referred back to any underlying rationality.[20]

Laclau's pronounced appeal to the "constitutive outside," the external factors that both decide and don't decide the formation of interest groups and their calls to action, is a far cry from the smug explanations and predications with which most political punditry fulminates. Laclau infuses his political discourse with unusual openness and even susceptibility to the outside chances, the wild cards, remote contingencies on which systemic "insiders" base their fundamental understandings of themselves. These outside factors, which smack of Deleuze and Guattari's deterritorialization, are conveniently overlooked by the partisans whose worldviews most significantly depend on them. Kafka regularly places his congenital but exemplary American outsider, Karl Rossmann, directly in the trajectory of the "constitutive outside." Karl experiences its uncanny rustling in the Stoker's subjugation and submission, in Therese's mock-tragic tale of woe, in the utopian promises of the Nature Theater of Oklahoma. This static, this interference, this telephone background noise is what, in Laclau's theory, both makes the situations of Kafka's characters intelligible and leaves them open to evolution, metamorphosis, effacement. There is great literary sense in Laclau's open and susceptible political theory.

But it is not too soon to draw attention to the first element in the complex signifier "constitutive outside." In several senses, in Laclau's political theory the outside is constitutive of what goes on inside. It constitutes. It defines a state; it operates within the framework of the State. It forms and configures. It affirms, in the sense of the constative, in no simple opposition to the performative. There are many senses in which we can understand why constitution, within the parameters of Laclau's political theory, is a pivotal figure. Constitution is constructive; it allows for some positive model of political discourse and processes even as Laclau moves them away from binary logic and positivist determinations. Constitutions are the founding legal texts of democratic republics. A compelling ethos of democracy underlies Laclau's optimal scenarios for political government: often chaotic, often transpiring under the umbrella of political leadership assertive enough to furnish social stability in the civil sphere and some degree of functional efficiency and focus, but diverse and inefficient enough to preempt take-over by means of the many options for authoritarian control, whether military, economic, bureaucratic, informational, or in some fashion combined. In many respects, *constitution* represents what Laclau might well regard as the viable result of political process: constituencies are configured and set into action; their interests over and against other groupings can be enunciated in a tolerant public sphere; the measures of democratic constitutions are instituted in order to protect the populace.

One of the telling sites at which literary artifacts, as politically nuanced as they may be, part ways with political theories, even one as open and light on its feet as Laclau's, is at such a term as *constitution*. We could say that, while literary works, even ones as incomprehensible as Joyce's *Finnegans Wake*, involve a constitutive process, the work of constitution is not, in the literary artifact, as compelling or definitive, or as endowed with aspirations to duration, as it is in the endeavor of politics. To be sure, *The Man Who Disappeared* may be said to be constituted by its language of hands, its rhythm of arrests and release, its outbreaks of pandemonium in the very abyss of communication and representation. But in their proliferation and chaos, these constitutive elements of the novel undermine the configuration in which they've played a role, whereas political theorists, by contrast, would be wary of relinquishing their constitution.

And yet the dance that Laclau choreographs between literature and political thought is a compelling one. Its aura is brightest where the literary artifacts involved are densest and have been most fatally marked by modernist and postmodern experimentation. "What one gets," Laclau sums up, from his panorama of a political space in which constituencies are seasoned by marginal factors, in which constitution coexists with objectification and negation:

> is a field of simply relational identities which never manage to constitute themselves fully, since relations do not form a closed system. This has two important consequences. The first is that the identities and conditions of existence form an inseparable whole. In the case of Christian thought, there was an infinite distance between the two; in that of rationalism, an essential unity, but which was simply the necessary unity of the whole of the real; in our case, there is a more subtle dialectic between necessity and contingency as identity depends entirely on conditions of existence which are contingent, its relation with them is absolutely necessary. What we find, then, is a relationship of complete imbrication between both; essence is nothing outside its accidents. But this means—and this is the second consequence—that the antagonizing force fulfills two crucial and contradictory roles at the same time. On the one hand, it "blocks" the full constitution of the identity to which it is opposed and thus shows its contingency. But on the other hand, given that this latter identity, like all identities, is merely relational and would therefore not be what it is outside the relationship with the force antagonizing it, the latter is also part of the conditions of existence of that identity.[21]

It is the relational aspect of antagonism, not the logical matrix under which relations transpire, that Laclau emphasizes. And the terrain on which relational identities coincide is quite specifically an open field. Whether characterized explicitly or not, the field in which identity contends with contingency, on which "relational semi-identities" interact, to no definitive conclusion, can only be understood and treated as a text: a text as explored and exploited by theoretically astute practitioners of literature such as Joyce and Kafka, and by philosophers of language, whether Plato, Nietzsche, Heidegger, Benjamin, or Derrida. The collective antagonists of sociopolitical life encounter one another in a space in which their collision is not preordained. They relate to one another indirectly, by means of factors specifically excluded from the terms of antagonism.

Laclau will read the epiphenomena of political deliberation and activity in the tracings of "relational semi-identities" across a field as indeterminate as it is definitive. There is a limit to which the specificity of a political outcome, whether democratic elections or apartheid, is predicated by hardcore socioeconomic realities. Contingencies of signification and decoding play a greater role in producing a particular outcome than the ostensible determinants.

> If a set of socio-political configurations such as apartheid, for example, are conditions of the existence of the economy and capitalist accumulation, then the economy cannot be constituted as an object separate from those conditions since we know that the conditions of existence of any contingent identity are internal to the latter. What we find then, is not an interaction or determination between fully constituted areas of the social, but a field of relational semi-identities in which "political," "economic," and "ideological" elements will enter into unstable relations of imbrication without ever managing to constitute themselves as separate objects. The boundary of essence between the latter will be permanently displaced. The combinatorial permutations between hypostasized entities . . . remind one most of those economic abstractions which Marx described as "an enchanted, perverted, topsy-turvy world in which *Monsieur le Capital* and *Madame la Terre*, who are social characters as well as mere things, do their *danse macabre*." This does not mean, of course, that an area of the social cannot become autonomous and establish, to a greater or lesser degree, a separate identity. But this separation and autonomization, like everything else, has specific conditions of existence which establish their limits at the same time.[22]

None of this—not even the orchestration of Laclau's unique call, in political theory, for contingency, undecidability, and acknowledgment of positions outside the province of representability with Kafka's textual acrobatics of the asystematic, the singular, and the incommensurable—prepares us for the bizarre acuity of language and vision making possible "The Nature

Theatre of Oklahoma" at the end of *Amerika*. On the one hand, the segment is in the mainstream of Kafka's plays on fragmentation, which became a staple of his fictive practice. The episode is another one of those heavy-handed, tacked-on endings, like the summons bringing Josef K. to the Prager Dom at the end of *The Trial* in time to hear the Priest's elucidation of the parable "Before the Law." It can be argued that this narrative event, bearing the multiple significations of the parable, itself a *mise-en-scène* of language's enigmas of representation, is, more than his subsequent murder by two grisly henchpeople, the sentence for his unknown and possibly nonexistent trespasses. In both *The Trial* and *The Man Who Disappeared*, the contrived appendage of an ending overstated in its finality in fact underscores the lacunae and discontinuities of which the novel is composed. Karl Rossmann, having endured in the course of his brief stay in the U.S. a demonic nightmare of rejection by his blood relative, exploitation by unsympathetic and unethical hangers-on, repeated scrapes with a Law bearing all of the Žižekian features of totalizing arbitrariness, predetermined guilt, an irrefutable logic of the double-bind, and projective identification, is only too well-primed for posters promising steady work, social acceptance, and advancement in Oklahoma.

> The great Theatre of Oklahoma is calling you! It's calling you today only! If you miss this opportunity there will never be another! Anyone thinking of his future, your place is with us! All welcome! Anyone who wants to be an artist, step forward! We are the theatre that has a place for everyone, everyone in his place! If you decide to join us, we congratulate you here and now! But hurry, be sure not to miss the midnight deadline! We shut down at midnight, never to reopen! Accursed be anyone who doesn't believe us![23]

The reception facility for the theater is in Clayton, a location presumably not far from the East Coast, where Karl has disembarked in the country and spent all his time. In uncanny anticipation of the Paris Vélodrome, a major collection site for the World War II deportations of Jews and other undesirables, depicted strikingly by Joseph Losey in "Monsieur Klein," Kafka sets the welcoming and sorting of the Nature Theatre applicants in a horse-racing track in Clayton, a day's train ride from Oklahoma, where Karl and the novel never arrive.

Writing from Prague in the 1910s and basing his images of America exclusively on secondhand accounts in journalism, literature, and cinema,

Kafka terminates Karl's diabolical encounter with the U.S. in what can only be described, with the benefit of historical hindsight, as a concentration camp, albeit the fictional embodiment of a "good concentration camp," one holding out promises for its internees more hopeful than near-certain death. Or perhaps there is a bizarre railroad turntable in the twentieth-century imaginary, at which the constructive image of Ellis Island, the main entry point into the U.S. for immigrants, even with its sifting and sorting and health testing, switches off into what were to become the death camps, with their simulated welcome and their fatal lineups either to the right or the left. This is how it plays near the termination of Kafka's novel: "As you've already seen from our posters, we can use everyone," declares the theater's director of personnel.

> "But of course we need to know what an applicant's previous occupation was, so that we can put him somewhere where his experience will be of use to us." But it's a theatre, Karl thought dubiously, and listened very closely. "Therefore," continued the head of personnel, "we have set up reception suites in the bookmakers' booths, one office for each type of profession. So I want you all to tell me your previous occupations, families generally go the office of the man, then I will lead you to your respective offices, where first your papers and then your qualifications will be tested by experts in the field—just a very short test, nothing to be afraid of. . . . All right, let's begin. Do there happen to be any engineers among you?" Karl stepped forward.[24]

With the irony of history, we know that the death meted out at places like Auschwitz and Bergen-Belsen, as throughout the long history of genocide in the twentieth century, whether in Cambodia or Rwanda, is similarly receptive and democratic vis-à-vis the targeted population. Kafka's imaginary becomes a site at which the unprecedented welcome to the Other unfurled at Ellis Island inches forward, under the fiction of an uncannily otherworldly welcome center, presided over by relays of oversized angels and devils, promising immediate artistic virtuosity to those who have never held a trumpet, toward what was to become, under authoritarian military administration, the Real of another sort of collection site for concentrations of people. Kafka would not be unmindful of the ironies attending the deployment of concentration technology by the major democratic powers, in the facilitation of their occasional purposes, whether in refugee camps that become human staging areas for decades or in preemptive holding centers for terrorists. So acutely attuned are Kafka's literary antennae—here I conflate him with Gregor—to the gathering flows and tendencies of twentieth-century politics that he anticipates by a quarter of a century the actuality of the industrially configured system of apprehension and collection, imprisonment, execution, and disposal of large populations first put into service by the Nazi regime. Laclau reminds us that even this horrific state of affairs resulted from a process of political antagonism, a not necessarily rational deliberation involving a nation's myths, representations of history, and marked signifiers, amid the play of hegemony and contingency.

> Social relations are always contingent relations. . . . Without power, there would be no objectivity at all. . . . Republican identity, the "people" are exclusively the denial of the forces opposed to it. Without that opposition, the elements constituting popular unity would disintegrate and its identity would fall apart." Bernstein rightly sustained that the unity of the German working class was simply the result of repression during the anti-socialist laws.[25]

We are not entitled, in other words, to pass off even the most egregious cases of political disaster as absolute.

The extraordinary instance of Kafka's literary synthesis and historico-political foresight in *The Man Who Disappeared* highlights the intense tango between politics and the literary. Kafka is obviously deeply interested in political process and acutely attuned to it. But for all its political themes, "The Nature Theatre of Oklahoma" episode also makes a splendid apotheosis to the novel, reiterating its major motifs on an epic scale, gesturing with an index and indexical finger to unresolved issues and energies. By the same token, hands definitely play within the novel's thematics of discovery and blasé recognition, release and arrest, welcome and enslavement. They comprise a marvelous shorthand figure for the novel's key movements and Karl's pivotal discoveries. Yet Kafka's insinuation of hands into every possible dramatic situation and linguistic context, an undergrowth of hands that overwhelms the semantic texture, is ultimately a literary epiphenomenon, annexing all kinds of concerns and apprehensions. Indeed, architectural, technological, ecological, and psycho-sexual as well as political tracks fan out from the novel's railroad station of thinking. The discourse of psychoanalysis might take up these hands as revolting, squirmy, extensions of the Real insinuating themselves into constructed American environments of administrative order and commercial exchange, if not malls, then the Hotel Occidental elevator and telephone systems.

But at a certain point political theory, even programmed as openly as in Laclau's practice, has to bid these uncannily proliferating hands a fond farewell or good riddance. Among their other gestures, the hands flaunt the Western philosophical operating system, with which political theory, and indeed any theoretical discourse with aspirations to conceptual rigor, cannot dispense entirely. Indeed, Laclau has no interest whatsoever in dissimulating the role of venerable and well-tested arguments and terms from the history of philosophy in his synthesis of a viable perspective from which political processes and phenomena can be analyzed: relations of contradiction, antagonism, objectivity, universalization, identity, and exclusion proliferate throughout his treatment. It is pivotal to Laclau that, at different points, the disputations of Plato, Aristotle, Hegel, St Just, and Derrida remain accessible and to some degree transferable to the scenarios of the exteriority or inexplicitness of the terms of political antagonism, the inseparability of political epiphenomena such as apartheid and death camps from "conditions of the economy and capitalist accumulation,"[26] and the unevenness of power between the undecidable and the choices that constitute subjectivity.[27] To the extent that philosophy comprises Western culture's cumulative conceptual and rhetorical resource for negotiating relations, whether of a logical, political, psychological, linguistic, sociological, economic, or even mathematical nature, Laclau would not want his recasting of a dynamic, context-specific, and contingent political theory to be extraneous to its operating system.

Literature is, by the same token, always attuned to the prevailing constellation of problems and concepts articulated and orchestrated by philosophy. Literature appeals to the current deliberations of philosophy to legitimate its own explorations. We might say that it is through philosophy that literature establishes the recognition of the more conceptual registers of its working through. But where literary aesthetics demands the effacement of any recognizable conceptual motive—demands this disabling and camouflage in any number of interests, including unpredictability, style, and formal contingencies of language—philosophy, even where it is playful, cannot definitively disavow the elaboration of properties within the archive of concepts and logical operations.

The tangible impacts of systems weigh heavier upon the programmers of political theory than upon the last-minute improvisers of literature. In different respects, epistolary, dialogic, and carnivalesque novels, the freewheeling poetic epics of the twentieth century, whether by Pound, Zukofsky, or Merrill, and Walter Benjamin's mammoth *Arcades Project* establish literature as a sticky Web site or chatroom to which all kinds of cultural materials get appended. Literature is inconsistent in the degree to which it processes, elucidates, or renders intelligible the materials that it assimilates or incorporates, by whatever principles of recognition, affinity, or association. This does not prevent it, as we have seen with Kafka, from being uncannily lucid in its political apprehensions. Literature is one of several media that put the materials of culture *out there*. To the extent that such a literary work as Kafka's *The Man Who Disappeared* encompasses and disguises serious political thought and the disturbing conclusions that might be drawn from it, it serves the multiple communicative, dissimulatory, and placatory functions of the Freudian dream.

In hegemonic terms, contemporary technological societies are more comfortable understanding political material in a literary format than in the discourse of political theory. The skills of literacy and their evaluative extension in "critical thinking" are widely understood to be integral to the efficiency and success of a whole range of socioeconomic enterprises, from the multinational corporation to the small private business. It seems possible to demonstrate that Kafka is a slippery fish indeed, that his bizarre prescience combined with his poetic gifts and a perverse gravitation toward the counterintuitive enable his writing to slip beyond the parameters of any theory, whether a psychoanalytical one by Lacan or a political one by Laclau. But such a demonstration limits itself to aesthetic celebration, to a definition of art as a neutral or "conflict-free" zone in which different media and discourses disguise themselves. More satisfying, it seems to me, at least at the present moment, when news broadcasts calibrated to different degrees of verisimilitude and entertainment value vie for TV market share, is renovating the literary classroom into a site for unscrambling the political messages embedded in the literature deemed salutary to teach. Here, it seems, Laclau's political theory and the political extensions of Lacanian psychoanalysis serve as invaluable resources in furnishing templates for the political decoding of aesthetic properties.

However much at certain points they pull apart, literature and political theory every bit as significantly pull together. They both take as their motive a constitutive incompletion. The space of literature is the horizon of forms, the Derridean *khōra*,[28] in which ideology is always confronted by possibility, in particular, the possibilities that totalization and exegetical irresponsibility have counted out. For Laclau, it is the very incompletion of the social that marks the spot whence its radical democratization can emerge:

> Society, then, is ultimately unrepresentable: any representation—and thus any space—is an attempt to constitute society, not to state what it is. But the antagonistic moment of collision between the various representations cannot be reduced to space, and is itself unrepresentable. It is therefore mere event, mere temporality. For reasons we have explained, this final incompletion of the social is the main source of our political hope in the contemporary world: only it can assure the conditions for a radical democracy.[29]

Laclau brings ultimately philosophical formats of spatiality, temporality, and representation to bear on an incompletion that is both a motive for art and a call for social activism. He is unusual in the degree to which he acknowledges the play of the incomplete within his project and even his thinking. In important respects, then, he is a brother-in-arms to Kafka, whose fictive sketches of incompletion, say, the Great Wall or the Castle, are legendary. No authority on signification could be emptier than the Old Commandant in the Penal Colony; no more banal evil could be supercharged with the force of law.

Of course, we can never reach an end to this topic, because its limitations and frustrations are endemic. Is literature fated simply to incorporate its sociopolitical surround, without comment, as it were, merely as another element in the landscape or ecology? Would this stance of neutrality amount to a political message in its own right, a "don't touch or go there" policy? Artists and writers are often partisans in an implicit cultural resistance to the ideological cant, and the misadventures calibrated to it, of their day. Are these the actions of literary producers or programmers, as operators, or is there something in linguistic codes themselves that is inimical to authoritarian oversimplification and generalization, that inherently partakes, irrespective of the author's "conscious" politics, in a politically edifying position? Or does the very intransigence of verbal, iconic, and musical notation systems preempt any clear political positionality and satisfaction?

Wouldn't such anomalies as Pound's synthesis of a radically inclusive poetic collage, one often taken to be the distinctive experiment of modernist verse inscription, or Céline's prosaic correlative, a fictive narrative that meanders anywhere by means of a ubiquitous copula of ellipses, frustrate the very possibility of criticism's messianic reform through the medium and institution of language?

I cannot pretend to resolve these age-old questions and anomalies. Others have devoted lifetimes to them. One example would be Bertolt Brecht's alienation effect (*Verfremdungseffekt*), the dramatic correlative to Benjamin's dialectical image:[30] a didactic education of the audience achieved by snaring it in the irremediably counterpoised social forces of the day, which have been, through many intellectual lenses and technical devices, projected on stage. Brechtian epic theater, according to Benjamin, performs the work of psychotherapy in the public sphere, in the venue of spectacle. As sleep is an enabling condition for the surprise of the Freudian dream, Brechtian drama lulls the spectator into a relaxation that is both conducive to and in stark contrast with the realities of political oppression and class conflict that the drama unfolds. The theater, not unlike the staging of "The Mousetrap" in *Hamlet*, becomes a lieu or *khōra* for public disclosure of the traumatic impasses besetting audience and society as they hurtle, in the actuality of the present, toward disaster. Brecht surely did not hold himself above the minute musical, scenographic, sartorial, and semiological calculations necessary to establish the spectacular intimacy capable of transforming of the theater into a dialectical mousetrap. With precision he planned and coordinated the poetry, song, stage props, signs, and other technological elements that would both create an intimate rapport with the spectator and amplify a calculated shock, one equally aesthetic and political in its impact. It is no accident that Brecht would have sought "Alienation Effects in Chinese Acting," or that in this essay he would have characterized the artistry as follows:

> The artist's object is to appear strange and even surprising to the audience. He achieves this by looking strangely at himself and his work. As a result everything put forward by him has a touch of the amazing. Everyday things are thereby raised above the level of the obvious and the automatic. . . . The Chinese artist's performance often strikes the Western actor as cold. That does not mean that the Chinese theatre rejects all representation of feelings. The performer performs incidents of utmost passion, but without his delivery becoming heated. At those points where the character portrayed is deeply excited the performer takes

a lock of hair between his lips and chews it. But this is like a ritual, there is nothing eruptive about it. . . . The performer shows that this man is not in control of himself, and he points to the outward signs.[31]

Any political bombshells directed at the audience from the Brechtian stage emerge through intricate loops of displacement, dissimulation, and indirection. Only through these feints do the arbitrariness and contingency of the political become Real. To be politically affected through the aesthetic in this way demands an act of submission by the audience, who may venture into the theater from the workers' suburban quarters. The experience of theater is a temporary incarceration in a medium that has embedded and performed the sociopolitical double messages and disconnects of the moment. Everything about theater, the medium as well as the spectator's experience, is a matter of domination and submission:

> The theatre can only adopt such a free attitude if it lets itself be carried along by the strongest currents in its society and associates itself with those most impatient to make great alterations there. The bare wish, if nothing else to evolve an art fit for the times must drive our theatre of the scientific age straight out into the suburbs, where it can stand as it were wide open, at the disposal of those who live hard and produce much, so that they can be fruitfully entertained there with their great problems. They may find it hard to pay for our art, and immediately to grasp the new method of entertainment, and we shall have to learn in many respects what they need and how they need it; but we can be sure of their interest.[32]

Brecht thought as long and as hard as anyone about the possibilities of a politically programmed theater. Arguably, some of his most striking aesthetic innovations have been successfully transferred to the domain of cinema. Such films as *Magnolia*, *American Beauty*, and *Short Cuts* come to mind. Given current levels of cultural literacy and engagement in the U.S., Brecht's confidence in the unassailable, widespread interest in his dramaturgy leaves me dubious. In the end, all I can leave you with is a something, rather, the trace or tatter of something, a residue, namely, a swath of textual material that another author, James Joyce, synthesized for his final major project, *Finnegans Wake*. As we noted in Chapter 3, the *Wake* is virtually unreadable. Its textual material is a "sufflosion" of ungrammatical sentences supersaturated with double entendres and other outrages of signification appended to a narrative structure—a loose myth of familial bonds, rivalries, sweet intimacies, and tragic eventualities—so minimal as to buttress up nothing. (Indeed, Finn McCool, its mythical prototype, is the casualty of a wall imploding upon him.) It is a work characterized by no national, ethnic, or ethical integrity. It is so saturated with interlinguistic puns that it scarcely occupies the pale of any national language, most of all its "native" English. Indeed, it ends up radically questioning the bases and viability of national languages in general. At a time when Joyce could, and should in many ways, have capitalized on the consummate success of *Ulysses*, arguably the ultimate novel to emerge from the global, not just Western history of the genre, he spent the last seventeen years of his life, 1922–39, almost to the time of his death, composing this embarrassment for literary convention. And he wasn't under contract to any of the major movie studios.

A postmodern work and comment on culture, *Finnegans Wake* devotes more of its resources to synthesizing a telling textual medium, a literary analogon to atonal music, than to arriving at a masterfully calibrated plot or perfectly formed segments or episodes. Any political work that *Finnegans Wake* undertakes consists in a productive embedding of the political in the very fabric or material of articulation, whether discourse, images, or musical notes. The discourse of *Finnegans Wake* is political in the relentlessness of thought and mindfulness it imposes on its readers, who, through the interface of its "soundsense" and "sensesound,"[33] are also its listeners. *Finnegans Wake* is a monument to the literary passive aggression that resists patent signification at every turn. It is the ultimate work of resistance, passive or not. It either drowns everyday sense and expectation in a cascade of puns, assonances, homonyms, double entendres, multilinguistic ambiguity, and other qualifications, or it thwarts the emergence of patterning and hence generalization through a belligerent dwelling in substandard plot, narrative development, characterization, chapters, sentence structure, and structure in general. *Finnegans Wake* resists, in a magnificent and unforgettable fashion, by compulsively switching off to either more or less than it's supposed to do. In the alternation, and sometimes simultaneity, of its compulsive excess and minimalism, it forces its audience, its community, to go into hyperthink at every turn. I leave you with the possibility of a political dimension in the signifying media in which we all truck, whether we write, program computers, compose music, or do video or film. If our own political moment is any example, the need and even responsibility, in Derrida's sense,

202   *Idylls of the Wanderer*

to upgrade the quality and level of public thought is endemic to all sociohistorical configurations. Bemoaning the current oversimplification of public thought will hardly garner votes or win popularity contests, but each of us favors certain registers of signification, as Joyce did. It is within the domain of our literacy, within the realm of our empowerment as language operators, to encrypt them with the notation of a politics of justice, *justesse* (a pun Derrida makes), and thoughtfulness.

I leave you with the following passage from chapter 1.1, the initiation of *Finnegans Wake*:

> What then agentlike brought about that tragoady thundersday this municipal sin business? Our cubehouse still rocks as earwitness to the thunder of his arafatas but we hear also through successive ages that shebby choruysh of unkalified muzzlenmiissilehims that would blackguardise the whitestone ever hurdleturtled out of heaven. Stay us wherefore in our search for tighteousness, O Sustainer, what time we rise and when we take up to toothmick and before we lump down upown our leatherbed and in the night and at the fading of the stars! For a nod to the nabir is better than wink to the wabsanti. Otherways wesways like that provost scoffing beduoueen the jebel and the jpsian sea. Cropherb the crunchbracken shall decide. Then we'll know if the feast is a flyday. She has a gift of seek on sight and she allcasually ansars helpers, the dreamydeary. Heed! Heed! It may have been a missfired brick, as some say, or it mought have been due to a collupsus of his back promises, as others looked at it. (There extand by now one thousand and one stories, all told, of the same).[34]

This passage intervenes just a few pages into the novel. It continues to expatiate on Finnegan's fall, or "pftjschute" on the first page, commemorated in the assonances of a hundred-letter thunder word composed of adjacent nonsense syllables, at the same time as it belongs to the overall process of disclosure by which the singular Wakean idiom comes into its own. There is a religious dimension to this passage, for it rises in prayer. Indeed, in the concatenation of the textual tricks and time bombs that the passage releases, it subjects organized religion, as it would respond to an event such as the death of Finnegan, to a devastating satire. The compulsively polymorphous idiom that Joyce has synthesized for this novel, whose elements include: strategic misspelling (e.g., "tragoady's," including "goad"); the unmarked splicing in of momentary submotifs, here related to Islam; compulsive punning, as when "between" becomes arabicized to "bedoueen"; and relentless interlinguistic fusions, as when "Thursday" appears in its Germanic articulation as "thundersday" and the composite "muzzlenimiisilehims" retains the German sense of "Musselmann," or Muslim. Not only does a torrent, or "coruysh" of hymns, Muslim or otherwise, take over this passage; the signifier *coruysh* grafts the episode onto the history of rivalry and strife between Shi'ite and Sunni Muslims, to the Karajihites, an early pious sect of Islam responsible for the death of Caliph Ali, the Prophet's son-in-law. The Wahabis, religious leaders of the Arabian peninsula over the past three-plus centuries, get a nod in the passage as well: "For a nod to the nabir is better than wink to the wabsanti."

In place of the sedimentary prose invoked so often by culture in its founding documents, constitutions, legal codes, and wills, Joyce compulsively substitutes the liquid medium of language as a river, all of whose stops have been pulled out. Amid the whirls and eddies of this river of language, different thematic motifs, whether religions, foods, letters, or geographical features—including rivers—surface, in spots, at the level of explicitness, only to be replaced by other riffs. References to Islam, words in Arabic, and a general openness to the Muslim world simply consolidate themselves in the course of the novel. It is clear that, to Joyce, Islam is closely linked, in the continuity of a Moebius strip and by appealing to a global composite of major world languages, to the other two major Abrahamic faiths.[35] In a discursive space configured by the continuity and contiguity of languages, there is simply no place for the marginalization of any bona fide site of cultural inscription. There is no motive for the declaration of rogues. The overall thrust is in the direction both of the dissemination of the seeds of meaning and the confluence of the formulations seeded by words.

The politics of literature may well eventuate in an impasse in which we each discover our medium, and then labor, for as many lifetimes as we can cram into a life, to implant the greatest radical, thought-engendering density into the medium we cultivate, serve, and in a limited sense command. We all struggle to calibrate the precise plane and venue of that improvisation. The linguistic contingencies in the design and delivery of our interventions are superordinant. Literary art concentrates and displays our primary weapons as we negotiate the continuum between private language and engaged intervention in the public sphere. "You too have weapons," is Kafka's last phrase in the *Diaries*.[36]

NOTES

PREFACE

1. Maurice Blanchot, "Literature and the Original Experience," in *The Space of Literature*, trans. Ann Smock (Lincoln: University of Nebraska Press, 1989), 238.
2. See, above all, the subsection of Blanchot's *The Space of Literature* titled "The Work's Space and Its Demand," 22, 52, 62. See also his *The Infinite Conversation*, trans. Susan Hanson (Minneapolis: University of Minnesota Press, 1993), 99, 176, 196, 240.
3. For the notion of the Open, see Martin Heidegger, *Poetry, Language, Thought*, trans. Albert Hofstadter (New York: Harper and Row, 1962), 39, 43, 45–47, 49, 55, 59–63, 65–66, 69–72 (from "The Origin of the Work of Art"); also 106–10, 112–23, 120–22, 125–28, 130–32, 136, 138, 140–41 (from "What Are Poets For?").
4. The present study would not exist were it not for the quality of the Philadelphia libraries, archives, and arts resources available to me as a young person simply by dint of my being a resident of its metropolitan area. I remember such rich cultural ports as the Free Library of Philadelphia, the Philadelphia Art Museum, the Franklin Institute, and the Academy of Music with particular vividness, warmth, and gratitude.
5. See, e.g., Jacques Derrida, *Rogues*, trans. Pascale-Anne Brault and Michael Naas (Stanford: Stanford University Press, 2005), 52–55, 62, 82–83, 91, 101, 112–14, 124–25, 150.
6. See Sigmund Freud, "The 'Uncanny'" (1919), in Freud, *Writings on Art and Literature* (Stanford: Stanford University Press, 1997), 193–233.
7. The idea that language is the home base for all cultural interactions is hardly a new one, and Martin Heidegger elaborates it with far more eloquence, philosophical depth, and rigor than I do. What sends my current discussion in a homeward direction is the notion of the classroom as temporary intellectual housing. Students epitomize the nomadic life, and those who instruct them

need to be adept both at building a firm foundation and at dismantling the pedagogical stage set in preparation for forthcoming dislocations and sit-ins. See Heidegger, "Building Dwelling Thinking," in *Poetry, Language, Thought*, 146, 153, 160–61.

8. Maurice Blanchot, "The Essential Solitude," in *The Station Hill Blanchot Reader*, trans. L. Davis, P. Auster, and R. Lamberton (Barrytown, N.Y.: Station Hill Press, 1999), 412.

9. A rich contemporary literature tracks the constitution, functions, and parameters of systems, the patterns they form and over which they preside, their relations to their surrounding contexts and environments, and the kinds of turbulence and chaos that either "opposes" them or can be illuminated in their wake. Systems theory is one of the clear directions for further study indicated by the present volume, with its circulation around inscriptive and exegetical parameters of interiority and exteriority. It is one I much look forward to pursuing. For basic and indispensable readings concerning systematic parameters, their closure and/or openness, their interplay with the environment, their patterning, and their accommodation of turbulence, see: Anthony Wilden, *System and Structure* (London: Tavistock Publications, 1972), 155–229; Niklas Luhmann, *Social Systems*, trans. John Bednarz, Jr. (Stanford: Stanford University Press, 1995), 12–102, 176–209; James Gleick, *Chaos* (New York: Penguin Books, 1987), 9–31, 81–153, 215–40; and Fritjof Capra, *The Web of Life* (New York: Anchor Books, 1996), 36–153. I'm indebted to N. Katherine Hayles and James H. Bunn for orienting me to this literature.

10. Franz Kafka, *Diaries 1914–1923*, ed. Max Brod (New York: Schocken, 1965), 200–201.

11. See, e.g., Harry Frankfurt's recent study *On Bullshit* (Princeton: Princeton University Press, 2005).

12. See, e.g., Ernesto Laclau, "Why Do Empty Signifiers Matter in Politics?" in his *Emancipation(s)* (London: Verso, 1996), 36–46; also Ernesto Laclau and Chantal Mouffe, *Hegemony and Socialist Strategy* (London: Verso, 1985), 111–14, 134–45, 152–59.

13. Henry Sussman, *The Aesthetic Contract: Statutes of Art and Intellectual Work in the Broader Modernity* (Stanford: Stanford University Press, 1997).

14. Kant's classic formulation, in *Critique of Judgment*, runs as follows: "Taste, like the judgment in general, is the discipline (or training) of genius; it clips its wings, it makes it cultured and polished; but, at the same time, it gives guidance as to where and how far it may extend itself if it is to remain purposive." In this pivotal passage, Kant invokes the socially legislated parameters of taste as a speed-governor or guardrail protecting both the artist and the communities in which she interacts against the potential excess and monstrosity of her aesthetic innovation and private language (Kant, *Critique of Judgment*, ed. J. H. Bernard [New York: Hafner Press, 1951], 163).

15. See Niklas Luhmann, *Art as a Social System*, trans. Eva M. Knodt (Stanford: Stanford University Press, 2000), 15–20, 22–26, 54–63, 74–76, 79–90, 102–11.

16. Marcel Proust, *Swann's Way*, in *Remembrance of Things Past*, trans. C. K. Scott Moncrieff and Terence Kilmartin (New York: Random House, 1982), 1:355–56.

17. Ibid., 1:377.

18. For the notion of smooth space, see Gilles Deleuze and Félix Guattari, *A Thousand Plateaus*, trans. Brian Massumi (Minneapolis: University of Minnesota Press, 1987), 478–500.

19. A seminal work in this movement, Stephen Pfohl's *Death at the Parasite Café: Social Science (Fictions) and the Postmodern* (New York: St. Martin's Press, 1992) takes a theoretical approach in achieving surreal narrative effects. Derek Sayer's *Going Down for Air: A Memoir in Search of a Subject* (Boulder: Paradigm Publishers, 2004) illustrates the full palette of possibilities at the intersection between sociological thinking and memoir. Allen Shelton's *Dreamworlds of Alabama* (Minneapolis: University of Minnesota Press, forthcoming), plumbs to the very roots of *engagé* sociological sensibility at the same time that it explores a perpetual hinterland in the eyes of the mainstream U.S. imaginary, but one currently in a jarring phase of transformation. A recent sociological work notable for the centrality of its author's firsthand experiences and perspectives is Jackie Orr's *Panic Diaries: A Genealogy of Panic Disorder* (Durham: Duke University Press, 2006). Shelton is a cross-town colleague of mine at Buffalo State College. I am considerably in his debt for his intellectual receptivity and for introducing me to such writers as Pfohl, Sayer, and Orr.

20. The visual materials of W. G. Sebald's *Vertigo*, for example, include: sketches by Stendhal; the title page to Franz Werfel's novel *Verdi*, with a dedication that the author presented to Franz Kafka; a postcard from the Hotel Sandwirth in Riva, Italy, where Kafka stayed during one of his rare escapes from Prague; and a replacement identity document furnished to Sebald by the German consulate in Milan during his Italian travels.

21. Sebald's *Austerlitz*, e.g., chronicles the gradual recollection of his wartime displacements and related traumatic events by a fictive character, Jacques Austerlitz, who recounts his story in different locations over several years to the narrator, who doubles as Sebald.

22. This is in sharp contradistinction, in the entertainment industry, journalism, and the governmental agencies of information and misinformation, to the current blurring of the lines between news, information, and marketing.

1. IDYLLS OF THE WANDERER

1. Franz Kafka, *The Castle*, trans. Willa and Edwin Muir (New York: Schocken, 1992), 138–39.

208   Notes to Pages 2–11

2. Although it is set in an undisclosed rural location known simply as "the Village," the inn has a name that coincides with one of the long-standing major coffeehouses of Vienna, a veritable temple of what Simmel would call sociability. It is against the backdrop of this sociability that K.'s senses of alienation and disorientation are to be measured.

3. Franz Kafka, "The Metamorphosis," in *The Complete Stories*, ed. Nahum N. Glatzer (New York: Schocken Books, 1970), 98.

4. For a fuller treatment of this story, see my "A Note on the Public and Private in Literature: The Literature of 'Acting Out,'" *Modern Language Notes* 104 (1989): 605–11.

5. This term attains prominence in Heidegger's "The Principle of Identity" ("Der Satz der Identität"). See Martin Heidegger, *Identity and Difference*, trans. Joan Stambaugh (New York: Harper and Row, 1969), 35–36, 38, 99, 100, 103, 105.

6. See Louis Althusser, "Ideology and the State," in *Lenin and Philosophy and Other Esaays*, trans. Ben Brewster (New York: Monthly Review Press, 1971), 175.

7. Jacques Derrida, "Ulysses Gramophone," in *Acts of Literature*, ed. Derek Attridge (New York: Routledge, 1992), 253–309; and "A Silkworm of One's Own," in Hélène Cixous and Jacques Derrida, *Veils*, trans. Geoffrey Bennington (Stanford: Stanford University Press, 2001), 21–92; rpt. in Jacques Derrida, *Acts of Religion*, ed. Gil Anidjar (New York: Routledge, 2002), 309–55.

8. Jacques Derrida, *Of Grammatology*, trans. Gayatri Chakravorty Spivak (Baltimore: The Johns Hopkins University Press, 1976).

9. Jacques Derrida, *Speech and Phenomena*, trans. and introd. David B. Allison (Evanston, Ill.: Northwestern University Press, 1973).

10. Jacques Derrida, *Writing and Difference*, trans. Alan Bass (Chicago: University of Chicago Press, 1978).

11. Ferdinand de Saussure, *Course in General Linguistics*, trans. Wade Baskin (New York: McGraw-Hill, 1966).

12. Derrida, *Of Grammatology*, 30.

13. Ibid., 35.

14. Ibid., 52.

15. Ibid., 35.

16. Jacques Derrida, "Des Tours de Babel," in Derrida, *Acts of Religion*, 102–34.

17. See Rodolphe Gasché's by now classic *The Tain of the Mirror: Derrida and the Philosophy of Reflection* (Cambridge: Harvard University Press, 1986), 142–251.

18. Derrida, *Of Grammatology*, 68–69.

19. This, of course, in *Beyond the Pleasure Principle* (1920), in Sigmund Freud, *The Standard Edition of the Complete Psychological Works of Sigmund Freud*, trans. James Strachey (London: Hogarth Press, 1953–74), 18:6–74.

20. Jacques Derrida, "Différance," in *Speech and Phenomena*, 129–60; rpt. in Derrida, *Margins of Philosophy*, trans. Alan Bass (Chicago: University of Chicago Press, 1982), 1–28; Derrida, "Ousia and Grammē," in *Margins of Philosophy*, 29–68.

21. Jacques Derrida and Maurizio Ferraris, *A Taste for the Secret* (Cambridge: Polity Press, 2002), 27.

22. Ibid., 85.

23. A phrase from Theodore Roethke's "Light Listened." See his *The Collected Poems of Theodore Roethke* (Garden City, N.Y.: Doubleday, 1966), 212.

24. A phrase from l. 48 of William Wordsworth's "Lines Composed a Few Miles above Tintern Abbey," in *Selected Poems and Prefaces by William Wordsworth*, ed. Jack Stillinger (Boston: Houghton Mifflin, 1965), 109.

25. The title of a short story collection by William H. Gass. See his *In the Heart of the Heart of the Country and Other Stories* (New York: Harper and Row, 1968).

26. J. Hillis Miller breaks new ground in his long-standing investigation into speech acts in literature in his *Literature as Conduct: Speech Acts in Henry James* (New York: Fordham University Press, 2005). The unpredictable moment at which the reader initiates the synthesis of writing (as far as I am concerned, as much a distinctive ontological state as a formal compositional process) is reminiscent of Miller's account of the vertigo surrounding decisions in de Man and James. See *Literature as Conduct*, 81–83.

27. In my *The Aesthetic Contract: Statutes of Art and Intellectual Work in Modernity* (Stanford: Stanford University Press, 1997), 165–205.

28. Georg Simmel, "Sociability as the Autonomous Form of Sociation," in *The Sociology of Georg Simmel*, trans. Kurt H. Wolff (New York: Free Press, 1950), 46–47.

29. Ibid.

30. Simmel, "The Isolated Individual and the Dyad," in *The Sociology of Georg Simmel*, 119.

31. Georg Wilhelm Friedrich Hegel, *Hegel's Phenomenology of Spirit*, trans. A. V. Miller (Oxford: Oxford University Press, 1977), 111–19.

32. Howard S. Becker, *Outsiders: Studies in the Sociology of Deviance* (New York: The Free Press, 1963).

33. This is the title of one of Goffman's major studies. See his *Interaction Ritual: Essays on Face-to-Face Behavior* (New York: Pantheon Books, 1967).

34. See Erving Goffman, *The Presentation of the Self in Everyday Life* (New York: Doubleday Anchor, 1959), 17–76; *Frame Analysis* (Boston: Northeastern University Press, 1986), 1–39.

35. This point is powerfully made by Zeev Sternhell in his overview of the ideological foundations of fascism in nineteenth-century science and thought. See his *Neither Left nor Right: Fascist Ideology in France* (Berkeley: University of California Press, 1986), 1–6, 11–12, 21–28, 32–43.

36. See, e.g., the notion of responsibility as Jacques Derrida develops it in "Faith and Knowledge: The Two Sources of 'Religion' at the Limits of Reason Alone," trans. Samuel Weber, in Jacques Derrida and Gianni Vattimo, eds., *Religion* (Stanford: Stanford University Press, 1998), 32, 37–38, 61; rpt. in *Acts of Religion*, 69, 72–73, 96. The "ethics of reading" is a notion developed by J. Hillis Miller in *The Ethics of Reading* (New York: Columbia University Press, 1987).

37. Friedrich Nietzsche, *Human, All Too Human: A Book for Free Spirits*, trans. R. J. Hollingdale (Cambridge: Cambridge University Press, 1996). References to this edition will be both by page and by volume (1 or 2), chapter, and numbered section.

38. The Benjaminian notion of the constellation denotes not only a historical compendium or aggregate of texts, each contributing to the other's significance and intelligibility, but also the only methodological practice—the assembly of the inevitable textual rhizome configured at any distinctive moment—capable of lending authenticity to historical oversight. *The Arcades Project* is a rhizomatic assemblage of textual resources regarding Paris during the Second Empire, interspersed with Benjamin's marginal observations and configured as a mega-textual constellation or print-medium Web site. It is a "natural" source for some of his comments regarding the constellation. See Walter Benjamin, *The Arcades Project*, ed. Howard Eiland and Kevin McLaughlin (Cambridge: Harvard University Press, 1999), 462–63, 477, 470, 475, 540.

39. Nietzsche, *Human, All Too Human*, 2.1.220, p. 266.

40. I am here punning on the connection between the underscoring or emphasis selected by a work and its signature. At the outset of his Kafka essay, in a parable called "Die Underschrift," Walter Benjamin explores the in part horrifying play between identity and alienation effected by the gesture of signature. See Walter Benjamin, *Selected Writings* (Cambridge: Harvard University Press, 1999), 2:794–95.

41. Nietzsche, *Human, All Too Human*, 1.1.3, p. 13.

42. Ibid., 2.2.243, p. 270.

43. See Martin Heidegger, "The Origin of the Work of Art," in *Poetry, Language, Thought*, trans. Albert Hofstadter (New York: Harper and Row, 1971), 36, 41, 46, 55, 57–64, 71–72; also, *Identity and Difference*, 36–39, 101–4. For the deconstructive notions of the event and the surprise, see, among other discursive sites, Jacques Derrida, *Specters of Marx*, trans. Peggy Kamuf (New York: Routledge, 1994), 10, 21, 28, 35, 42–43, 57–60, 62–66, 69–70, 73, 104, 117, 167–70.

44. For an account of the formation and composition of the Athenaeum group, see Philippe Lacoue-Labarthe and Jean-Luc Nancy, *The Literary Absolute*, trans. Philip Barnard and Cheryl Lester (Albany: State University of New York Press, 1988), 7–12.

45. With "shock," I am referring to Benjamin's problematic of the traumatic concussion characteristic of modern commerce and human relationships,

a motif he gleans from the poetry of Baudelaire, the fiction of Poe, the lithographs of Senefelder and Daumier, and the interweaving of prostitution and gambling in the cosmopolitan city, among other sources. See his "On Some Motifs in Baudelaire," in *Selected Writings*, vol. 4, *1938–1940*, trans. Edmund Jephcott and others, ed. Howard Eiland and Michael W. Jennings (Cambridge: Harvard University Press, 2003), 319–24, 327–32.

46. Nietzsche, *Human, All Too Human*, 2.1.219, p. 265.

47. See, above all, Jacques Derrida, *Spurs: Nietzsche's Styles / Éperons: Les Styles de Nietzsche*, trans. Barbara Harlow (Chicago: University of Chicago Press, 1979).

48. Nietzsche, *Human, All Too Human*, 2.2.111, p. 337.

49. Ibid., 2.2.87, p. 332.

50. Ibid., pp. 26–27, 33, 253, 329, 343, 351, 367.

51. Ibid., 1.6.358, p. 143.

52. Ibid., 1.6.368, p. 145. Nietzsche's comments on friendship in *Human, All Too Human*, particularly his attention to the discretion that is for him the irreducible foundation of this relationship, form the basis of Jacques Derrida's wide-ranging exploration of these linguistic as well as sociological conventions in *Politics of Friendship*, trans. George Collins (London: Verso, 1997).

53. The suggested link here between the implied writer of *Human, All Too Human* and the remains of our old friend Gregor Samsa of Kafka's "The Metamorphosis" is not entirely gratuitous.

54. Nietzsche, *Human, All Too Human*, 1.4.208, p. 97.

55. Jorge Luis Borges, "The Circular Ruin," in *Collected Fictions*, trans Andrew Hurley (New York: Viking, 1998), 96. Note that the structure of a doubled literary creation, in this case arising out of intimacy with women, who are at once the author's interlocutors, image, and other, prevails in Maurice Blanchot's "Death Sentence," in *The Station Hill Blanchot Reader*, trans. Lydia Davis, Paul Auster, and Robert Lamberton (Tarrytown, N.Y.: Station Hill, 1999), 129–88.

56. Very much in the spirit of Margot Norris's *Beasts of the Modern Imagination: Darwin, Nietzsche, Kafka, Ernst, and Lawrence* (Baltimore: The Johns Hopkins University Press, 1985).

57. Nietzsche, *Human, All Too Human*, 1.9.638, p. 203.

58. "No fixed abode" is a key phrase throughout the present study. It derives from Franz Kafka's "The Cares of a Family Man" and reiterates composite creature Odradek's response to inquiries concerning his address. See Kafka, *The Complete Stories*, 428.

59. See Nietzsche, *Human, All Too Human*, 1.2.266, p. 374: "*The Impatient*—It is precisely he who is becoming who cannot endure the state of becoming: he is too impatient for it."

60. Ibid., 1.2, p. 301.

61. "The Limit-Experience" is the title of an extended essay on literary effects by Maurice Blanchot. See his *The Infinite Conversation*, trans. Susan Hanson (Minneapolis: University of Minnesota Press, 1993), 83–281.

62. Nietzsche, *Human, All Too Human*, 1.9.638, pp. 203–4.

63. Ibid., 1.2.49, p. 38. Also see, with respect to benevolence, pp. 45, 51, 179–80, 203, 229–30, 239, 332–33, 348, 391, 393.

64. Hegel, *Phenomenology of Spirit*, 90–91.

65. In his doctoral thesis at SUNY Buffalo, Christopher Devenney wrote powerfully about the "Detours of Writing." I look forward to the appearance of this work with much anticipation.

66. I am here playing off the notion of "racespeak" as it has been developed by Paul Gilroy.

67. See Heinrich von Kleist, "The Earthquake in Chile," in *The Marquise von O—and Other Stories* (New York: Penguin, 1978), 51–67. And see Melville's novella *Benito Cereno*, in Herman Melville, *The Piazza Tales and Other Prose Pieces, 1839–1860* (Evanston, Ill.: Northwestern University Press, 1987), 46–117.

68. This is, of course, the protagonist of Albert Camus's *The Stranger*, trans. Matthew Ward (New York: Vintage, 1988).

69. Emmanuel Levinas, *Totality and Infinity*, trans. Alfonso Lingis (Pittsburgh: Duquesne University Press, 1990), 37–38.

70. In "The Joke and Its Relation to the Unconscious"; See Freud, *Standard Edition*, trans. James Strachey (London: Hogarth Press, 1955–74), 8:12–13, 49, 145–55, 185–87, 194, 208–12, 26–36.

71. The threat posed by Franz Kafka's occupation as a workman's compensation attorney and by possible long-term domestic arrangements to his writing remained a persistent obsession throughout his adult life. It registered, among other sites, in the *Diaries*, ed. Max Brod (New York: Schocken Books, 1965), 1:211, 222–23, 275–76, 292–93; 2:92–95, 109, 197–201, 212, 216–17. Rainer Stach explores this theme persistently and with striking results in his groundbreaking Kafka biography; see *Kafka: The Decisive Years* (Orlando: Harcourt, 2005), 29–31, 39, 45–46, 70, 94–95, 113, 126, 146–49, 151, 237–39, 295, 326–32, 336, 358.

72. Martin Heidegger, "Building Dwelling Thinking," in *Poetry, Language, Thought*, trans. Albert Hofstadter (New York: Harper and Row, 1971), 161.

73. Derrida and Ferraris, *A Taste for the Secret*, 57–58.

2. ON THE BUTCHER BLOCK: A PANORAMA OF SOCIAL MARKING

1. Citations of the novel refer to Patrick McCabe, *The Butcher Boy* (New York: Dell Publishing, 1992).

2. See Henry Sussman, *The Aesthetic Contract: Statutes of Art and Intellectual Work in Modernity* (Stanford: Stanford University Press, 1997), 202–4, 246, 258–59.

Notes to Pages 45–59   213

3. Gilles Deleuze and Félix Guattari, *Anti-Oedipus*, trans. Robert Hurley, Mark Seem, and Helen R. Lane (Minneapolis: University of Minnesota Press, 1983), 245.

4. Gilles Deleuze and Félix Guattari, *A Thousand Plateaus*, trans. Brian Massumi (Minneapolis: University of Minnesota Press, 1987), 229–31, 241–43, 247–49, 287, 294–97.

5. McCabe, *Butcher Boy*, 89–90.

6. Ibid., 15.

7. Ibid., 16.

8. Ibid., 18.

9. Ibid., 53.

10. Ibid., 40.

11. Ibid., 41.

12. Ibid.

13. Ibid., 4.

14. Deleuze and Guattari, *A Thousand Plateaus*, 242–43, 257–59.

15. "Making things happen" is J. Hillis Miller's overall moniker for the effect of speech acts and performatives, in and outside of literature. See his *Literature as Conduct: Speech Acts in Henry James* (New York: Fordham University Press, 2005), 4, 8, 10, 22, 28, 171–72, 203, 259.

16. On the virtuality of the literary spaces that readers address and in which characters are set loose, see ibid., 50, 155–56, 166, 169–76, 178, 182, 184.

17. See Roland Barthes, *Mythologies*, trans. Annette Lavers (New York: Noonday, 1972), 114–17; *Writing Degree Zero and Elements of Semiology*, trans. Annette Lavers and Colin Smith (Boston: Beacon, 1967), 92–94; *Critical Essays*, trans. Richard Howard (Evanston, Ill.: Northwestern University Press, 1972), 272–77.

18. See Henry Sussman, *Psyche and Text: The Sublime and the Grandiose in Literature, Psychopathology, and Culture* (Albany: State University of New York Press, 1993), 22–23.

19. Cf. Genesis 4.

20. Cf. Deleuze and Guattari, *A Thousand Plateaus*, 63, 68, 134–37, 140–43.

21. Barthes, *Mythologies*, 11–12, 109–37, 155–59.

22. McCabe, *Butcher Boy*, 65.

23. Ibid., 66–67.

24. Organized by Charles Manson, the Tate-LaBianca murders took place on consecutive evenings in August 1969. Victims included Sharon Tate, who was pregnant by film director Roman Polanski, Abigail Folger, Voyter Frykowski, and Leno and Rosemarie LaBianca. Manson Family members participating in the crimes included Charles "Tex" Watson, Susan Atkins, Patricia Krenwinkel, and Linda Kasabian.

25. At the moment of writing, no element of cultural criticism within "advanced, technological society" seems more pivotal to me than discerning the

complex interplay, a movement of mutual collusion as well as undermining, between explicit, "official" religion or civil ideology and its more understated, cynical, and violent counterpart or shadow religion. The stringently racist and homophobic "surround" by which the exemplary Whittaker family finds itself judged and condemned in the U.S. during the 1950s in the recent film *Far from Heaven* may constitute the most powerful current instance of this shadow religion in the popular media. Forty years ago, Louis Althusser elaborated this duplicity in systematic terms. It arises in the tension inevitably prevailing between the ideological state apparatus and the human and material conditions that it in turn presumably regulates. See his *Lenin and Philosophy and Other Essays*, trans. Ben Brewster (New York: Monthly Review Press, 1971), 136, 143–49, 165–73.

26. One major appeal of the work that Gilles Deleuze and Félix Guattari synthesized together, including their "Capitalism and Schizophrenia" diptych and *Franz Kafka: Toward a Minor Literature*, trans. Dana Polan (Minneapolis: University of Minnesota Press, 1986), may well be its orientation toward the systematic margin, hinterland, or borderline at which hegemonic or authoritarian control is displaced, undermined, or, in their terms, deterritorialized. There can be no scenario of deterritorialization, whether staged in a sociopolitical or semiological setting, without some credence placed in the outside, if only as a dimensional hypothesis. The ambition to fuse the discourses of social systems and textuality drives Deleuze and Guattari in this direction. To the degree that deconstruction treats sociological determinants and processes as yet another instance of language, it does not endeavor to merge these theaters of representation. Hence it devotes far more energy to questioning hypothetical parameters or thresholds separating putative systemic outsides and insides. Such spatial dimensions serve indeed as a paradigm on which far-reaching logical categorization is founded. For instances of the rhetoric of deterritorialization in Deleuze and Guattari's work, see their *A Thousand Plateaus*, 40, 61–63, 87–89, 140–45, 174–75, 306–9, 333–37; *Franz Kafka: Toward a Minor Literature*, 13–15, 18–21, 35, 67–68, 85–88.

27. See Walter Benjamin, "The Task of the Translator," in *Selected Writings*, vol. 1, *1913–1926*, ed. Marcus Bullock and Michael W. Jennings (Cambridge: Harvard University Press, 1999), 256–57, 259–61.

28. Cf. Sussman, *The Aesthetic Contract*, 178–202.

3. EXILES IN WRITING: JOYCE AND BENJAMIN

1. Paul de Man, *Allegories of Reading* (New Haven: Yale University Press, 1979).

2. Ibid., 15.

3. Joseph Conrad, *Lord Jim* (Boston: Houghton Mifflin, 1958), 153.

4. This is the death knell and concatenation under whose aura the dual readings of Hegel and Genet coincide in Jacques Derrida's *Glas*, trans. John P. Leavey, Jr., and Richard Rand (Lincoln: University of Nebraska Press, 1990).

5. Italo Calvino, *Cosmicomics*, trans. William Weaver (New York: Harcourt Brace Jovanovich, 1976), 3–18.

6. Ludwig Wittgenstein, *Tractatus Logico-Philosophicus* (London: Routledge & Kegan Paul, 1964), 150–51: "6.54 My propositions serve as elucidations in the following way: anyone who understands me eventually recognizes them as nonsensical, when he has used them—as steps—to climb up beyond them. (He must, so to speak, throw away the ladder after he has climbed up it.)"

7. For a theoretical overview of language poetry, see "Prolegomena to any Present and Future Language Poetry," in my *The Task of the Critic* (New York: Fordham University Press, 2005), 37–55.

8. James Joyce, *Portrait of the Artist as a Young Man* (New York: Penguin, 1985), 117–24.

9. As iterated, in one of Derrida's most powerful ethical and political as well as aesthetic position pieces, "The Law of Genre." In this essay, on Maurice Blanchot's prose poem "La folie du jour," Derrida links the logic by which art forms as well as categories are formed to the most basic acts of naming and categorization at the core of Western values. See Jacques Derrida, "The Law of Genre," in *Acts of Literature*, 221–52. I comment on the importance of this essay in my "The Fourth Abrahamic Religion?" in *The Task of the Critic*, 176–241.

10. Benjamin, "The Task of the Translator," in *Selected Writings*, vol. 1, *1913–1926*, ed. Marcus Bullock and Michael W. Jennings (Cambridge: Harvard University Press, 1999), 262.

11. Jacques Derrida, "Des Tours de Babel," in *Acts of Religion*, 108–9.

12. Ibid., 121.

13. I owe these tangible implications of the interface between the deconstructive approach to translation and the realities of publishing to Helen Tartar, editor of the present volume, who has added many significant dimensions to its purview.

14. Benjamin, "On Some Motifs in Baudelaire," in *Selected Writings*, vol. 4, *1938–1940*, trans. Edmund Jephcott and others, ed. Howard Eiland and Michael W. Jennings (Cambridge: Harvard University Press, 2003), 328.

15. Ibid., 324.

16. See, e.g., James Campbell, *Exiled in Paris: Richard Wright, James Baldwin, Samuel Beckett, and Others on the Left Bank* (Berkeley: University of California Press, 2003).

17. James Joyce, "Araby," in *Dubliners* (New York: Penguin, 1977), 29–35.

18. James Joyce, *Finnegans Wake* (New York: Viking, 1986), 107.

19. On the problem of the material or materiality of twentieth-century poetic texts, see my *High Resolution: Critical Theory and the Problem of Literacy* (New York: Oxford University Press, 1989), 115–31.

20. Benjamin, "The Task of the Translator, in *Selected Writings*, 1:261.

21. Joyce, *Finnegans Wake*, 118.

216   *Notes to Pages 76–86*

22. Ibid., 121.
23. Ibid., 111.
24. Ibid., 118.
25. Ibid., 119–20.
26. See Henry Sussman, *Afterimages of Modernity* (Baltimore: The Johns Hopkins University Press, 1990), 161–75.
27. Joyce, *Finnegans Wake*, 120.
28. Ibid.
29. Ibid., 1.1, pp. 8–10.
30. Ibid., 3.
31. Ibid., 196.
32. Ibid., 196–97.
33. Ibid., 197.
34. Ibid., 198.
35. See Walter Benjamin, *Selected Writings*, 1:444–88; vol. 2, *1927–1934*, trans. Rodney Livingstone and others, ed. Michael W. Jennings, Howard Eiland, and Gary Smith (Cambridge: Harvard University Press, 1999), 595–637; vol. 3, *1935–1938*, trans. Edmund Jephcott, Howard Eiland, and others, ed. Howard Eiland and Michael W. Jennings (Cambridge: Harvard University Press, 2002), 344–413.
36. Walter Benjamin, *The Origins of German Tragic Drama*, trans. John Osborne (London: New Left Books, 1977).
37. Benjamin, "The Right to Use Force" and "Critique of Violence," in *Selected Writings*, 1:231–34, 236–52.
38. An English approximation of the Hebrew phrase *tikkun olam*, the messianic call for a literal correction (or reform) of the world toward the end of one of the mainstays of the Jewish liturgy, the "Aleynu" prayer, which is included in all three daily prayer services as well as their counterparts on holidays. The "Aleynu" is an affirmation of submission to the deity. A pivotal element of this service is the ongoing labor of *tikkun olam*.
39. See my "Walter the Critic," in *The Task of the Critic*, 56–98.
40. See: Benjamin, "Goethe's Elective Affinities," in *Selected Writings*, 1:297–360; Benjamin, "The Lisbon Earthquake," in *Selected Writings*, 2:536–40; and Benjamin, "Announcement of the Journal *Angelus Novus*," in *Selected Writings*, 1:292–96.

4. JAMES BALDWIN'S EXILE: THEORY, CIRCUMSTANCE, AND THE REAL OF LANGUAGE

1. James Baldwin, *Notes of a Native Son* (Boston: Beacon Press, 1984), 3.
2. Franz Kafka, "A Crossbreed [A Sport]," in *The Complete Stories* (New York: Schocken Books, 1976), 426–27.

3. Baldwin, *Notes of a Native Son*, 5.
4. Ibid.
5. Ibid., 9.
6. Ibid., 6.
7. Ibid.
8. Ibid.
9. Wikipedia attributes this phrase to German sociologist Robert Michels. At the time he devised it, he "was an anarcho-syndicalist (he later became an important ideologue of Mussolini's fascist regime in Italy)." The entry lists Gustav Wagner's "Robert Michaels und das eherne Gesetz der Oligarchie," in Graswurzel Revolution ( ) as a useful source. See http://en.wikipedia.org/wiki/Iron_Law-of_Oligarchy. Also see http://www.spunk.org/texts/places/germany/sp000711.txt. The phrase, according to this entry, dates from 1911.
10. Baldwin, *Notes of a Native Son*, 6.
11. For an elaboration of the complexities confronted in plumbing the depths to a "hard bottom" of language, in relation to Henry David Thoreau, see Walter Benn Michaels, "Walden's False Bottoms," in *Glyph 1*, ed. Samuel Weber and Henry Sussman (Baltimore: The Johns Hopkins University Press, 1977), 132–49.
12. One of Derrida's most masterly demonstrations of the ultimately linguistic formation and pretext to a near-universal sociological phenomenon is his treatment of hospitality. In "Hostipitality," he meticulously traces out the full fluctuations between aggression and generosity in the rhetoric and terminology, as well as in the phenomenon. See his *Acts of Religion*, 356–420.
13. At present, it seems clearly within the compass of history, anthropology, sociology, linguistics, and cognitive science to perform this survey of the permeable membrane between the infrastructural orientation of culture and its material conditions. In its current orientation toward experimental procedure and design, psychology seems to fall out of this grouping.
14. A site of intense convergence between the Lacanian rhetoric of the Real and deconstruction's attention to the intractable, and often microscopic, features of language is J. Hillis Miller's work on speech acts and performatives. This work lends a new coherence to Derrida's initial explorations of the performative in Austin and Searle. One of deconstruction's most striking demonstrations of the materiality of language is Miller's insistence on the virtual reality of the fictive settings of novelists as diverse as Johann David Wyss (*The Swiss Family Robinson*) and Henry James. To insist that places in narrative are virtual is to make them materially tangible. With regard to *The Wings of the Dove's* virtual existence, Miller writes in *Literature as Conduct* (New York: Fordham University Press, 2005), 162: "The novel, it follows, refers to an entire world to which James alone has access, but which he has not invented, except in the sense of discovering it. The evidence for this is the way he says he fails to bring all of it to light." For other passages on fictive virtual reality in this study, see 155–56, 166, 169–71, 174–78, 182, 184.

15. Needless to say, as the productive dialogue between Lacanian psychoanalysis and deconstruction has long ago realized, the foreclosure of articulation ascribed to the Lacanian Real is made possible by classical Western attributes of subjectivity, and therefore the Lacanian transformation of the Id into the Real doesn't quite rise to the challenge of retrofitting all three of the Freudian intrapsychic agencies as modalities of articulation. But even as Lacan mobilized the substantial and long-standing Western onto-theology of the sublime in characterizing the Freudian Id, he calibrated this hypothetical entity in terms of a relation to language. This relation emerges, in terms of the Western conventions of silence in the face of awe and magnificence, as linguistic paralysis or foreclosure. Hence, the Lacanian Real is prelinguistic and mute, while the Symbolic and Imaginary are engaged in particular forms of representation and figuration.

16. See Samuel Weber, *Return to Freud: Jacques Lacan's Dislocation of Psychoanalysis* (Cambridge: Cambridge University Press, 1991), 106.

17. The seminars are entitled, respectively, *The Ego in Freud's Theory and in the Technique of Psychoanalysis 1954–55* and *The Four Fundamental Concepts of Psychoanalysis*, trans. Alan Sheridan (New York: W. W. Norton, 1988 and 1978). They justly occupy prominent places in the literature that has emerged from Lacan's thinking.

18. Lacan, *The Four Fundamental Concepts*, 55.

19. Ibid., 57.

20. Lacan, *The Ego in Freud's Theory*, 237.

21. Ibid., 238.

22. Ibid., 239.

23. Jacques Lacan, *Ecrits: A Selection*, trans Alan Sheridan (New York: W. W. Norton, 1977), 106.

24. Walter Benjamin, *The Origin of German Tragic Drama*, trans. John Osborn, (London: New Left Books, 1977).

25. For the intense semiological nuance even a subsyllabic element such as the *gl* in *glas* is capable of producing, see Jacques Derrida, *Glas*, trans. John P. Leavey, Jr., and Richard Rand (Lincoln: University of Nebraska Press, 1990), 47–52, 119–20, 139–40, 235–36. For the buzz or stammer of semiological elements that Derrida places at the fictive threshold of "Plato's Pharmacy," see the essay of that title in *Dissemination*, trans. Barbara Johnson (Chicago: University of Chicago Press, 1981), 169–70. In reference to the role of *gl* in *Glas*, see also my "Hegel, Glas, and the Broader Modernity," in *Hegel after Derrida*, ed. Stuart Barnett (New York: Routledge, 1998), 282–89.

26. For the "noise" (or static) a system is capable of producing, often related to "traces" it cannot assimilate, see Anthony Wilden, *System and Structure* (London: Tavistock, 1972), 36–37, 131–32, 138, 168–70, 218–20, 230–36, 407–12, 433–35, 492–94.

27. See, e.g., James Joyce, *Ulysses*, The Corrected Edition, ed. Hans Walter Gabler (New York: Vintage, 1986), 186–87.
28. Baldwin, *Notes of a Native Son*, 5.
29. Ibid., 6.
30. Ibid., 9.
31. I employ the term *deterritorialization* as it has been developed by Gilles Deleuze and Félix Guattari in such works as *Kafka: Toward a Minor Literature*, trans. Dana Polan (Minneapolis: University of Minnesota Press, 1986), 13–15, 18–21, 35, 67–68, 85–88, and *A Thousand Plateaus*, trans. Brian Massumi (Minneapolis: University of Minnesota Press, 1987), 32–33, 40, 54, 61, 67, 70, 87–88, 99–100, 109, 112, 117, 129, 133–35.
32. James Joyce, *Portrait of the Artist as a Young Man* (New York: Penguin, 1985), 27–39, 117–35.
33. James Baldwin, *Go Tell It on the Mountain* (New York: Delta, 1981), 3.
34. Ibid., 7.
35. Ibid.
36. Ibid.
37. Ibid.
38. Ibid.
39. Ibid., 198.
40. This dimension of aesthetico-religious awe is suggestively explored in relation to the poetry of Paul Celan by Jacques Derrida in *Sovereignties in Question*, ed. Thomas Dutoit and Outi Pasanen (New York: Fordham University Press, 2005), 111, 115–18, 124–25, 151–54.
41. See Jacques Derrida, *Specters of Marx: The State of the Debt, the Work of Mourning, and the New International*, trans. Peggy Kamuf (New York: Routledge, 1994), 10, 40–47, 93, 97–102, 110.
42. Baldwin, *Go Tell it on the Mountain*, 198.
43. Ibid., 99–100.
44. Ibid., 11.
45. Ibid., 19–20.
46. Lacan, *Four Fundamental Concepts*, 17–18, 62, 76–77, 83, 103–5, 112–13, 116, 118, 142–43, 145–48, 151, 159, 168, 180, 182–86, 194–96, 198, 209, 239, 242–43, 256–58, 265–70, 272–76, 282.
47. Baldwin, *Go Tell it on the Mountain*, 25.
48. Ibid., 40.
49. Ibid., 16.
50. Ibid., 41.
51. Ibid., 99–102.

5. WILLIAM FAULKNER AND THE ROMANCE OF THE AMERICAN DRIFTER

1. William Faulkner, *Absalom, Absalom!* (New York: Vintage International, 1990), 4.

2. William Faulkner, *The Hamlet* (New York: Vintage International, 1991).
3. Faulkner, *Absalom, Absalom!*, 4–5.
4. Ibid., 26.
5. Ibid., 28–29. Note that Borges appropriates "amazement" as a quintessential feature of literature in his "Tlön, Uqbar, Orbis Tertius." See Borges, *Collected Fictions*, trans. Andrew Hurley (New York: Viking, 1998), 74.
6. See Jacques Derrida, "Plato's Pharmacy," in *Dissemination*, trans. Barbara Johnson (Chicago: University of Chicago Press, 1981), 128–34.
7. See William H. NcNeill, *A World History*, 4th ed. (New York: Oxford University Press, 1999), 3–47, 113–19, 194–209, 239–55, 273–82.
8. The two works comprising the diptych are Gilles Deleuze and Félix Guattari, *Anti-Oedipus*, trans. Robert Hurley, Mark Seem, and Helen R. Lane (Minneapolis: University of Minnesota Press, 1996), and *A Thousand Plateaus*, trans. Brian Massumi (Minneapolis: University of Minnesota Press, 1987). With regard to antiquated political formations always hovering *in potentia* in sociopolitical space, see the former work, 139–45, and the latter, 53–57, 133–45, 380–403, 427–37.
9. Deleuze and Guattari, *A Thousand Plateaus*, 14, 115–16, 176, 187, 232–52, 259–60, 308–9.
10. It is possible to think of the overall crisis initiated by the arrival of the outsider either as a Freudian repetition-compulsion or in terms of the dormant persistence of archaic political formations that enables them, according to Deleuze and Guattari, to reconfigure themselves at any given juncture.
11. Férnand Braudel, *Capitalism and Civilization: 15th-18th Century* (Berkeley: University of California Press, 1992), 2:265–72.
12. Roland Barthes, *S/Z*, trans. Richard Howard (New York: Hill and Wang, 1986), 11–20, 106–26.
13. Faulkner, *The Hamlet*, 76–77.
14. I review the aesthetic and certain of the semiological implications of the emergent Protestant theology in *The Aesthetic Contract: Statutes of Art and Intellectual Work in Modernity*, 34–70.
15. For Braudel's assessment of the importance of the peasantry in world history, particularly since the fifteenth century, see his *Capitalism and Civilization*, 1:49, 283; 2:254–55, 265–67, 269.
16. On the constitution and action of the pack, see Deleuze and Guattari, *A Thousand Plateaus*, 241–47, 251–52, 275–78, 280, 292.
17. Faulkner, *The Hamlet*, 235–36.
18. For Deleuze and Guattari's distinction between "smooth" and "striated" space, see *A Thousand Plateaus*, 474–500.
19. Faulkner, *The Hamlet*, 4–5.
20. Ibid., 300.
21. Ibid., 330.

22. Friedrich Nietzsche, *Thus Spoke Zarathustra*, trans. Walter Kaufmann (New York: Penguin, 1966), 28–29, 47, 74, 182.
23. Ibid., 302.
24. Ibid., 302–3.
25. Ibid., 303.
26. Ibid., 303–4.
27. Ibid., 317–18.
28. Ibid., 332–34.
29. Deleuze and Guattari, *A Thousand Plateaus*, 243.
30. Ibid.
31. Ibid.
32. Ibid.
33. Ibid., 245.
34. J. M. Coetzee, *Life and Times of Michael K* (New York: Viking, 1984).
35. Richard Wright, "The Man Who Lived Underground," in *Eight Men* (New York: Thunder's Mouth Press, 1987).
36. Coetzee, *Life and Times of Michael K*, 23–25, 39–40, 68–69, 97–98, 100, 107, 115.
37. Ibid., 31, 43, 78, 137–42.
38. Ibid, 71, 113–17.
39. Wright, *Eight Men*, 92.

6. THE AFTERLIFE OF JUDAISM: THE ZOHAR, BENJAMIN, MILLER

1. The notion of three core Abrahamic religions, Judaism, Christianity, and Islam, is a conceptual matrix and platform that Derrida uses to culturally far-reaching effects in his writings on religion of the past three decades. This construct reminds us that the major Western religions, studied from a rigorous philosophical point of view, are in more intimate exchange and communication than the history of religious persecutions, expulsions, and genocide would allow us to suspect. For some of Derrida's major writings in this sphere, see his *Acts of Religion*, ed. Gil Anidjar (New York: Routledge, 2002); also his *On the Name*, ed. Thomas Dutoit (Stanford: Stanford University Press, 1995). See also Hent de Vries, *Philosophy and the Turn to Religion* (Baltimore: Johns Hopkins University Press, 1999).

2. A useful overview of Jewish positions on the afterlife is to be found in "The Domain of Heaven and the Domain of Hell," a chapter in Ben Zion Bokser, *Judaism: Profile of a Faith* (New York: Alfred A. Knopf, 1963), 131–60.

3. My own efforts to come to some productive terms with modernity are contained in *The Aesthetic Contract: Statutes of Art and Intellectual Work in Modernity* (Stanford: Stanford University Press, 1997).

4. Among the many contributions furnished by Derrida's writings on Western religions is a full extrapolation of the otherworldly, spectral, abyssal,

ghostly, and uncanny constructs and figures, including the revenant appearing in this very paragraph, upon which the edifice of the Abrahamic religions stands. Derrida places this underside of our canonical faiths in relief, and this in turn allows us to question their claim to have initiated an age of rationality, principle, and disinterest in religion and the communities of Judeo-Christianity and Islam. Derrida's highly nuanced recognition of the spectral dimension of the core Western religions had helped me instrumentally in discerning the traits of the Jewish afterlife as it is staged in the Zohar. See Derrida, *Acts of Religion*, 62, 83–84, 87, 91–92, 100, 141, 151, 191, 198–203, 208, 210, 213–18, 222–23, 252–53, 258–59, 276–79, 296, 382, 384, 387, 399, 405, 413.

5. In sheer scholarly terms, Gershom Scholem's annotations and elucidations are indispensable to any approach to the Kabbalah. The fact that Scholem was an intimate and lifelong friend of Benjamin, having met him in 1912, at the age of seventeen, means that there is an important imaginary confluence of their views, even though their opinions diverged on many theological points. This citation, as well as others helpful to me in launching the present exploration, comes from Scholem's *Kabbalah* (New York: Meridian, 1978), 11.

6. Ibid., 23.

7. Ibid., 57.

8. I have explored the Talmud's status as a multi-register text, above all in relation to Benjamin's *Arcades Project*, but also in conjunction with Derrida's *Glas*, in "Between the Registers: The Allegory of Space in Benjamin's Arcades Project," in "Benjamin Now: Critical Encounters with The Arcades Project," ed. Kevin McLaughlin and Philip Roseu, special issue, *boundary 2* 30 (2003): 169–90, reprinted in *The Task of the Critic* (New York: Fordham University Press, 2005), 101–28.

9. J. Hillis Miller, "Border Crossings, Translating Theory: Ruth," in *Topographies* (Stanford: Stanford University Press, 1995), 336.

10. Ibid., 330–31.

11. Ibid., 333.

12. Ibid., 334.

13. I appropriate here a suggestive term of Maurice Blanchot, one that has intrigued me for a long time, and give it a more crassly historical deployment than he perhaps might countenance. "The Limit Experience" is the title of an extended essay taking up almost half of Blanchot's *The Infinite Conversation*, trans. Susan Hanson (Minneapolis: University of Minnesota Press, 1993). A limit experience is both a borderline experience verging on the systemic boundaries of Western thought and culture and a compositional process setting limits to the broader ideological pronouncements of that tradition. In his proposal of the limit experience, Blanchot weaves together an ahistorical constellation of writers whose articulations resonate with one another. These writers include Heraclitus, Pascal, Nietzsche, Hölderlin, Kafka, Weil, Camus, and Foucault. The limit experience, like Derridean deconstruction, then seems to entail a performance proceeding through all memorable theaters and scenes of cultural

production. The term nevertheless seems most resonant to me in characterizing the broad retrofitting and refitting of Western concepts and intellectual operations that coincided with European Romanticism. Do we have a way of considering the ongoing constellation of philosophical and literary interests that might indicate, if nothing else, the exquisite refinement of Blanchot's taste? Do we have a way, in the interest of literary periodization in the broadest sense, of classifying the major elements in Blanchot's literary network as Romantics before the fact, Romantics in and of themselves? I find this a worthwhile intellectual exercise. It may help when we grope for general formulations regarding Romanticism.

14. Michel Foucault, *The Order of Things*, trans. Richard Howard (New York: Vintage, 1973), 54–58, 71–76, 117, 130–31, 137–38, 167–68, 203–11, 316–19, 346–48.

15. This is, admittedly, a theoretically "over-the-top take" on *tikkun olam*, the Hebrew liturgical phrase for the reform or reconfiguration of the world along messianic lines.

16. Scholem, *Kabbalah*, 15.

17. For the notion of the dialectical image, see Walter Benjamin, *The Arcades Project*, ed. Howard Eiland and Kevin McLaughlin (Cambridge: Harvard University Press, 1999), 13, 70, 150, 317, 388–89, 391–92, 396, 406, 417, 459–70, 473–76.

18. "The Talmud has been compared to the sea; you never enjoy swimming anywhere until you have gotten used to the water." Robert Goldenberg, "Talmud," in *Back to the Sources*, ed. Barry W. Holtz (New York: Simon and Schuster, 1984), 168.

19. Gershom Scholem, ed., *Zohar: The Book of Splendor: Basic Readings from the Kabbalah* (New York: Schocken, 1963), 72–73. Scholem's selection and editing of this slim compilation of Zoharic tales and elucidations have made my own extrapolations possible. The choice of texts in this volume is indeed selective: it narrows the five-volume Soncino Edition down to fewer than a hundred pages. The folktales that Scholem included must have enjoyed a special resonance for this groundbreaking elucidator of Jewish mystical literature.

20. For a comprehensive and compelling account of this prayer, one intertwining pivotal aspects in the Judaic approach to death, see Leon Wieseltier, *Kaddish* (New York: Alfred A. Knopf, 1998), xiii, 4–11, 96–124, 264–95, 355–68.

21. The *Athenaeum Fragments* are a privileged site, one whose significance Benjamin fully recognized, for the theoretical working through of the poetic figurations of key philosophical issues explored in Jewish mysticism, among other literatures. Benjamin's aspirations to an integration of Judaic images and narratives and German letters were not merely the stuff of dreams. They were founded on the work of Fichte, the Schlegels, and their peers. See, above all, Friedrich Schlegel's *Lucinde and the Fragments*, trans. and introd. Peter Firchow (Minneapolis: University of Minnesota Press, 1971), 175–77, 191–98.

22. Scholem, ed., *Zohar*, 74–75.

23. In *The Order of Things*, Michel Foucault earmarks analogical thought and imagery, capable of spanning vast distances of plane, realm, and category, a thinking not incompatible with the author(s) of the Zohar, with the *épistème* (or linguistically configured worldview) of the European Renaissance. This cultural moment is for him a domain saturated with radical similitudes. See Foucault, *The Order of Things*, 17–77.

24. See Gershom Scholem, *Major Trends in Jewish Mysticism* (New York: Schocken, 1961), 217–35; see also his *On the Kabbalah and Its Symbolism* (New York: Schocken, 1965), 130–53.

25. Scholem, *Zohar*, 75.

26. Ibid., 29.

27. Given that Kafka did so much to dramatize and perform the twentieth-century cultural imaginary of texts and textually configured environments and institutions, it can be no accident that Deleuze and Guattari dedicated a book to his fiction and the philosophical notions that can be extracted from it. Two of Kafka's novels, *Amerika* and *The Trial*, and an extended late animal fable, "The Burrow," devote particular attention to the construction and performance of extended, interconnected, involuted, self-enclosing environments and architectures. Dedicated readers of Kafka and of Deleuze and Guattari owe much of their sense of a rhizomatic, schizo (that is, nonhierarchical) interconnected cultural landscape to Kafka's projections and imaginings. See Franz Kafka, *Amerika*, trans. Edwin Muir and Willa Muir (New York: Schocken, 1974), 4, 11, 41, 74–75, 108–10, 196–99; *The Trial*, trans. Edwin Muir and Willa Muir (New York: Schocken, 1974), 34–35, 63–67, 99, 116, 119–21, 142–45, 155, 213–14; "The Burrow," in Kafka, *The Complete Stories*, ed. Nahum N. Glatzer (New York: Schocken, 1971), 326–28, 337, 339–40, 343–49. Deleuze and Guattari, above all in their Capitalism and Schizophrenia diptych, translate, in a Benjaminian sense, Kafka's images and tropings into a rhetoric of rhizomes and an architecture of "planes of consistency" and assemblages. For an introduction to this rhetoric, see Deleuze and Guattari, *A Thousand Plateaus*, 3–18, 40–45, 49–57, 141–48, 208–27, 351–74.

28. For the Sefiroth, see Scholem, *Major Trends in Jewish Mysticism*, 204–15, 268–73; see also his *On the Kabbalah and Its Symbolism*, 94, 96–105.

29. Scholem, *Zohar*, 39.

30. Foliage figures prominently in other roughly contemporary literatures with epic or mystical dimensions. I think, for example, of the flower imagery reaching a crescendo in the later cantos of Dante's *Paradiso* (30.124–26, 32.22–24, 33.1–18; Dante Alighieri, *Paradiso*, in *The Divine Comedy*, trans. Charles S. Singleton [Princeton: Princeton University Press, 1975], 3:342–43, 360–61, 370–71). There are also the leaves in John Milton's *Paradise Lost*, 9.1080–125, that Adam and Eve, in the wake of the Fall, use to conceal themselves (Milton, *Complete Poems and Major Prose*, ed. Merritt Y. Hughes [New York: Odyssey

Press, 1957], 403–4). Perhaps these marks of sin are foreshadowed by the famous simile in which the fallen angels "lay intrans't / Thick as Autumnal Leaves that strow the Brooks / In *Vallombrosa*," (1.301–3, Hughes p. 219); widely taken to be an allusion to Dante's spirits numberless as autumn leaves on the verge of the Styx (*Inferno*, 3.112–14; Singleton, 33). In a secular context, note echoes in the leaf and tree imagery in Wallace Stevens, *An Ordinary Evening in New Haven*, sections 12 and 29–30 (in Stevens, *The Palm at the End of the Mind*, ed. Holly Stevens (New York: Random House, 1972), 338, 349–51.

31. Scholem, *Zohar*, 40.

32. Ibid.

33. Irony is a trope and ethos on which J. Hillis Miller has shed light with unusual persistence and radiance. Among many sites in Miller's work in which he pays careful attention to irony, see, e.g., *Versions of Pygmalion* (Cambridge: Harvard University Press, 1990), 43–46, 59, 75–76, 90–93, 157–60. Miller's intuitions of the privileged affinity between reading, writing, interpretation, and death—as negotiated by the rhetorical figure of prosopopoeia—reaches an apotheosis in this volume.

34. I here revert to the "J" conference, held at the University of California, Irvine, on April 18–19, 2003. The senior scholars at this colloquium, which in this passage I reinvent as a Talmudic conference, were J. Hillis Miller, whose work the occasion celebrated and extended, and Jacques Derrida. I thus figure Miller as Rabbi Yose and Derrida as Rabbi Eliyahu or Eli. (Derrida elaborates on this play on his name in "Ulysses Gramophone," in *Acts of Literature*, 277.) In *The Task of the Critic*, I explore the effect of occasionality on literary and cultural criticism over and against commitments to a conceptual operating system and to particular texts shaping, respectively, philosophical discourse and what has constituted itself as "close reading."

35. I refer here, of course, to the character of the Angelus Novus, culled from Klee's drawing (once owned by Benjamin), a figure for the cultural redemption attainable only through the "tasks" of close exegesis, translation, collecting, dedicated archival work, and even urban cruising. This image, as its possibility, attains its full aura and eloquence in section 9 of Benjamin's "On the Concept of History," in Walter Benjamin, *Selected Writings*, vol. 4, *1938–1940*, ed. Howard Eiland and Michael W. Jennings (Cambridge: Harvard University Press, 2003), 392–93.

36. Rochelle Tobias's recent work on the figure of the stars in the work of Celan is suggestive about the culmination of this "line of imagery." See her *The Discourse of Nature in the Poetry of Paul Celan: The Unnatural World* (Baltimore: The Johns Hopkins University Press, 2006).

37. Georg Büchner, *Complete Works and Letters*, trans. Henry J. Schmidt, The German Library 23 (New York: Continuum, 1986), 161.

38. Ibid., 142.

39. Ibid., 143.
40. Ibid.
41. My translation of Paul Celan, "Gespräch im Gebirge," in Celan, *Gesammelte Werke* (Frankfurt am Main: Suhrkamp, 1983), 3:169.
42. Benjamin, *The Arcades Project*, 25–26, 64–65, 112–19, 337, 339–40, 343, 347–49, 357, 462–64, 466, 470, 475, 540.
43. Walter Benjamin, "Goethe's *Die Wahlverwandschaften*," in *Selected Writings*, vol. 1, *1913–1926*, ed. Marcus Bullock and Michael W. Jennings (Cambridge: Harvard University Press, 1997), 354–56, 357n.
44. Benjamin, "On the Concept of History," *Selected Writings*, 4:397.
45. Ibid., 331.
46. Ibid.
47. Ibid.

7. MODERNIST NIGHT: DISTORTION, REGRESSION, AND OBLIVION IN THE FICTION OF BRUNO SCHULZ

1. Bruno Schulz, *Sanatorium under the Sign of the Hourglass*, trans. Celina Wieniewska, introd. John Updike (New York: Penguin, 1979), 72.
2. See Gilles Deleuze and Felix Guattari, *Kafka: Pour une littérature mineure* (Paris: Minuit, 1975), 29–50.
3. Schulz, *Sanatorium*, 116–17.
4. Franz Kafka, *The Complete Stories*, ed. Nahum N. Glatzer (New York: Schocken, 1976), 429.
5. The term, familiar to developmental and cognitive psychologists, was coined by William James.
6. See Henry Sussman, "The All-Embracing Metaphor: Reflections on Kafka's 'The Burrow,'" in *Glyph 1* (Baltimore: The Johns Hopkins University Press, 1977), 99–131; rpt. in Henry Sussman, *Franz Kafka: Geometrician of Metaphor* (Madison: Coda Press, 1979), 148–81.
7. Schulz, *Sanatorium*, 20–23.
8. Walter Benjamin, "Franz Kafka: On the Tenth Anniversary of His Death," in *Selected Writings*, vol. 2, *1927–1934*, trans. Rodney Livingstone and others, ed. Michael W. Jennings, Howard Eiland, and Gary Smith (Cambridge: Harvard University Press, 1999), 802.
9. The "strange interlude" between Joseph K.'s exegetical sentencing and between his execution is situated between chapters 9 and 10 in *The Trial*. Franz Kafka, *The Trial*, trans. Willa and Edwin Muir (New York: Schocken, 1974), 222–23.
10. Thomas Bernhard, *Correction*, trans. Sophie Wilkins (New York: Vintage, 1983), 61, 115, 130–32, 242, 261–63, 266.
11. Schulz, *Sanatorium*, 40.
12. Ibid., 40–43.

13. Kafka, *Complete Stories*, 9.

14. Martin Heidegger, "The Origin of the Work of Art," in *Poetry, Language, Thought*, trans. Albert Hofstadter (New York: Harper & Row, 1975), 69–78.

15. Schulz, *Sanatorium*, 42–43.

16. Marcel Proust, *Combray*, trans. F. Scott Moncrieff and Terence Kilmartin (New York: Vintage, 1989), 4, 9–10, 18–19, 46–50, 55, 63–65, 90–94, 123, 142, 151–53, 184–85.

17. Schulz, *Sanatorium*, 43–44.

18. I have discussed the endless semiological ambiguity in the late Joyce in terms of a strategy of work stoppage in the conventional representational expectations surrounding the novel. See Henry Sussman, "A Broken Contract: The Discourse of Half-Reference," in *Afterimages of Modernity* (Baltimore: The Johns Hopkins University Press, 1993), 161–75.

19. Schulz, *Sanatorium*, 43.

20. Johann Wolfgang von Goethe, "Faust II," in *Faust*, trans. Walter Arndt, Norton Critical Edition (New York: W. W. Norton, 1976), 178–79 ("On the Upper Peneios," ll. 7080–98); 189–92 ("On the Upper Peneios," ll. 7496–581); 300–2 ("Mountain Gorges," ll. 11843–88).

21. Schulz, *Sanatorium*, 43.

22. Ibid.

23. Ibid., 44.

24. Walter Benjamin, "Franz Kafka," in *Selected Writings*, 2:807.

25. Ibid., 808–9.

26. Ibid., 809–10.

27. Ibid., 810–11.

28. Schulz, *Sanatorium*, 45.

29. Immanuel Kant, *Critique of Judgment*, trans. J. H. Bernard (New York: Macmillan, 1951), 85–95.

30. Michel Foucault, *The Order of Things*, trans. Richard Howard (New York, Vintage, 1973), 17–44.

31. There are multiple instances of Derrida's articulation and staging of textuality. The most memorable include "Ellipsis," in *Writing and Difference*, trans. Alan Bass (Chicago: University of Chicago Press, 1980), 294–300; "Plato's Pharmacy" and "The Double Session," in *Dissemination*, trans. Barbara Johnson (Chicago: University of Chicago Press, 1981), 65, 168–84, 208–22, 227–37, 274–86; and, "Tympan," in *Margins of Philosophy*, trans. Alan Bass (Chicago: University of Chicago Press, 1982), ix–xxix.

32. Schulz, *Sanatorium*, 85.

33. The fireworks link the scene to another moment of sexual apotheosis in a marginal cultural backwater, namely, Leopold Bloom's ejaculation at the end of the "Nausicaa" episode of *Ulysses*. See James Joyce, *Ulysses*, The Corrected Edition, ed. Hans Walter Gabler (New York: Random House, 1986), 299–301.

34. For the notion of "poetic prose," see Benjamin's "On Some Motifs in Baudelaire," in *Selected Writings*, vol. 4, *1938–1940*, trans. Edmund Jephcott and others, ed. Howard Eiland and Michael W. Jennings (Cambridge: Harvard University Press, 2003), 320.

35. Schulz, *Sanatorium*, 85–86.

36. Ibid., 16.

37. Franz Kafka, *The Trial*, 141–42.

38. For the notion that the histories of literature and art in general transpire through a series of aesthetic contracts, see Henry Sussman, *The Aesthetic Contract: Statutes of Art and Intellectual Work in Modernity* (Stanford: Stanford University Press, 1997), 165–205.

39. Schulz, *Sanatorium*, 4.

40. Ibid., 14.

41. For a compilation of modernistic contracts or "complex art-games" whose emptying or rendering indifferent becomes the base position for postmodernism, see my *Afterimages of Modernity*, 1–57.

42. Schulz, *Sanatorium*, 59–63, 72–82.

43. Joyce, *Ulysses*, 90, 171, 175, 177, 183, 196, 269, 274, 348, 362, 373, 414, 611.

44. Schulz, *Sanatorium*, 174–78.

45. Ibid., 4.

46. Ibid., 1.

47. Ibid., 5.

48. For the crucial notion of aura, see Benjamin, "On Some Motifs in Baudelaire," in *Selected Writings*, 4:336–39, 342–43.

49. Schulz, *Sanatorium*, 7.

50. Ibid., 31–32.

51. Ibid., 32.

52. Ibid., 46.

53. Ibid.

54. Ibid., 46–47, 56, 63, 65–67.

55. Ibid., 101–2.

56. Ibid., 102.

57. Ibid., 103.

58. Ibid., 174.

59. See Sigmund Freud, "Totem and Taboo," in *The Standard Edition of the Complete Psychological Works of Sigmund Freud*, trans. James Strachey (London: The Hogarth Press: 1953–74), 13:19–22, 133–55.

60. Schulz, *Sanatorium*, 178.

61. Ibid., 152.

8. INCARCERATED IN *AMERIKA*: LITERATURE ADDRESSES THE POLITICAL, WITH THE HELP OF ERNESTO LACLAU

1. Franz Kafka, *Amerika (The Man Who Disappeared)*, trans. Michael Hoffmann (New York: New Directions, 1996).

2. Franz Kafka, "The Cares of a Family Man," in *The Complete Stories*, ed. Nahum N. Glatzer (New York: Schocken, 1971), 427.
3. See Slavoj Žižek, *The Ticklish Subject* (London: Verso, 1999), 25–30; *The Fragile Absolute* (London: Verso, 2000), 46–51, 107–13, 117–27.
4. Kafka, *Amerika*, 22.
5. Ibid., 25.
6. Ibid., 37.
7. Ibid., 135.
8. Ibid., 168.
9. See Gilles Deleuze and Félix Guattari, *A Thousand Plateaus*, trans. Brian Massumi (Minneapolis: University of Minnesota Press, 1987), 26–30, 120–21, 146–47, 165, 273, 403.
10. Kafka, *Amerika*, 102.
11. In his recent biography, Rainer Stach affords us unprecedented access to Kafka's work as a high official in worker's compensation insurance firms as well as in the familial enterprise in which Herrmann Kafka helped open the first asbestos factory in Czechoslovakia. See his *Kafka: The Decisive Years* (Orlando: Harcourt, Inc., 2005), 23–24, 26–29, 35–41, 66–67, 94, 125–32, 140–41, 147–48, 284–91, 294–95, 350–51, 364–67.
12. Kafka, *Amerika*, 104.
13. Ibid., 170.
14. See Deleuze and Guattari, *A Thousand Plateaus*, 149–54, 157–59, 165–66, 243, 270, 285.
15. Kafka, *Amerika*, 172.
16. See Jacques Derrida, "Faith and Knowledge: The Two Sources of 'Religion' at the Limits of Reason Alone," in *Acts of Religion*, ed. Gil Anidjar (New York: Routledge, 2002), 67–77.
17. See Martin Heidegger, "The Origin of the Work of Art" and "What Are Poets For?" in *Poetry, Language, Thought*, trans. Albert Hofstadter (New York: Harper & Row, 1971), 37–39, 70–71, 74, 103–7, 13–39.
18. Ernesto Laclau, *New Reflections on the Revolution of Our Time* (London: Verso, 1990), 16.
19. Ibid., 17.
20. Ibid.
21. Ibid., 20–21.
22. Ibid., 24.
23. Kafka, *Amerika*, 202.
24. Ibid., 208.
25. Laclau, *New Reflections on the Revolution of Our Time*, 31–32.
26. Ibid., 24.
27. Ibid., 39–40.
28. See Jacques Derrida, *On the Name*, ed. Thomas Dutoit (Stanford: Stanford University Press, 1993), 56–58, 89–127.
29. Laclau, *New Reflections on the Revolution of Our Time*, 82.

30. For the highly suggestive notion of the dialectical image, see Benjamin, *The Arcades Project*, trans. Howard Eiland and Kevin McLaughlin (Cambridge: Harvard University Press, 1999), 13, 70, 150, 317, 388–92, 396, 406, 417, 459–62, 463–70, 473–76.

31. Bertolt Brecht, *Brecht on Theatre*, ed. John Willett (New York: Hill and Wang, 1992), 92–93.

32. Ibid., 186.

33. James Joyce, *Finnegans Wake* (New York: Viking, 1986), 121.

34. Ibid., 5.

35. See my "The Fourth Abrahamic Religion?" an exploration of the cultural and theoretical implications of Jacques Derrida's grouping of the three major Western faiths within a common paradigm in *The Task of the Critic: Poetics, Philosophy, Religion* (New York: Fordham University Press, 2005), 176–241.

36. Franz Kafka, *Diaries 1914–1923* (New York: Schocken Books, 1965), 233.

INDEX

Abrahamic religions, 14, 68, 90, 97, 104, 130, 131, 133, 140, 143, 146, 203, 221*n*1, *n*4. *See also* Judaism; Christianity; Islam
À la recherche du temps perdu: *See* Proust: *Remembrance of Things Past*
allegory 18, 31, 45, 51, 57, 58, 62, 63, 65, 100, 118–19, 126–27, 135, 138, 149
Althusser, Louis, 5–6, 213*n*25
Aristotle, 196
Aura, xviii, 2, 24, 101, 106, 118, 225*n*35
Austen, Jane, 57

Babel, 9, 68, 69, 74, 75, 76, 105
Baldwin, James, 32, 85–109; and exile, 73, 85–89, 99; *Go Tell It on the Mountain*, 73, 98–109; *Notes of a Native Son*, 73, 86, 88, 89, 101; in relation to other writers, 85, 86, 87, 88, 92, 98, 100, 104; in relation to Joyce, 100–2; and exile, xxiv, 85–89, 99; and reading, 86; "Autobiographical Notes," 86, 87, 89, 98, 99; and the Real, 87, 91–109
Barrie, J. M., 171
Barthes, Roland, 4, 35, 53, 54, 213, 220; *S/Z*, 117
Baudelaire, Charles, xx , 4, 62, 100, 150
Becker, Howard S., 18; *Outsiders: Studies in the Sociology of Deviance*, 18
Beckett, Samuel, 37, 164, 215
Being, xxiii, 11–19 passim, 40, 91, 157, 177, 205*n*4

Benjamin, Walter, vii, xx, xxiii, 4, 106, 154, 166, 167, 192, 210*n*40
and constellation, xxiii, 21, 146, 210*n*38
and exile, 68–74, 81–84
and translation, 61–62, 68–71
"The Task of the Translator," 61, 68, 69, 75, 215
The Origin of German Tragic Drama, 62, 95
The Arcades Project, 68, 73, 81, 150, 151, 197, 210*n*38
and criticism, 71, 81–83, 138, 150, 151
"One-Way Street," 81
"Berlin Chronicle," 81
"A Berlin Childhood, circa 1900," 81
"The Right to Use Force," 82
"Critique of Violence," 82
and shock, 106, 210*n*45
and stars, 138, 146, 150–51
"On Some Motifs in Baudelaire," 150, 151
"On the Concept of History," 150–51
and Judaism, 131, 138–51 passim, on Kafka, 156, 161–62
on Brecht, 199
Bergson, Henri, 154
Bernstein, Charles, 181
Bible, the, 53, 54, 68, 103, 135, 159, 165; Genesis, 9, 54, 68, 143, 163, 183; Cain, 53, 105, 135; Exodus, 139, 183; Tower of Babel: *See* Babel; Book of Ruth: *See* Book of Ruth. *See also* Talmud

231

Blanchot, Maurice, x, xi, xiv, 221*n*55; and the outsider, xiv; "Literature and the Original Experience" x, 205; *The Infinite Conversation*, 62
Book of Ruth, the, 133–37
Book of Splendor, the: See Zohar
Borges, Jorge Luis, 32, 44, 62, 70, 71, 83, 221*n*55; "The Circular Ruin," 32, 211
Braudel, Fernand, 116
Brecht, Bertolt, 199–200
Büchner, Georg, 33, 131, 147–49; "Lenz," 33, 147–49; *Woyzeck*, 147,
Buddhism, xiii, xxii, 30, 32, 33, 180

Calvino, Italo, 44, 65, 71, 215; "The Chase," 71; *Cosmicomics*, 65
Camus, Albert, 222*n*13; *The Stranger*, 38
Cannetti, Elias, xxi
Celan, Paul, 131, 147, 149, 150
Celine, Louis-Ferdinand, 199
Cervantes, Miguel de, *Don Quixote*, 2
Chaplin, Charlie, 183, 184
Chaucer, Geoffrey, 127
Childhood, 51–52, 86, 152–55, 159, 166, 168–69
Christianity, 53, 59, 130, 131, 135, 137, 140, 141, 148, 149, 191, 221*n*1, *n*4. See also Abrahamic religions; Bible
Cinderella, 183–84
Coetzee, J. M., 127, 128
Cohen, Tom, xxiii
Conrad, Joseph, 65; *Lord Jim*, 63
Courbet, Gustav, 147
Crane, Hart, 92
criticism, 15, 62, 132, 147, 199, 213*n*25, 225*n*34; outsider status of, xi, xiii, xiv, xx, 3, 4, 18, 44, 60, 71, 72; and deconstruction, 6, 90, 93, 102; conditions for, 29, 31, 32, 35, 36, 40, 43, 44; and Nietzsche, 31, 35; and Benjamin, 71, 81–83, 138, 150, 151
critique: outsider status of, x, xx, 59–61; cultural, x, 24, 27, 40, 59, 61; and writing, xv, xxiii; political, 5, 174, 179; and deconstruction, 7, 64, 100, 179, 222*n*13; and Nietzsche, 24–27, 34; sociological, 34, 60, 62

Dante Alighieri, 127, 224, 225
death, ix, 10–11, 31, 35, 42, 46, 82, 91, 95, 104–5, 119, 136, 138–40, 143–46, 154, 158
deconstruction, xxiv, 11; and the inside-outside binary, 6, 63, 64, 70; and language, 7, 10, 90, 98, 102, 214*n*16, 217*n*14; and writing, 11, 30, 33, 164, 180; and Nietzsche, 23, 24, 30, 33; and Lacan, 92, 93, 217*n*14, 216*n*5; and critique, 100, 179, 222*n*13
Defoe, Daniel, 67; *Robinson Crusoe*, 67, 127, 183
Deleuze, Gilles, 184; and Félix Guattari, xx, 46, 54, 91, 119, 220*n*10; Capitalism and Schizophrenia, 45, 115, 118, 186, 214*n*26; on animals, 52, 118, 121, 125, 128, 224*n*27; on deterritorialization, 190, 214*n*26, 219*n*31
de Man,
Derrida, Jacques, 23, 36, 42, 62, 63, 68, 69, 70, 86, 90, 131, 136, 164, 192, 196, 201, 202, 211*n*52
autoimmunity, xii
and exile, 6–15
"Ulysses Gramophone," 6, 9, 208, 225
"A Silkworm of One's Own," 6, 208
on Lévi-Strauss, 7
on Saussure, 7–8
Of Grammatology, 7, 10, 208
and language, 7–11
the hinge in, 8, 10–12, 70, 108, 119
différance, 9, 11, 21, 209
"Des Tours de Babel," 9, 68, 208, 215
"Différance," 11
"Ousia and Gramme," 11, 12
on *khora*, 23, 198, 199
and Lacan, 91–96, 104, 217*n*14, 216*n*5
"Plato's Pharmacy," 95, 115, 218
"Faith and Knowledge," 187
textuality, 188
dialectical image, 138, 151, 199

Dickens, Charles, 57, 127; *Great Expectations*, 62
Dostoyevsky, Fyodor, 2, 60, 127, 185
Dreiser, Theodor, 92
DuBois, W. E. B., 85

Einstein, Albert: *See* relativity
Eliot, George, 57; *Middlemarch*, 62
Escher, M. C., 183
exile: and Kafka, 1–5; and Derrida, 6–15; and sociology, 17–20; and Nietzsche, 21–35; and Joyce, 63, 74–81; and Benjamin, 68–74, 81–84; and Baldwin, 73, 85–89, 99. *See also* outsider; wanderer

Faulkner, William, vii, 32, 87, 100, 110–29; *Light in August*, 60; *Absalom, Absalom!*, 110, 111, 112, 127; *The Hamlet*, 111, 116–28
Ferraris, Maurizio, 13, 42, 209, 212
flâneur, xx, 4, 83. *See also* Baudelaire; Benjamin
Flaubert, Gustave, *Emma Bovary*, 37
Foucault, Michel, xvi, 136, 163, 222, 223, 224, 224, 227; *The Order of Things*, 163
Frankenstein, xx, 147
Friedrich, Caspar David, 147, 148
Freud, Sigmund, 11, 12, 27, 40, 93, 95, 154, 176, 197, 199, 218n15, 220n10; and the uncanny, xiii, 38, 61; and the death drive, 11, 31, 35; *Beyond the Pleasure Principle*, 31; *The Interpretation of Dreams*, 93. *See also* Lacan; psychoanalysis
"Fugitive, The," 50, 59

Gasché, Rodolphe, xxiii, 9, 208
Gilgamesh, 60
Goethe, Johann Wolfgang von, 24, 147, 150, 160; *Electiive Affinities*, 84, 86, 136, 147, 150, 216; *Egmont*, 147
Goffman, Erving, xxi, 19, 36, 209
Gogol, Nikolai, 127

Gombrowicz, Witold, 172
Guattari, Félix, and Gilles Deleuze, xx, 45, 46, 52, 54, 186, 190, 207, 213, 214, 219, 220, 221, 224, 226, 229; *Capitalism and Schizophrenia*, 115, 118; on animals, 118, 121, 125, 128

Hegel, G. W. F., xix, 9, 18, 93, 95, 189, 196; "Force and the Understanding," 36
Heidegger, Martin, 23, 86, 188, 192, 205n7; and the Open, xi; on dwelling, xiv, 41, 72; on Being, 11–12, 157, 179; *Poetry, Language, Thought*, 42; "The Origin of the Work of Art," 157
Hemingway, Ernest, 92
Herder, Johann Gottfried von, 24
hinge: *See* Derrida
Husserl, Edmund, 7, 8, 27

Islam, 6, 130, 131, 141, 202, 203, 221n1, n4. *See also* Abrahamic religions

Jacobs, Carol, xxiii
James, Henry, 57, 209n26, 217n14
Jordan, Neil, 43, 56; *The Butcher Boy*, 43–62; *The Crying Game*, 56
Joubert, Joseph, 151
Joyce, James, 32, 44, 74–81, 83, 100–2, 192, 200–3
"Araby," 74, 153, 166; *Ulysses*, 71, 72, 73, 74, 75, 98, 102, 160, 168, 201, 227n33
Dubliners, 74
and exile, xxiv, 63, 69, 74–81
Finnegan's Wake, 9, 68, 69, 73–81, 160, 191, 200, 201, 202, 216, 230
Portrait of the Artist as a Young Man, 67, 74, 75, 100–6 passim, 166, 169
in relation to James Baldwin, 100–2
in relation to Bruno Schultz, 154–69 passim
the political in, 200–3.

See also Derrida: "Ulysses Gramophone"
Judaism, 13, 82, 130–51, 176; afterlife in, 130–32, 138, 151, 221n2, 221n4; influence on German Romanticism, 131, 136, 141, 147, 150, 223n21. *See also* Abrahamic religions; Kaballah; mysticism, Talmud; Zohar
Just, Saint, 196

Kabballah, 131–32, 136–37, 141, 142, 143, 146, 148, 149, 151. *See also* Judaism; mysticism
Kafka, Franz, 31, 33, 44, 62, 64, 71, 121, 125, 127, 131, 144, 172, 178–203, 210n40, 211n58, 212n71, 214n26, 219n31, 222n13, 224n27, 229n11
and writing, xv–xvi, xxii
"The Judgment," xvi
The Castle, 1–3, 4, 62, 71, 180, 198, 208n2 208n2
and exile, 1–5
The Trial, 4, 71, 156, 161, 166, 184, 193
"The Metamorphosis," 4, 37, 168, 173–74
Amerika, 4, 178–203
"The Hunger Artist," 33
"A Crossbreed [A Sport]," 86, 88
in relation to Baldwin, 86, 88
"Josephine, the Mouse Singer," 125
"Children on a Country Road," 153
"A Common Confusion," 153
in relation to Bruno Schultz, 153–58, 161–66, 168, 172–75
as seen by Benjamin, 156, 161–62
"Description of a Struggle," 157
"Cares of a Family Man," 162, 180, 211n58
"Before the Law," 175
the political in, 178–203
"The Great Wall of China," 188, 198
"In the Penal Colony," 188, 198
Diaries, 203
The Man Who Disappeared: see *Amerika*
Kant, Immanuel, xviii, 17, 38, 45, 121, 206n14; and creativity, 155, 163, 164

Keats, John, 135–36
Kierkegaard, Søren, 23
Kleist, Heinrich von, 131, 136, 186
Kracauer, Sigfried, xxi

La Rochefoucauld, François de, 23
Lacan, Jacques, 87, 91–96, 103, 104, 107, 118, 197, 217; *Seminar 2*, 93, 94; *Seminar 11*, 93; the Real, 87, 92–95, 195, 200, 218; and deconstruction, 92, 93, 217n14, 216n5; the Symbolic, 93, 106; the Imaginary, 93, 103; "Function and Field of Language," 95; *objet petit à*, 107, 109, 180; *Four Fundamental Concepts of Psychoanalysis*: See *Seminar 11*. *See also* Freud; psychoanalysis
Laclau, Ernesto, xvi, 187–98; hegemony, 187; constituitive outside, 189–90
Levinas, Emmanuel, 24, 38, 39, 70, 212
Lévi-Strauss, Claude, 7
"Lone Ranger, The," 49, 55, 59
Losey, Joseph, 193; "Monsieur Klein," 193
Luhmann, Niklas xviii

Mallarmé, Stéphane, 12, 15, 100
Marcuse, Herbert, xxi
Marx, Karl, xxi, 180, 192; *Communist Manifesto*, 183
McCabe, Patrick, 43, 45, 49, 50, 56, 212, 213. *See also* Jordan: *The Butcher Boy*
McNeill, William, 115
Melville, Herman, 2, 65, 100, 109, 127, 212; *Moby Dick*, 65, 126
memory, xxi–xxii, 71, 119, 125, 128, 130
Merrill, James, 197
messianism, ix–xi, 24, 25, 69, 73, 82–83, 116, 146–47, 150–51
Miller, J. Hillis, xxiii, 21, 130, 209n26; on The Book of Ruth, 133–37
modernism, xvii, xx, 25–26, 44, 68, 71, 111–12, 128, 154, 158–59, 161–68, 173, 179
modernity, xvii–xviii, 17, 25, 27, 31, 68, 81, 83, 91, 111–12, 116, 119, 131, 136–38, 140–41, 151, 163

Moses ben Shem Tov de Leon, 32, 132. *See also* Kabbalah; Zohar

Murasaki, Shikibu, 57; *The Tale of Genji*, 57, 62

mysticism, 33, 131–32, 137–50 passim, 223*n*19, 121

Nietzsche, Friedrich, x, xx, 2, 21–34, 35, 36, 40, 62, 64, 121, 192, 210, 211*n*52; *Human, All Too Human*, x, 11, 21–34, 40, 62, 210, 211, 212, 32; the Wanderer, x, xx, 2, 31–35; and exile, 21–35; and deconstruction, 23, 24, 30, 33; friendship, 28–29, 211*n*52; *Thus Spake Zarathustra*, 62, 121

Novalis, 23, 131

Oberlin, Johann Friedrich, 147–49

Odysseus, 24, 60

Odyssey, 75, 79, 224

Orr, Jackie, xxi

outsider, 24, 31, 36, 48, 67, 102, 116, 190, 220*n*10; and writing, x–xiv passim, 2–5, 20–21, 37, 64; in Kafka, 1–2, 190; and Derrida, 6, 12–14, 63; the writer as, 16, 30, 67; in sociology, 16–20, 43, 44, 62; in relation to insiders, 18–20, 39, 114–16; and De Man, 63–65; in Faulkner, 119–29. *See also* exile; wanderer

parabasis, 141

Pfohl, Stephen, xxi, 207–19

Plato, 9, 12, 36, 62, 95, 192, 196, 218, 220, 227; *Phaedrus*, 95; Derrida on, 95

Poe, Edgar Allan, 2, 62, 100, 211

Pound, Ezra, 158, 197, 199

Proust, Marcel, 101, 155, 157; *Remembrance of Things Past*, xviii–xx, 51, 53, 57, 62, 153, 158, 166, 169; in relation to Bruno Schultz, 153–55, 157–58, 163–66, 169

psychoanalysis, 7, 11, 21, 27, 85, 91–96, 179, 180–84, 195–99 passim, 218*n*15. *See also* Freud; Lacan

Pynchon, Thomas, 87; *Gravity's Rainbow*, 71

Rabbi Abba, 139–40. *See also* Judaism; mysticism

Rabbi Eleazar, 139–40. *See also* Judaism; mysticism

Real, the, 87, 92–95, 105, 218, 189, 191; in Lacan, 87, 92–95, 217, 218; of language, 91–92, 95–101, 104–6, 109; of social circumstance, 96–99, 108–9, 194

Recherche: *See* Proust: *Remembrance of Things Past*

relativity, 139, 153–54

Romanticism, 17, 23, 25, 31, 34, 135, 137, 171; influence from Judaism, 131, 136, 141, 147, 150, 223*n*21

Rousseau, Jean-Jacques, 7, 64

Saint-Saëns, Camille. 76; "Carnival of the Animals," 76

Saussure, Ferdinand de, 7, 8, 10, 208

Sayer, Derek, xxi, 151, 207*n*19

Schlegel, Friedrich, 141

Schlegels, the, 23, 32, 131, 155, 223

Schleiermacher, Friedrich, 23

Scholem, Gershom, 131, 132, 137–39, 143, 151, 222, 223. *See also* Judaism; mysticism

Schulz, Bruno, vii, xxv, 32, 139, 152–77, 226, 227, 228; *Sanatorium under the Sign of the Hourglass*, 139, 152–77; relation to Modernism, 152–77; in relation Kafka, 153–79 passim; in relation to Proust, 153–55, 157–58, 164–66, 169; in relation to Joyce, 153–54, 158, 160, 166–69

Sebald, W. G., xxii, 207*n*20, *n*21, *n*22

Sefer ha-Zohar: *See* Zohar

shadow, x, xvii, xx, 24–33 passim

Shakespeare, William, xvii, 104; *Hamlet*, xvii, 104, 199

Shelton, Allen, xxi, 207*n*19

Simmel, Georg, xxi, 17, 18, 208*n*2. *See also* sociability

Simonides, 23, 24
Skinner, B. F., 35
sociability, 17, 18, 90, 208, 208n2. *See also* Simmell
sociology, xvi–xviii, 16, 17, 18, 19, 43, 44, 62, 96, 120, 168, 207n 19, n20, n21, n22; and memoir, xxi–xxii; view on art, 16, the outsider in, 16–20, 43, 44, 62; and mobility, xx; and exile, 17–20
Stein, Gertrude, 44, 100, 158, 168,
Sterne, Laurence, 24; *Tristam Shandy*, 68
Stevens, Wallace, 158
Sussman, Henry: *The Aesthetic Contract*, xvii, 44; *The Task of the Critic*, xxiv, 215n9, 222n8, 225n34, 230n35
Swift, Jonathan: *Gulliver's Travels*, 127
systems theory, xv, 206n9

Talmud, the, 132–41 passim, 225n34. *See also* Bible; Judaism; mysticism
Tartar, Helen, xxiv
teaching, xii–xiii
Tieck, Ludwig, 23
Tolstoy, Leo, 127
Turner, J. M. W., 147
Twain, Mark, 51; *Huckleberry Finn*, 47, 49

Underground man, 2, 60, 127, 128. *See also* Dostoyevsky; Wright
Upanishads, the, 95

Vertov, Dziga, 71; "I Am a Camera," 71

Wagner, Gustav, 217
Wagner, Richard, 25, 31, 160
wanderer, the: outsider status of, 41, 42, 73, 125; and writing, x, 31, 32, 41, 71; in Büchner, 147–49; in Nietzsche, x, xx, 2, 24, 27, 32–34; in Schultz, 157–65 passim, 176–77; in Kafka, 180–84. *See also* exile; outsider
Weber, Max, xxi
Weber, Samuel, 93
West, Nathanael, 187; *The Day of the Locust*, 187
Whitman, Walt, 100
Wieland, Johannes, 24
Wilder, Thorton, 67; *Our Town*, 65
Wittgenstein, Ludwig, 62, 65, 215; *Tractatus Logico-Philosophicus*, 65
Woolf, Virginia, 100
Wright, Richard, 85, 92, 98; "The Man Who Lived Underground," 60, 127, 128, 129; *Native Son*, 108; *Black Boy*, 108

Žižek, Slavoj, 183, 193
Zohar, the, vii, xxv, 32, 130–33, 136–51, 222n4, 223n19, 224n23; date of composition, 132; author, 132. *See also* Judaism; mysticism; Moses ben Shem Tov de Leon
Zola, Emile, xxi, 62; *Nana*, 62; *Ladies' Paradise*, 71
Zukofsy, Louis, 197